GEOFFREY HODSON was born and educated in England. During the first World War he served with distinction in the British Army and after the war he became actively interested in theosophical studies. He has carried out occult research in collaboration with medical men, physicists, anthropologists and archeologists.

For some forty years Mr. Hodson has been a lecturer for the Theosophical Society, speaking in America, England, Europe, South Africa, India, New Zealand, Australia and the Far East. He is also the author of some thirty-five theosophical and other books, dealing with such topics as meditation, the spiritual life, health and disease, and the life and powers of the occultist.

Mr. Hodson has three times occupied the position of Director of Studies at the School of the Wisdom at Adyar, Madras, India, the International Headquarters of the Theosophical Society.

Mr. Hodson was awarded the Subba Row Medal in 1954 for his contributions to theosophical literature.

THE HIDDEN WISDOM IN THE HOLY BIBLE, VOL. I

BY THE SAME AUTHOR

THE ANGELIC HIERARCHY

    Fairies at Work and at Play.   French Translation.
    The Kingdom of Faerie.
    The Brotherhood of Angels and of Men.
    Be Ye Perfect.
    The Angelic Hosts.
    Man, The Triune God.
    The Coming of the Angels.
    The Kingdom of the Gods.   Illustrated.
    The Supreme Splendour.

THE SPIRITUAL LIFE

    First Steps on the Path.
    Thus Have I Heard.
    Meditations on the Occult Life.
    The Pathway to Perfection.
    Destiny.
    The Inner Side of Church Worship.

THE POWERS LATENT IN MAN

    The Science of Seership.   French Translation.
    Clairvoyance and the Serpent Fire.
    Occult Powers in Nature and in Man.
    Man's Supersensory and Spiritual Powers.
    The Soul's Awakening.   American Edition.
    A Yoga of Light.
    Some Experiments in Four-Dimensional Vision.

THE THEOSOPHICAL PHILOSOPHY OF LIFE

    Theosophy Answers Some Problems of Life.
    Vital Questions Answered.
    Reincarnation—Fact or Fallacy?
    The Miracle of Birth.
    The Spiritual Significance of Motherhood.   English and Spanish Editions.
    Through the Gateway of Death.
    The Seven Human Temperaments.
    The School of the Wisdom Lecture Notes, Vols. I and II.

INTERPRETATIONS OF SCRIPTURES AND MYTHS

    The Hidden Wisdom in the Christian Scriptures.   American Edition.
    The Divine Wisdom in the Christian Scriptures.   New Zealand Edition.

HEALTH

    Health and the Spiritual Life.
    New Light on the Problem of Disease.
    An Occult View of Health and Disease.

ANIMAL WELFARE

    An Animals' Bill of Rights.
    The Humanitarian Cause, Its Extreme Urgency.
    Animals and Men, The Ideal Relationship.
    Authentic Stories of Intelligence in Animals.
    Our Friends the Animals.
    Radiant Health From a Meat-free Dietary.
    The Case for Vegetarianism.
    Plant Foods, Their Nutrient Properties.

THE HIDDEN WISDOM IN THE HOLY BIBLE

AN EXAMINATION OF THE IDEA THAT THE CONTENTS
OF THE BIBLE ARE PARTLY ALLEGORICAL

BY

GEOFFREY HODSON

VOLUME I

An Introduction to the Sacred Language
of Allegory and Symbol

1970

THE THEOSOPHICAL PUBLISHING HOUSE

ADYAR, MADRAS 20, INDIA

68, Great Russell Street, London, W. C. 1., England

Wheaton, Illinois 60187, U.S.A.

© The Theosophical Publishing House, 1963

First Edition   1963
Revised and enlarged Second Edition,   1970

SBN 7229-7350-0   (U.K.)
ISBN 0-8356-7350-2 (U.S.A.)

PRINTED IN INDIA

At the Vasanta Press, The Theosophical Society, Adyar, Madras 20

DEDICATION

This work is dedicated to Philo Judaeus,
the great Alexandrian Sage.

ACKNOWLEDGEMENTS

I gratefully acknowledge the valued assistance in the production of this work received from my wife, Sandra, my valued literary assistant, Myra G. Fraser and my friend, Nell K. Griffith.

THE HIDDEN WISDOM AND WHY
IT IS CONCEALED

THE greatest degree of power which occult science can bestow is to be derived from knowledge of the unity and interaction between the Macrocosm and the microcosm, the Universe and man. " The mystery of the earthly and mortal man is after the mystery of the supernal and immortal One ", wrote Eliphas Levi. Lao Tzu also expresses this truth in his words: " The Universe is a man on a large scale."

The whole Universe with all its parts, from the highest plane down to physical Nature, is regarded as being interlocked, interwoven, to make a single whole—one body, one organism, one power, one life, one consciousness, all cyclically evolving under one law. The " organs " or parts of the Macrocosm, though apparently separated in space and plane of manifestation, are in fact harmoniously inter-related, intercommunicative and continually interactive.

According to this revelation of occult philosophy the Zodiac, the Galaxies and their component Systems, and the planets with their kingdoms and planes of Nature, elements, Orders of Beings, radiating forces, colours and notes, are not only parts of a co-ordinated whole and in " correspondence " or mutual resonance with each other, but also—which is of profound significance—have their re-presentations within man himself. This system of correspondences is in operation throughout the whole of the microcosm, from the Monad to the mortal flesh, including the parts of the mechanism of consciousness, or vehicles and their *chakras*,[1] by means of which the Spirit of man is manifested throughout his whole nature, varying in degree according to the stage of evolutionary development. *The human being who discovers this truth could enter the power aspect of the Universe and tap any one of these forces. He would then become endowed with almost irresistible influence over both Nature and his fellow men.*

[1] q.v. Glossary.

H. P. Blavatsky writes: [1]

" The danger was that such doctrines as the Planetary Chain, or the seven Races, at once give a clue to the seven-fold nature of man, for each principle is correlated to a plane, a planet, and a race, and the human principles are, on every plane, correlated to seven-fold occult forces, those of the higher planes being of tremendous power. So that any septenary division at once gives a clue to tremendous occult powers, the abuse of which would cause incalculable evil to humanity; a clue which is, perhaps, no clue to the present generation —especially to Westerns, protected as they are by their very blindness and ignorant materialistic disbelief in the occult—but a clue which would, nevertheless, have been very real in the early centuries of the Christian era to people fully convinced of the reality of occultism, and entering a cycle of degradation which made them rife for abuse of occult powers and sorcery of the worst description.

" The documents were concealed, it is true, but the knowledge itself and its actual existence was never made a secret of by the Hierophants of the Temples, wherein the MYSTERIES have ever been made a discipline and stimulus to virtue. This is very old news, and was repeatedly made known by the great Adepts, from Pythagoras and Plato down to the Neo-Platonists. It was the new religion of the Nazarenes that wrought a change—for the worse—in the policy of centuries."

In his *Yoga Aphorisms*, Patanjali writes: [2]

" The [successful] ascetic acquires complete control over the elements by concentrating his mind upon the five classes of properties in the manifested universe; as, first, those of gross or phenomenal character; second, those of form; third, those of subtle quality; fourth, those susceptible of distinction as to light, action, and inertia; fifth, those having influence in their various degrees for the production of fruits through their effects upon the mind.

" From the acquirement of such power over the elements there results to the ascetic various perfections, to wit, the power to project his inner-self into the smallest atom, to expand his inner-self to the size of the largest body, to render his material body light or heavy

---

[1] q.v. *The Secret Doctrine*, Vol. I, (Adyar Ed.), pp. 54-58, H. P. Blavatsky.
[2] q.v. *Yoga Aphorisms of Patanjali*, Book III, slokas 45-47.

at will, to give indefinite extension to his astral body or its separate members, to exercise an irresistible will upon the minds of others, to obtain the highest excellence of the material body, and the ability to preserve such excellence when obtained.

"Excellence of the material body consists in color, loveliness of form, strength, and density."

This knowledge of the relationship between Universe and man is also part of the secret wisdom of Kabbalism, which teaches that in the chain of being everything is magically contained within everything else. Where one stands, there stand all the worlds; what is below is above, what is inside is outside and, in addition, ceaselessly acts upon all that exists. Kabbalism thus stresses the interrelationship of all worlds and levels of being according to exact, though unfathomable, laws. All things, moreover, possess their infinite depths which from every point may be contemplated.

Such is a portion of the wisdom which is said to be implicit— and, indeed, revealed under the veil of allegory—in the *Torah*.[1] This sacred book is for Kabbalists a revelation of the laws of the Cosmos and the intimate and active relationship between the parts of the Cosmos, the Spirit of man, and the vehicles in which that Spirit is incarnate. The history of the Jews forms a foundation upon which the edifice of this secret knowledge is erected. Modern Christian theology would seem to have fallen into the grievous error of regarding the sub-structure of metaphoricised history as a total and divinely inspired revelation of God's guidance to mankind.

The mission of the Jews and the purpose of the erudite and initiated authors of the Bible was, I submit, to preserve, to enunciate and to deliver to humanity this wisdom of the Chaldeo-Hebrew Sanctuaries. It is for this and not for lordship over the Earth, I suggest, that the Jews were a chosen people, a nation or " kingdom of priests "[2] in very truth. May not their tribulations have partly arisen from their neglect of this mission, and may not their earthly wanderings and centuries of physical homelessness have followed upon and resulted from their departure from their true Sanctuary and the real purpose for which they were " chosen " ?[3] Happily

---

[1] *Torah* (Heb.): "Law". The *Pentateuch* or Law of Moses.
[2] *Ex.* 19:6.   [3] *Gal.* 6:7.

the light still shines, however deeply veiled, in and through this marvellous record of the Scriptures of the Hebrew Race.

The task of unveiling the hidden truth demands some knowledge of Cosmogenesis, of the emanation of the Universe from the Absolute, the finite from the Infinite, and of the successive cycles, major and minor, of involution and evolution. In addition, both knowledge of the Symbolical Language, its purposes, methods and classical symbols, and the faculty of analysing and interpreting historical metaphors, are necessary to open the casket containing the treasures of concealed wisdom—the Holy Bible itself.

INTERPRETATION OF TEXTS

" Every text relates to, and has to be rendered from, one of the following standpoints:

1. The Realistic Plane of Thought
2. The Idealistic
3. The purely Divine or Spiritual

" The other planes too far transcend the average consciousness, especially of the materialistic mind, to admit of their being even symbolized in terms of ordinary phraseology. There is no purely *mythical* element in any of the ancient religious texts; but the mode of thought in which they were originally written has to be found out and closely adhered to during the process of interpretation. For it is symbolical, the archaic mode of thought; emblematical, a later though very ancient mode of thought; parabolical or allegorical; hieroglyphical; or again logogrammical, the most difficult method of all; every letter, as in the Chinese language, representing a whole word. Thus, almost every proper name, whether in the *Vedas*, the *Book of the Dead*, or, to a certain degree, in the *Bible*, is composed of such logograms. No one not initiated into the mystery of the Occult religious logography can presume to know what a name in any ancient fragment means, before he has mastered the meaning of every letter that composes it. How is it to be expected that the merely profane thinker, however great may be his erudition in orthodox symbolism, so to say—i.e., in that symbolism which can never get out of the old grooves of solar myth and sexual worship—how is it to be expected that the profane scholar should penetrate into the arcana behind the veil? One who deals with the husk or shell of the dead-letter, and devotes himself to the kaleidoscopic transformation of barren word-symbols, can never expect to get beyond the vagaries of modern Mythologists."

The Secret Doctrine, H. P. BLAVATSKY

"WHERE the Word found that things done according to the history could be adapted to these mystical senses, he made use of them, concealing from the multitude the deeper meaning; but where in the narrative of the development of super-sensual things, there did not follow the performance of those certain events which were already indicated by the mystical meaning, the Scripture interwove in the history the account of some event that did not take place, sometimes what could not have happened; sometimes what could, but did not."

> *De Principiis*, Origen, Christian philosopher and Biblical scholar, famed for his teaching at Alexandria and Caesarea (c. 185—C. 254 A. D.).

"What man of sense will agree with the statement that the first, second and third days in which the *evening* is named and the *morning*, were without sun, moon, and stars, and the first day without a heaven? What man is found such an idiot as to suppose that God planted trees in Paradise, in Eden, like a husbandman, and planted therein the tree of life, perceptible to the eyes and senses, which gave life to the eater thereof; and another tree which gave to the eater thereof a knowledge of good and evil? I believe that every man must hold these things for images, under which the hidden sense lies concealed."

> Origen: Huet., *Origeniana*, 167, Franck, p. 142.

"Every time that you find in our books a tale the reality of which seems impossible, a story which is repugnant to both reason and common sense, then be sure that the tale contains a profound allegory veiling a deeply mysterious truth; and the greater the absurdity of the letter, the deeper the wisdom of the spirit."

> Moses Maimonedes, Jewish theologian, historian, Talmudist, philosopher and physician (1135-1205 A. D.).

"Woe. . . to the man who sees in the Thorah, i.e., Law, only simple recitals and ordinary words! Because, if in truth it only contained these, we would even today be able to compose a Thorah much more worthy of admiration. . . . The recitals of the Thorah

are the vestments of the Thorah. Woe to him who takes this garment for the Thorah itself! ... There are some foolish people
who seeing a man covered with a beautiful garment, carry their
regard no further, and take the garment for the body, whilst there
exists a still more precious thing, which is the soul. ... The Wise,
the servitors of the Supreme King, those who inhabit the heights
of Sinai, are occupied only with the soul, which is the basis of all
the rest, which is Thorah itself; and in the future time they will be
prepared to contemplate the Soul of that soul (i.e. the Deity) which
breathes in the Thorah."

Zohar III, 152b. (Soncino Ed. Vol. V, p. 211).

"Rabbi Simeon said: 'If a man looks upon the Torah as merely
a book presenting narratives and everyday matters, alas for him!
Such a Torah, one treating with everyday concerns, and indeed a
more excellent one, we too, even we, could compile. More than
that, in the possession of the rulers of the world there are books of
even greater merit, and these we could emulate if we wished to compile
some such Torah. But the Torah, in all of its words, holds supernal
truths and sublime secrets.'"

Zohar III, 152a.

"Like unto a beautiful woman hidden in the interior of a palace
who, when her friend and beloved passes by, opens for a moment a
secret window, and is only seen by him: then again retires and disappears for a long time; so the doctrine shows herself only to the elect,
but also not even to these always in the same manner. In the beginning, deeply veiled, she only beckons to the one passing, with her
hand; it simply depends (on himself) if in his understanding he perceives this gentle hint. Later she approaches him somewhat nearer,
and whispers to him a few words, but her countenance is still hidden
in the thick veil, which his glances cannot penetrate. Still later
she converses with him, her countenance covered with a thinner
veil. After he has accustomed himself to her society, she finally
shows herself to him face to face, and entrusts him with the innermost
secrets of her heart (Sod)."

Zohar II, 99a (Soncino Ed. Vol. III, p. 301).

"The shell, the white, and the yolk form the perfect egg. The shell protects the white and the yolk, and the yolk feeds upon the white; and when the white has vanished, the yolk, in the form of the fledged bird, breaks through the shell and presently soars into the air. Thus does the static become the dynamic, the material the spiritual.

"If the shell is the exoteric principle and the yolk the esoteric, what then is the white? The white is the food of the second, the accumulated wisdom of the world centring round the mystery of growth, which each single individual must absorb before he can break the shell. The transmutation of the white, by the yolk, into the fledgling is the secret of secrets of the entire Qabalistic philosophy."

The Secret Wisdom of the Qabalah, J. F. C. Fuller.

"Having taken the Upanishad as the bow, as the great weapon, let him place on it the arrow, sharpened by devotion! Then having drawn it with a thought directed to that which is, hit the mark, O Friend, namely, that which is Indestructible! Om [1] is the bow, the Self is the arrow, Brahman [2] is called the aim. It is to be hit by a man who is not thoughtless, and then as the arrow becomes one with the target, he will become one with Brahman."

Mundaka Upanishad, II.

"Know the Self as the Lord of the chariot and the body as, verily, the chariot; know the intellect as the charioteer and the mind as, verily, the reins.

"The senses, they say, are the horses; the objects of sense the paths (they range over); (the self) associated with the body, the senses and the mind—wise men declare—is the enjoyer.

"He who has no understanding, whose mind is always unrestrained, his senses are out of control, as wicked horses are for a charioteer.

"He, however, who has understanding, whose mind is always restrained, his senses are under control, as good horses are for a charioteer.

[1] OM or AUM: The name of the triple Deity. A syllable of affirmation, invocation and divine benediction.

[2] Brahman (Sk.): The impersonal, supreme and incognisable Principle of the Universe from the Essence of which all emanates and into which all returns.

" He, however, who has no understanding, who has no control over his mind (and is) ever impure, reaches not that goal but comes back into mundane life.

" He, however, who has understanding, who has control over his mind and (is) ever pure, reaches that goal from which he is not born again.

" He who has the understanding for the driver of the chariot and controls the rein of his mind, he reaches the end of the journey, that supreme abode of the all-pervading."

> The *Kathopanishad* 1-3-3 to 1-3-9, Dr. Radha-krishnan's translation from *The Principal Upanishads.*

" And the disciples came, and said unto him, Why speakest thou unto them in parables?

" He answered and said unto them, Because it is given unto you to know the mysteries of the kingdom of heaven, but to them it is not given. . . .

" But blessed are your eyes, for they see: and your ears, for they hear."

> *Matt.* 13: 10, 11 and 16.

" Whoso eateth my flesh, and drinketh my blood, hath eternal life; and I will raise him up at the last day.

" For my flesh is meat indeed, and my blood is drink indeed.

" He that eateth my flesh, and drinketh my blood, dwelleth in me, and I in him.

" As the living Father hath sent me, and I live by the Father: so he that eateth me, even he shall live by me."

> *Jn.* 6: 54-57.

" The early Genesis accounts of the creation, Adam and Eve and the Fall of man contain truths of a religious nature which do not depend for their validity upon historical or scientific confirmation. Such accounts expressed truths of a timeless nature. They were myths, teaching spiritual truths by allegories."

> From a Sermon by The Most Reverend Dr. Frank Woods, Anglican Archbishop of Melbourne, speaking at St. Paul's Cathedral on the 18th February, 1961.

Support for a symbolical reading of the Bible is gained by comparison of the promises of perpetual prosperity and divine protection[1] made by God to Abram and his successors with the subsequent defeats by invaders, exile under their commands in Babylon and Egypt, and the destruction of the Temples of King Solomon and King David. To these misfortunes may be added the later fate of the Hebrew people, including their miseries and homelessness since the *Diaspora* and the holocaust of German Jews under Nazi rule. This marked divergence between divine assurances and promises on the one hand and what actually happened on the other provides strong grounds for a non-literal reading of the Scriptures.

The alternative of a total rejection of the *Pentateuch* as being, on the surface, unworthy of serious consideration would, I suggest, involve the loss of invaluable treasures of wisdom which are revealed when the veil of allegory and symbol is removed.

GEOFFREY HODSON

[1] *Gen.* 17:2,5-8; 26:2-5; 28:13-16.

This work is founded upon the King James Bible and all quotations and references are taken from that version.

AUTHOR'S PREFACE

In common, I believe, with the majority of fellow Christians, in my early years I accepted the Bible as the inspired word of God, a direct message from Deity to man. Later, however, a more critical approach to the Scriptures revealed incredibilities, impossibilities, and even obscenities, which both shocked and repelled me. Finding myself unable either to ignore these barriers to belief or to adopt a tolerant, uncritical acceptance of Holy Writ, two alternatives presented themselves to me. One was to discard entirely the orthodox concept of the Bible as an error-free and infallible source of spiritual wisdom and moral counsel, and the other to undertake a detailed study of the whole text. This latter course was chosen, and in this decision I was largely influenced by the discovery that many of the difficulties arising from a literal reading disappeared if much of the Bible was regarded as allegorical.

Many erudite scholars, I found, affirmed that the authors of World Scriptures deliberately concealed beneath cleverly constructed veils of allegory and symbol the profound truths which they had discovered by direct research. This enveiling was enforced upon them because such knowledge would inevitably bestow very great spiritual, intellectual, psychical and super-normal physical powers. Since these were, and still are, subject to grave misuse—the evils of priestcraft and mental domination, for example—it became necessary to do all possible to make available to the trustworthy and to conceal from the profane the wisdom and knowledge of which the authors had become possessed. For this purpose they invented a special category of literature which differs from ordinary writing in that, with some historical fact as foundation, it is largely composed of allegories, symbols and certain key words. These were given an agreed universal significance, the whole constituting a cipher by means of which the ageless Wisdom Religion,[1] theoretical and practical, was with reasonable safeguards made available to mankind. Such, I learned, were the origin, the nature and the purpose of the Sacred Language.[2]

On making the discovery that parts of the Bible are allegorical,[3] I began to apply the various keys—also to be found in ancient and modern literature on the subject—to many of the books of the Bible. The rewards—the resolving of many textual difficulties and the gaining of a philosophy of life, spiritual, intellectual and pre-eminently practical—have been so immeasurably rich that I have felt moved to share them in book form. This first Volume is largely devoted to a consideration of the Sacred Language itself and the presentation of certain classical keys of interpretation, with some of the results of their application to Scriptural stories, including especially the life of Christ. Naturally, no claim is made for anything like a complete and error-free presentation. Care has, however, been taken neither to overstress a possible symbolical significance, nor to read into a narrative more than is inherent within it or was presumably present in the minds of the authors. Major interpretations have been both suggested by and compared with the writings of Sages and philosophers, including Hebrew scholars. This comparison was made in order to test the validity of such an approach, and its value in providing a key to the Scriptures and mythologies of ancient peoples. The quotations which precede this Preface will indicate some of these literary sources, whilst the Introduction and the first chapter give a fuller exposition of the central idea and its applications to modern theological and world problems.

One of the most readily available of such sources, I have found, is the literature of the Theosophical Society and, indeed, Theosophy itself so far as it has been made available to mankind. The Neo-Platonists of the early centuries of the Christian era, notably Ammonius Saccus and his disciples, coined the word *Theosophia*, meaning Divine Wisdom.[4] For them, Theosophy connoted the totality of the

---

[1] The one religion which underlies all creeds.

[2] q.v. *A Dictionary of The Sacred Language of All Scriptures and Myths*, G.A. Gaskell. George Allen & Unwin Ltd.

[3] q.v. *Mk.*, 4:11, *Gal.* 4:24.

[4] *Sk. Brahma Vidya*, the wisdom of *Brahma*.

revealed wisdom and discovered knowledge allotted to man throughout the ages. The use of this source is mentioned here to explain,
should it be necessary, the constant reference to theosophical literature, ancient and modern, and the adoption of some of its terminology.
For both brevity and accuracy of presentation Sanskrit words are
occasionally employed, but in all cases brief expositions of doctrines
and full translations of Sanskrit words are given as footnotes.

Thus studying the Bible, I have found that many of the difficulties and discrepancies which had hitherto proved so perplexing
no longer exist. May those who are similarly perplexed and similarly seeking find in these Volumes solutions of their problems and
the restoration of their faith.

GEOFFREY HODSON

AUCKLAND,
New Zealand.
1963.

INTRODUCTION

A LARGE number of writers in both ancient [1] and modern times have affirmed that spiritual wisdom and a practical philosophy of life have always been available to mankind and that, however deeply hidden, they are to be found in the Scriptures of the great World Faiths. Man, they state, has but to remove the concealing veils of allegory, parable and symbol to discover a knowledge which can bestow serenity of mind and heart and lead to spiritual illumination.

Mere folk tales and primitive superstitions apart, the Scriptures and mythologies of ancient peoples may, it is claimed, be similarly approached. At least two views exist, however, concerning their origin. According to one of these, world myths gradually developed as explanations of the phenomena of Nature. Primitive races, who possessed little or no scientific knowledge, personified the forces of Nature and dramatised their interactions. Such tales may be thought of as folk myths in contra-distinction to those based upon historical, or presumedly historical, foundations.

The second view is that many of these ancient stories were given deep cosmogonical, religious, psychological and moral significance by poets, seers and prophets who later arose within the nations. Aeschylus, for example, thus relied upon Greek myth and legend for many of his plots, as also did Sophocles and Euripides, amongst others. In this way many archaic legends were both preserved and vitalised, having become imbued with religious or philosophic meanings. Initiates [2] of the various occult schools and the Mystery Religions

[1] St. Paul, Origen and other early Church Fathers; Kabbalists, ancient, medieval, and modern. The Neo-Platonic School, founded in 193 A.D. by Ammonius Saccus, included Alexandrian philosophers who sought to interpret the Bible according to a system of allegory and symbol and were, in consequence, named Analogeticists.

[2] Initiate. From the Latin *Initiatus*. The designation of anyone who was received into or had revealed to him the secrets and mysteries of occult philosophy. q.v. Part VI of Volume I.

of the older civilisations are also said to have deliberately refashion-
ed the stories into vehicles for the transmission to later races of
their knowledge of cosmogony, cyclic involution and evolutions,[1] and
the true nature and destiny of man. Modern scientists have also
found in ancient myths appropriate symbols for the subtle mental processes they study and attempt to elucidate. Freud, for example, used
the phrase "Oedipus complex", whilst the term "Achilles' Heel"
is sometimes employed to indicate vulnerability. Jung, in his turn,
found in the ancient stories symbolic archetypes of human responses.

In these various ways the religions and philosophies of the
ancients prove profitable to the modern student, whilst those possessed
of knowledge of the Sacred Language and the keys of interpretation[2]
recognise ideas which are found to be common to all World Faiths,
exoteric and esoteric. The universal use of symbols with which to
portray those ideas makes them readily available; for the meaning
of the symbols used are found to be constant, as constant also are the
doctrines which they reveal. Thus, whilst ancient superstitions and
magical practices, and the instinctive personification and dramatisa-
tion of natural phenomena by primitive peoples, are recognised,
World Scriptures and mythologies may legitimately be regarded
as rich mines of the Ageless Wisdom. On occasion throughout this
work, therefore, parallels are drawn between Biblical statements and
the same ideas appearing in different forms in other sacred writings.

The value of this approach to World Scriptures becomes evident
when the keys of interpretation are applied to the Bible. Success
has, however, been rendered difficult by at least three prevalent
practices. The first of these is to mistake the veils for the truths
which they both conceal and reveal. The second is to require the
acceptance as fact of much that is purely allegorical and, indeed,
in some cases incredible.[3] The third is the insistence by some Christian denominations upon unquestioning belief in dogmas, based
upon a literal reading of certain passages of the Bible, as essential to
the salvation of man here and hereafter. Unfortunately this is
carried to still greater lengths by *ex cathedra* pronouncements that

[1] q.v. Part IV of Volume I.
[2] q.v. Part II of Volume I.
[3] q.v. Pp. 93-97 of Volme I.

failure to affirm implicit belief in stated dogmas may lead to excommunication, and even to eternal damnation.

These trends observable in orthodox Christianity may be regarded as particularly harmful at the present period in world history; for as a result of them the attention of Christians is diverted from eternal verities. These especially include the supreme importance of the search for and discovery of the Divine Presence *within* man, " Christ in you, the hope of glory," [1] and of the fact that *the Divinity in all men is one and the same*. When the spiritual unity between all members of the human Race is fully recognised aggressive competition, organised crime and wars of conquest become impossibilities. The spiritually darkened, war-threatened and competitively divided condition of humanity today may well be amongst the tragic consequences of the long continued imposition by the spiritual Heads of the Christian Faith—doubtless with the highest motives and out of consideration for the spiritual welfare of the people—of dogmas based upon the literal reading of Biblical allegories; for when accepted and applied to life such dogmas inevitably affect international, national and personal relationships. They may be partly responsible for the divided condition of Christianity and even of humanity itself.

How, then, may the veils of allegory and symbol be drawn aside and the hidden wisdom revealed? This work—amongst many others upon the subject in ancient and modern literature—offers both general and detailed answers to that most vital question. Briefly stated, those who seek to discover the wisdom underlying inspired allegories should proceed somewhat as follows:—

(*a*) Determine to discover essential truths.

(*b*) Mentally utter a cry for interior light,[2] with the single motive of becoming an ever more efficient servant of humanity.

(*c*) Clear the mind of the tendency to regard the literal reading as the only true and ecclesiatically permissible one.

[1] *Col.* 1 : 27.

[2] *Lk.* 11 : 9, 10.

"And I say unto you, Ask, and it shall be given you; seek, and ye shall find; knock, and it shall be opend to you.

" For every one that asketh receiveth; and he that seeketh findeth; and to him that knocketh it shall be opened."

(*d*) Practice meditation in order to develop the intuitive per- ception necessary for the discovery of the successive layers of revelation concealed beneath Scriptural alle- gories, ancient myths and some traditional fairy tales.

(*e*) Study the writings of notable exponents of the Sacred Language.

(*f*) Learn the major keys and the method of interpretation, and practice until proficient the science of their appli- cation to the elucidation of world Scriptures and mythologies. As stated in the Author's Preface, care must always be taken neither to overstress a possible symbolical significance, nor to read into a narrative more than is inherent within it or was presumably present in the minds of the authors.

The task of unveiling was undertaken in this age with great insight and erudition by Madame H. P. Blavatsky, co-Foundress of the Theosophical Society. Her aptly titled books, *Isis Unveiled* and *The Secret Doctrine*,[1] give the traditional keys and many inter- pretations of world allegories. G. A. Gaskell has made a magnificent contribution to the subject by producing a *Dictionary of the Sacred Language of All Scriptures and Myths*.[2] Fabre d'Olivet's *The Hebrew Tongue Restored*[3] and F. J. Mayers' *The Unknown God*[4] advance the Kabbalistic keys and apply them to the Book of *Genesis*. Indebted- ness is here acknowledged to these and other standard works.

The literature which proceeded from the Neo-Platonists of Alexandria, especially the writings of Philo Judaeus (approximately 30 B.C. to 45 A.D.) to whom this work is dedicated, is also a valuable source of information. The interpretations of the symbolism of the Bible which he gives are very remarkable. The animals, birds, reptiles, trees and places mentioned in the Bible are all said by him to be " allegories of conditions of the soul, of faculties, dispositions or passions; the useful plants were allegories of virtues, the noxious of the affections of the unwise, and so on through the mineral kingdom;

---

[1] Theosophical Publishing House, Adyar, Madras, India.

[2] Geo. Allen & Unwin Ltd.

[3] C. P. Putnam's Sons, New York and London.

[4] Thomas's Publications Ltd., Birmingham, England.

through heaven, earth and stars; through fountains and rivers, fields and dwellings; through metals, substances, arms, clothes, ornaments, furniture, the body and its parts, the sexes, and our outward condition." [1]

As previously stated, the disciples of Ammonius Saccus were called Analogeticists because of their practice of interpreting sacred Scriptures and mythologies by a principle of analogy and correspondence, also found in both the kabbalistic system and the esoteric philosophy of the East. Thus studied, many books of the Old and New Testaments are found to contain hidden knowledge of the greatest value to mankind; for, in addition to its content of metaphysical teachings of profound significance, the Bible also indicates the existence of a pathway of hastened evolution and the means by which special powers for the service of humanity may be attained. These powers can, however, be misused to bring grave harm upon their possessors and their victims. The more metaphysical teachings in the Bible are therefore, as also previously stated, written in an allegorical language which conceals, even while it reveals, power-bestowing knowledge. The Lord Christ referred to this pathway of hastened evolution as " the narrow way " which is entered through " the strait gate ".[2] Isaiah wrote of " The way of holiness ".[3] Hinduism similarly teaches of the " Razor-edged Path " and Buddhism of the " Noble Eightfold Path ". This is the Path of discipleship and Initiation which leads within a relatively short space of time to Salvation,[4] *Moksha*,[5] *Nirvana*.[6]

Since the essentials, the procedures and the pitfalls on the narrow way, as also the powers attained by those who tread it, are portrayed by the authors of the Bible, interpretations of Biblical allegories from the point of view of the path of hastened unfoldment are included in this work. Volume I contains an introduction to the Symbolical Language, some keys of interpretation and some examples of their

---

[1] *Dictionary of Christian Biography.*

[2] *Matt.* 7: 13, 14.

[3] *Is.* 35 : 8.

[4] *Salvation*—realization of oneness with God. (Christianity).

[5] *Moksha*—Liberation from the delusion of self-separateness. (Hinduism).

[6] *Nirvana*—conscious absorption in the one Life of the Cosmos or absolute consciousness. (Buddhism).

application to various Scriptural passages. In Volumes II and III interpretations of the Book of *Genesis* are offered, whilst in succeeding Volumes most of the remaining Books of the Bible will be similarly considered.

CONTENTS

PART ONE

MANKIND'S QUEST FOR LIGHT

PART TWO

THE MYSTERIES OF THE KINGDOM

XXX

PART THREE

AN ALPHABET OF
THE SACRED LANGUAGE

PART FOUR

THE CYCLIC PATHWAY OF FORTHGOING
AND RETURN

THE PARABLE OF THE PRODIGAL SON AS AN EXPOSITION OF THE
LAW OF CYCLES

PART FIVE

THE LIFE OF CHRIST SPIRITUALLY
INTERPRETED

xxxi

PART SIX

" THE STRAIT GATE " AND " THE NARROW WAY "

PART ONE

MANKIND'S QUEST FOR LIGHT

CHAPTER I

CHRISTIANITY AND THE MODERN WORLD

THE decision taken by orthodox Christianity to concentrate upon the Bible as history rather than as a blend of history and allegory has, it is submitted, been responsible for disastrous results. When, furthermore, despite affronts to the intellect and a sense of propriety, it is insisted that the Bible is divinely inspired from beginning to end, then the adverse results become far-reaching indeed. Many moral evils may not unjustly be regarded as consequences of this choice. Indeed, such continued affronts cause some people to turn away from the Bible, from the religion founded upon it and, unfortunately, from the morality which Christianity inculcates. When faced with the piling of the incredible upon the impossible in the Old Testament, and its portrayal of the Supreme Deity as an arrogant, ruthless and cruel despot,[1] many people fall into atheism, agnosticism, cynicism and indulgence in vice. When, in addition, the Bible is found to contain accounts of frequent indulgence in illicit, and even incestuous, sexual relationships, the Christian Faith can come to be regarded as encouraging such practices, gross immorality being the unfortunate result.

The existence of the above evils, amongst many others, points to the urgent necessity for a greatly revised reading of the Bible. If, however, many of the anomalies in the Old Testament can be shown to be revelations, under the veil of symbology, of profound spiritual, metaphysical and psychological truths, then the importance of the study of the Scriptures from this point of view at once emerges.

Ignoring impossibilities and accounts of moral delinquencies, blind faith in the Bible, together with the fear of damnation and the hope of salvation after death, bring large numbers of people to religion.

[1] See footnote 3, p. 88.

Nevertheless, truly thoughtful minds cannot fail to be repelled by scriptural affronts to reason and propriety. These considerations accentuate the great need for an interpretation of the Bible as a repository of profound wisdom symbolically portrayed. Such an interpretation would meet the objections inevitably aroused by a literal reading with all its consequences, so obviously harmful to mankind.

Certain portions of the text of the Bible, if taken literally, cannot possibly be regarded as in any way conducive to a high moral standard. In *Genesis* XII:10-20, for example, Abraham passes his wife off as his sister that Pharaoh may possess her. His motive in doing so was that his life might be spared and he be greatly rewarded. Isaac transgresses similarly and for the same reason, as stated in *Genesis* XXVI:6-11. In this latter case the Lord God blessed Isaac and he becomes rich and prospers. *Genesis* XXVII:1-45, recounts a most deplorable example of deliberate deceit by Jacob, who later becomes a favoured patriarch under the inspiration of the Lord.

In *Judges* IV:17-22 Jael, the wife of Heber, invites Sisera to enter her tent on the pretext of hiding him, and whilst he slept she took a hammer and with it drove a tent peg right through his temple and into the ground, thereby slaying him. In 2 *Samuel* XI: 2-27, is related the all too familiar story of the adultery of David, the Lord's anointed, with Bathsheba, the wife of Uriah. In Chapter XII the Lord pardons David, and King Solomon is born of this union.

Passages are also to be found which portray the Lord God as capable of anger and Himself ready to destroy, and to encourage his servants to destroy, whole peoples other than Israelites. One such example is to be found in *Deuteronomy* IX:14:

The suggestions in verses five, six and seven of the sixth Chapter of *Genesis* that the Supreme Deity could conceive of an imperfect plan which failed, experience wrath at that failure, revengefully decide to destroy with insensate cruelty " both man, and beast, and the creeping thing, and the fowls of the air ",[1] in their literal reading are surely quite unacceptable. The assertion that God could be guilty of such actions and could be moved to make the later promise

[1] *Gen.* 6:7.

not to " curse the ground any more for man's sake" [1] or " again smite any more every thing living ",[1] is either an erroneous attribution to the Deity of conduct of which even man would not be guilty, or else a deliberately constructed blind for the concealment of an underlying truth.

The concept is inconceivable, surely, that there could be in existence a single, extra-cosmic, personal God Who could fail and then be destructively wrathful at the wicked conduct of the products of His own work.   Such a conclusion is strengthened by the affirmation that man was created in God's own image.[2]   It is similarly, inconceivable that the conjoined *Elohim* (translated as God in *Genesis*) could be capable either of error in the planning and fulfilment of Their cosmic functions or of wrath at a failure which was solely attributable to Themselves.   In the presence of such affronts to human reason, the concept of the use of a special category of literature known as the Sacred Language, as previously defined, is surely preferable to total unbelief in such Biblical inconsistencies and errors as a literal reading necessitates.   The consequent possible rejection of the Bible as a whole, with its affirmation of the existence of a Supreme Being as the Directive Intelligence in Nature would indeed be a very great loss.   The great scientist, Dr. Albert Einstein, evidently felt himself to be under no necessity to make the latter rejection, expressing his view that " That deeply emotional conviction of the presence of a *superior reasoning power* [italics mine, author] which is revealed in the incomprehensible Universe, forms my idea of God." Nevertheless, the actions attributed to the Deity in the verses under review certainly do not present Him in the guise of a " superior reasoning power ".

Since the episodes are unacceptable in their literal form, the idea receives support that the authors of the Pentateuch were spiritually instructed men, writing to evoke wonder and so to start enquiry, to preserve, to conceal from the profane, and yet to reveal to the worthy, the wisdom which they had been taught.

These and other passages are considered in later volumes of this work. Interpretations are there offered which, if accepted,

[1] *Gen.* 8: 21.
[2] *Gen.* 1: 26, 27.

remove the indications of guilt and reveal a profound wisdom concealed beneath the veil of allegory, and even incongruity.

Those who regard the Scriptures and Mythologies of the world
as a combination of history, allegory and symbol, point out that full
answers to these and other pressing questions concerning human
life, experiences and destiny are contained beneath the surface of
scriptural writings. They further state that such answers are there
fully given as under-meanings, and that the relative impotence in the
presence of world evils so evident in the orthodox Christianity of
today is due to the official insistence upon belief in the Bible as divine,
verbal, revelation from *Genesis* to *Revelation*. Had orthodoxy been
willing to examine the Scriptures as parables revealing profound
spiritual truths and laws, instead of insisting that the text in its literal
reading is divine utterance and, therefore, absolute truth, it would
not have been subject to the charges made against it. When, furthermore, implicit belief in the letter of the Bible is stated to be essential
to the salvation of the soul, a natural repulsion from the acceptance
of dogmas, some of which contravene both fact and possibility, is
intensified.

SOME CRITICISMS LEVELLED AT CHRISTIANITY

A further charge levelled against modern Christianity is that
it fails to grip the mind and direct the life and conduct of modern
man; that it has proved impotent to influence favourably either
human conduct or the progress of world events in the first half of the
twentieth century, tragic as they have been for humanity. Is this
criticism justified? If it is, what then is wrong with the Christian
teaching and practice of today?

Whilst even the most devout Christians must admit—and surely
may do so without impiety—certain limitations, nevertheless there is
unquestionably a great deal to applaud in modern Christianity and
the conduct of Christian peoples, though there is also much to deplore.
In this twentieth century nations nominally Christian have, for
example, embarked upon unprovoked aggression. Other nations,
however, guided by a truly Christian spirit and at immeasurable
cost to themselves in men and material, have successfully resisted two
major attempts to conquer, impoverish and enslave humanity.

Furthermore, with the co-operation of non-Christian nations two great World Organisations have been formed to resist such wanton aggression, to preserve world peace, to combat vice and to give assistance to peoples in need. Both the League of Nations and U.N.O., formed for these purposes, have rendered very great service to humanity.

In addition to these far-reaching international and national activities on behalf of the human Race, an increasing number of individuals have embarked upon the search for truth, wisdom, knowledge and an understanding of the laws of life, material and spiritual. Many men of science are leading humanity in this search. In physics, astronomy, medicine, biology and psychology, the mechanistic view is giving place to vitalism, to affirmations of belief in the existence of both a Directive Intelligence in Nature and in a plan or aim in the evolution of life and form. Human conduct is, however, justly under criticism and Christianity as a great world religion cannot escape some responsibility for the conduct by which that criticism is aroused. Christian apologists reply that the responsibility is less with the Christian Faith than with modern man. They point out that it is impossible to assess the full value of Christianity because, in fact, it has never yet been collectively and thoroughly tried.

MAN'S MORAL DECLINE

This brings us to man himself. What are the chief charges brought against modern man, and more particularly against those six hundred and ninety millions or so living within the fold of Christendom? In addition to the one already stated, it is pointed out that in this period humanity has displayed a marked decline in morality. This decline has been made evident by aggressive wars, political corruption, and widespread criminality and vice. In economic and industrial fields also, in monopolies, trusts and cartels, in cut-throat competition based on the doctrine of " each for himself and the Devil take the hindmost ", modern man has adopted the law of the jungle. There are those who sell for profit raw materials and armaments to potentially hostile nations, and destroy greatly needed food in order to keep up prices. In addition, deliberate incitement to narcotic addiction and to alcoholic and sexual excesses has become almost universal.

Sir Richard Livingstone, a distinguished British scholar and educationalist, lecturing in Australia under the auspices of the National University in 1951, said: "This age has sex on the brain. It is decaying in consequence . . . . . . Today's students too often stumble through their education as if they were drunk, not knowing where they are, where they are going, or what they are doing. . . . . . Men no longer have moral driving force. Moral driving force— a belief in principles and a willingness to accept discipline and make sacrifices for them—is far more important to the survival of humanity than either knowledge or intelligence." Sir Richard continues: "If the world is ever to recover from its present sick uncertainty, it must be prepared to accept again principles which, in the broadest sense of the term, are Christian principles. Christianity is a doctrine of individual responsibility. The man who lives by it chooses a hard way, but a happy one. There is far too much emphasis on preparing young people to earn a living, and not nearly enough on teaching them how to live."

Such are some of the maladies afflicting modern man. Such is part of the problem confronting human beings, Christians and non-Christians alike, as a family of people on Earth. These are not only physical evils—they are also sicknesses of the soul. Living in the midst of them, man naturally seeks the appropriate source of healing, which ought to be found in religion. Most Western peoples turn, therefore, to the Christian religion and its official representatives. When the body is sick a doctor is consulted, and when the soul is sick hope lies with the priest and what he prescribes, namely spiritual light, healing grace and practical guidance in the conduct of life.

HAS CHRISTIANITY BEEN FULLY TRIED?

Critics say that this is where modern Christianity fails; that neither orthodox forms of Christianity nor their officials successfully answer the cry of the human soul for spiritual and intellectual light and understanding. The spiritualising and purifying influences which could cause man to forsake his evil ways are, it is claimed, not found in Western religion. This is severe criticism but, wherever the fault may lie, it cannot be truthfully denied that wickedness is indeed rampant upon Earth. One answer has already been advanced. It is that the Christian ideal had not been fully tried; that it is, in fact, constantly denied by the mode of life followed by many profess-ing Christians. The counsel and the example of Christ embodied in His life and in His words: " These things I command you, that ye love one another ",[1] and " as ye would that men should do to you, do ye also to them likewise ",[2] are ignored. In the economic and industrial fields it must be admitted that Christian civilisation is founded upon the satanic doctrines: " Each for himself and the Devil take the hindmost " and " I am not my brother's keeper." Few, indeed, accept and ratify Einstein's noble dictum: " Man is here for the sake of other men."

This indictment might be regarded as too sweeping, however, for whilst it is true of much collective action it is definitely not true of individual practice, which includes " the multitude of unparaded charities of men." Nevertheless it is still true that, apart from cer-tain religious Orders, Christianity has not been tried collectively. The modern world has, for example, been confronted with the pheno-mena of Hitler, Mussolini, and their successors in the international field; prevalent dishonesty in trading, including the peddling (espe-cially to young people) of narcotics, not infrequently given without charge to induce addiction; prostitution and white slavery; the open and almost exclusive pursuit of temporal pleasures; radio and movie entertainments and advertisements which, deliberately and for profit, incite to lawlessness, sensuality, sexuality and artificial standards of living—all these are widespread characteristics of modern Western civilisation.

The frank and deliberate choice of these evil practices as means of gaining power and wealth is, indeed, a denial of that spirituality which was taught by precept and example by the Founder of the Christian Faith. In the Sermon on the Mount He inculcated self-surrender, and exemplified it in His Nativity in poverty and by His voluntary acceptance of rejection, scorn and cruel death. The highest moral law, Our Lord said, imposed a complete surrender of self. This personal disinterestedness constitutes the tremendous

[1] *Jn.* 15:17.
[2] *Lk.* 6:31.

dynamic of the teaching of Jesus; but the modern mental attitude—
" self first and God afterwards, if I have time "—is indeed the reverse
of this ideal of Christlike selflessness.

Thomas á Kempis, even in his day,[1] saw this difficulty and
wrote these wonderful words:—" Know that the love of self doth
hurt thee more than anything else in the world.   With it everywhere
thou shalt bear a cross.   If thou seekest only thine own will and
pleasure, thou shalt never be quiet nor free from care, for in everything something shall be wanting."[2]   How true these words prove
to be today! In everything we possess (and how much we do possess)
something is wanting.   In all our wealth, our scientific progress,
inventions   and   mechanical   developments,   something   is   indeed
wanting.   That " something " is happiness, health, serenity and
peace based upon selflessness and obedience to moral law.

Associated with the decline in morality is the growth of cynicism,
deepening to bitterness, both of which stem from lost faith and broken
ideals.   Those who meet adversity with bitterness and who, when
tragedy and loss touch their lives, feel that there can be no God;
those who cry out for help and, failing to find it, in their despair
sink into disbelief in their religion, and even deny the existence of
God—all these people have not found in orthodox religion that
immovable rock upon which their beliefs and their lives can be sec-
urely founded.   This is a tragedy which Christianity—particularly
its doctrines of impersonal law [3] and of the divine Presence within
man,[4] and its ideal of universal love [5]—might have averted.   So far
it has not done so, at least for very large numbers of its followers.

MAN'S CRY FOR AID UNANSWERED

What answer has orthodox Christianity to offer to the natural
question: " Where has God been during the tragic events of our
times? Why did He not protect and save us from the afflictions with
which we have been visited? In what way have we deserved the
immeasurable sufferings which have been inflicted upon us in an age

[1] 1380-1471.
[2] The Imitation of Christ.
[3] Matt. 5: 18, Gal. 6:7.
[4] Jn. 14:20, 1 Cor. 3: 16 & 6: 19, 2 Cor 6: 16, Phil. 2: 13, Col. 1:27.
[5] Matt. 5:44, Jn. 15: 12, 13 & 17, 1 Peter 1: 22.

which has been so black with horrors? Where is the justice meted out by God to His children? Millions who were tortured and died prematurely were loving and good-living men and women. What had they done that they should have suffered so?" The orthodox reply, "It is God's will", makes of Him a monster to be adored through fear and potent to destroy. Receiving such an answer the modern mind, nurtured upon the science of the day, is inevitably repelled, and so rejects such a Deity and such answers to legitimate enquiries. Yet orthodox Christianity has no other answers to give and this, its critics say, is the reason for its impotence and for humanity's moral decline. If, as the Archbishop of Canterbury, Dr. Geoffrey Fisher, stated on November the 14th, 1958, half of the world is agnostic, the Church cannot escape some responsibility for this situation. Whilst government provides laws and means of ensuring obedience to them, and education provides knowledge and instruction concerning the ways in which further knowledge may be obtained, orthodoxy, except in certain closed Orders, does not encourage the interior search for direct experience of spiritual truths and laws. Christians are not taught systematic self-purification and elevation of consciousness as in *yoga*, or the science of realised union with God.

What else is charged against the Christian Faith and its Officials? In addition to the criticisms already noted, grave misgivings are also being expressed concerning the prevalent decline in the qualities of holiness and reverence. This is very tragic; for when a nation loses the sense of holiness and the quality of reverence, that nation becomes subservient to a stronger nation. In these days the decline in respect for womanhood and for the parental (especially the maternal) functions, and in reverence for the sacrament of marriage, is very marked. Sensuality and sexuality constitute very grave dangers to modern civilisation; for the loss in the active majority of a nation of the moral sense, and of the sense of the holy, leads to the downfall of that nation and to its subjection to a foreign power. This moral decline must be regarded as a very dangerous symptom. So fell Egypt, Greece and Rome.

A further adverse symptom consists of the division of Christian thought and conduct of life into two compartments, sacred and secular, Sunday and weekday, which is responsible for many ills. Ideally all life, with its work and achievement, is spiritual and this fact should be recognised day by day and hour by hour.

TREASON DARKENS THE TIMES

The greatest casualty of the Second World War has been described as the decline of loyalty. One quality of human nature, disloyalty, has manifested itself in an unusual degree in recent times. Indeed, a special term has come to be used for it, one with very evil connotations. That term is " fifth column ", meaning treason as a chosen policy. When, in 1936, General Emilio Mola announced that he would capture Madrid because he had four columns outside the city and a fifth column of sympathisers within, the world pounced on the phrase with the eagerness of a man who had been groping for an important word. The phrase was, in fact, a tocsin of calamity, as the subversion which followed demonstrates. What General Mola had done was to indicate the dimension of treason in our time. Other ages have had their individual traitors—men who, from faint-heartedness or hope of gain, betrayed their causes—but in the twentieth century, for the first time in history, men have banded together in millions in Movements like Nazism, Fascism and totalitarian Communism, dedicated to the purpose of betraying the institutions under which they live. Treason has become a vocation whose modern form is specifically the treason of ideas. This is indeed part of the darkness of these years.

Faithlessness in this and other forms finds expression in the prevalent low moral standard in public life, marked as it is by corruption. This is particularly evident in the sphere of politics, national and international. In a speech delivered during September 1951, Herbert Hoover, ex-President of the United States, said: " I sometimes wonder what the 56 Founding Fathers, from their invisible presence in our Congressional halls, would say about the procession of men in responsible offices who have come before its committees of this day . . . . of those who coquette with traitorship. . . . We have a cancerous growth of intellectual dishonesty in public life which is mostly behind the law. The issue today is decency in public life against indecency. . . . Our greatest danger is not from invasion by foreign armies. Our dangers are that we may commit suicide from within by complaisance of evil or by public tolerance of scandalous behaviour."

Whilst it is true that human nature is itself prone to these evils which, it is admitted, are not confined solely to Christendom, it is also true that one function of religious teaching and practice is to reduce them to a minimum by inspiring men to rise above them. If, however, instances of the prevalence of these evils are recorded in the Bible, and in a literal reading the Deity or His inspired representatives are there found to be encouraging some of them, those who inculcate a dead-letter reading of these and other passages cannot escape some responsibility for similar actions indulged in by people whose religion is founded upon the Bible. The author here repeats the opinion, however, that although it is not sufficiently followed, many Christian Institutions do inculcate a high morality. Christendom has, in fact, produced large numbers of magnificent men and women, many of whom have become great servants of humanity. It can safely be affirmed that many Churches and their Pastors, Sunday Schools and their teachers, Christian workers, parents and school teachers, do exercise moral restraint and, in particular, tend to encourage Christlike conduct and a high moral standard amongst their young people.

BLIND FAITH OR SPIRITUAL KNOWLEDGE?

Nevertheless the prevailing conditions referred to do, indeed, indicate that modern Christianity is in need of revitalisation. What, then, is absent? What is needed? The subject is immense, but in advance it may be said that Christianity suffered an irreparable loss when Gnosticism, in the *true* meaning of the word,[1] was proscribed. What is wanted is the gnosis, *i.e.*, direct knowledge. The emphasis in religion upon direct, interior spiritual experience and the interpretative reading of the Scriptures must be restored to replace blind faith, the literal reading of the Bible, dependence upon priests for salvation and for communion with God, and reliance upon lip service and outward observance. Direct interior experience—personal knowledge of the Divine within all Nature and all men—is of supreme

[1] *Gnosticism:* Esoteric, spiritual knowledge.

importance.   Direct guidance in its attainment is not easily available
in modern Christianity, which (save perhaps in certain closed Orders)
has lost much of its mystical element in these days.   Men and women
of prophetic vision are rare.   The appeal is rather to blind faith,
despite what has been described as " the piling of the incredible upon
the impossible " in both literal Scripture and imposed dogma.   If
laymen cannot believe, they are told to " try to believe ".   If they
still cannot believe, they can come to be regarded as ungodly.   The
paramount importance of interior illumination, of direct spiritual
experience, of teaching in the technique of meditation, greatly needs
to be recognised and stressed; their absence is a grave weakness of
modern Christianity.

DOES CHRISTIANITY SPEAK WITH ONE VOICE ?

The dividedness of the Christian Faith is regarded as another
of its great weaknesses.   In 1951 President Truman told a large
audience, the Washington Pilgrimage of American Churchmen,
that he had been unable to obtain agreement among religious groups
on a common statement of faith in order to meet the Communist
threat.   " I have asked them," said Mr. Truman, " to join in one
common act which will affirm those religious and moral principles
on which all agree.   I am sorry to say that it has not yet been possible
to bring the religious faiths together for this purpose of bearing witness
that God is the way of truth and peace.   Even the Christian churches
have not yet found themselves able to say with one voice that Christ
is their Master and Redeemer and the source of their strength against
the hosts of irreligion and the danger of world catastrophe."   However, in 1959 Pope John XXIII issued an invitation to the Churches
of the Catholic Faith to collaborate with him in removing barriers
which divide them and drawing together in a spirit of co-operation
for the service of humanity.   It is fervently hoped that such efforts
will succeed, for Christianity cannot reach its highest effectiveness
as long as it continues to be divided into so many sects that, despite
the formation and the efforts of the World Council of Churches, whole-
hearted collaboration for the common good is difficult to obtain.
This weakness is increased when the claim is made for certain denominations that they alone represent true, authoritative Christianity,

that their Priests are the only real Priests, and that they possess exclusively the divinely appointed right to mediate between God and man. These claims are direct contradictions of the words of Our Lord, Who said: " And other sheep, I have, which are not of this fold; them also I must bring, and they shall hear my voice; and there shall be one fold, and one shepherd." [1]

Two further difficulties in making Christianity effective in healing the ills of man consist of the variability of Christian doctrines [2] and the insistence that belief in them is essential to salvation. A study of Christian origins and of the history of the Church since the first century reveals that many changes have occurred in the number and nature of beliefs held as essentials of the Christian religion by certain Christian bodies. The geocentric system is an example of a firmly held Article of Faith, disbelief in which, as in the case of Galileo, was regarded as heretical. Other beliefs have either undergone changes or have disappeared, evolving man having outgrown them. It is clear, therefore, that they never were beliefs necessary for salvation, and that some of them simply were not true.

CHRISTIAN ORTHODOXY AND ITS LIMITATIONS

This leaves in a very fluid state the whole question of what does and what does not constitute Christian orthodoxy. Indeed, many people at the present time are finding difficulty in accepting as literally and finally true such dogmas as: the infallibility of the Old and New Testaments; that all mankind descended from one pair of original parents and that their procreative act constituted a fall, or grave sin, which has been handed down to the whole human Race as " original sin " by which every single member of the Race has ever since been stained; that after some thousands of years the Supreme Deity sent—once, and once only—His only Son down to Earth in order that the harm done by the iniquity of the first parents of men might be undone, mankind thus being ransomed from the wrath of God; that to prevent this original sin from reaching the Lord Christ, Who was both man and God, He was born of a virgin who

---

[1] *Jn.* 10 : 16.

[2] Contraception, referred to as family planning, proscribed as utterly immoral until 1958, then became accepted, and even advocated, by the Anglican communion as pronounced at the Lambeth Conference of that year.

had miraculously conceived; that the consummation of the redemptive process consisted of His crucifixion at the insistence of the Jews, after which His body was raised from the tomb and later ascended into heaven; that in consequence of this sacrifice all those—and presumably only those—who were able before they died to affirm belief in this group of ideas, would after death be washed white and clean " in the blood of the Lamb ";[1] furthermore, that the normal operation of the law of cause and effect, so strongly insisted upon by the Lord Christ[2] and by the apostle Paul,[3] would be abrogated in the case of such believers, and that all who did not so affirm were in all probability condemned to eternal damnation, one concomitant of which is to be perpetually burned in the fires of hell *without being destroyed*,[4] and another to become outcasts from God's love of the human Race.

Indeed, it must be admitted that modern doctrinal Christianity, thus objectively considered, does not meet the need of the modern mind, which says with the Psalmist: " Give me understanding, and I shall keep thy law; yea, I shall observe it with my whole heart ",[5] and with Paul: " Prove all things; hold fast that which is good."[6] A religion which offers no answers to the problem of justice for man on Earth, for example, cannot possibly grip and hold minds which in this age of rapid scientific development have become accustomed to logic, cause and effect, and demonstration of propounded ideas. The inequalities of human birth, the continuance of apparently undeserved human suffering, the happiness and success of evildoers and the misery and failure of kindly and good-living people—these pose intellectual questions which modern Christianity, bereft of the gnosis, is unable to answer. Enquirers find that dogmatism stifles the human intellect, which demands both that religious teaching be consistent with the scientific method of enquiry and thought, and that man be granted complete freedom to exercise the mind as fully

---

[1] *Rom.* 5 : 9, *Eph.* 1 : 7, *Col.* 1 : 14, *Rev.* 9 : 12-15.

[2] *Matt.* 5 : 18, 7 : 1, 2 & 12.

[3] *Gal.* 6 : 7.

[4] The concept of the existence in the superphysical worlds of physical fire which can burn, and so punish, is indeed an anomaly.

[5] *Ps.* 119 : 34.

[6] 1 *Thes.* 5 : 21.

in religious and spiritual enquiry as in every other activity of the intellect. This necessity was affirmed by Professor Einstein in these words: " Only if outward and inner freedom are consciously and constantly pursued is there a possibility of spiritual development and perfection and of improving man's outer and inner life."

Christian orthodoxy, however, demands a measure of blind faith, insisting upon belief amongst other things that man, though a temple of the living God, is innately depraved; that Deity is to be placated by sacrifices, observances by rote, donations and petitions; that God condemns His sons to eternal damnation for sins committed in time; and that vicarious atonement ensures forgiveness and the abrogation of causative law for even the greatest, most deliberate and continually committed crimes against humanity and God. This last mentioned doctrine of the remission of sins can have sapped the moral fibre of many orthodox Christians. The Apostle Paul makes it very clear, moreover, that the redeeming principle is *within* man; for he wrote: " Christ in you, the hope of glory ";[1] " work out your own salvation with fear and trembling. For it is God which worketh in you . . .";[2] " Till we all come in the unity of the faith, and of the knowledge of the Son of God, unto a perfect man, unto the measure of the stature of the fulness of Christ ";[3] " My little children, of whom I travail in birth again until Christ be formed in you." [4] From these and similar utterances we can legitimately assume that Paul believed that nothing *outside* of man can save him.

THE BIBLE—SOURCE OF INSPIRATION, KNOWLEDGE, WISDOM

Such is part of the indictment justly or unjustly levelled against the modern form of Christianity. Those who have recognised the present limitations of the Christian Faith and the restrictive barriers placed around it by an artificially erected orthodoxy, may well ask where the necessary knowledge is to be found which will lead Christians to the discovery of their own light and their own truth. The

[1] *Col.* 1:27.
[2] *Phil.* 2:12, 13.
[3] *Eph.* 4:13.
[4] *Gal.* 4:19.

2

title of these volumes gives us the author's answer—*in the Bible itself*. As long, however, as the Scriptures continue to be read either as the inspired word of God from beginning to end, or literally as history, the discovery will continue to be elusive, if not impossible. The idea that the Bible in its present forms, and in all the languages in which it may be printed, is divinely and verbally inspired from beginning to end, and that it is an accurate chronological and historical record of the period of world history with which it deals, must be greatly modified, if its hidden wisdom is to be discovered. This does not in the least imply the abandonment of the Bible itself. Far from it, but the literal reading of some passages of the Bible must be replaced by the study of them as revelations, by means of allegory and symbol, of eternal, spiritual truths.

The all-illuminating and power-bestowing truth concerning the nature of man, that the divine Presence is within him as a Ray of the Supreme Deity, is revealed in the Bible both directly and under a veil of allegory, symbol and parable. The purpose of man's existence, which is evolution to Christhood, the method of its fulfilment, the rule of law which ensures strict justice, the way of communion between the human and the divine aspects of human nature and the illumination and empowerment which follow—all these and far more, it is submitted, are both revealed and concealed within the allegories of which the Scriptures of the world so largely consist.

REVELATION BENEATH THE VEIL

The veil, however, must first be removed. Using the age-old keys whereby symbols may be interpreted, the under-meanings, the half-hidden and yet sometimes clearly revealed directions for self-illumination,[1] and the all-essential knowledge concerning the whole of man's nature,[2] must be sought. The keys are indeed age-old, as is the language in which every truly inspired Scripture is written. When these keys are applied and the Scriptures intuitively read, an inexhaustible treasure of pure wisdom, lofty morality, guidance in the healing of individuals and nations, and the sure way to personal, national and international peace, are revealed. Admittedly,

[1] 1 *Kings* 19:11, 13, *Ps.* 46:10, *Phil.* 2:12-13, *Matt.* 6: 9-13.
[2] 1 *Cor.* 15: 44, *Col.* 1: 27.

restrictive dogmas, enforced acceptance in blind faith of unprovable and definitely erroneous assertions, the assumption by orthodoxy of the supremacy of the Christian religion over all other Faiths— all these, in so far as they are present, must cease to fetter the mind if " the true Light, which lighteth every man that cometh into the world " [1] is to be realised.

Self-discovery and God-consciousness are parts of the oldest science in the world, the science of the Soul of man. Just as a physical scientist begins and continues his researches with an unrestricted mind, as free as possible from preconceptions, so those who would successfully study the science of the Spirit must do so with unfettered minds determined upon truth itself, and truth alone. Only with difficulty will man find either the Supreme Deity of a Universe or that same divine Principle within himself if he begins and continues his search holding to those Biblical conceptions of God which in the Old Testament portray Him as jealous, cruel, showing favouritism, condoning the greatest wickedness, and as deliberately being responsible for gross injustices. [2] Undertaken under such conditions, the essential search for God and truth is almost certain to fail.

THE ALL-IMPORTANT " STILL SMALL VOICE "

Nevertheless, the true method is described directly, as in the words of the Psalmist, " Be still, and know that I am God ", [3] and allegorically in such stories as that of Elijah standing upon the mount and over-riding the limitations symbolised by wind, earthquake and fire; for thereafter Elijah entered that stillness in which the " voice of the silence " is heard. [4] The pathway to Light which every man may tread is symbolically described in this, as in many other Scriptural passages. In the succeeding Chapters and Volumes of this work on the symbolism of the Bible, guidance which it is hoped will prove helpful is offered in treading that way which leads to " the Light that never was on sea or land ", [5] " the true Light, which lighteth

---

[1] *Jn.* 1: 9.

[2] See footnote 3, p. 88.

[3] *Ps.* 46:10.

[4] 1 *Kings* 19:11-13. For an interpretation of this passage see Part One, Chapter IV, p. 46.

[5] *Wordsworth.*

every man that cometh into the world "[1]—the inner Light personified
by Jesus Christ as the Light of the World.

These considerations bring one to the conclusion that modern
Christianity needs to offer to the world a deep, religious philosophy
of life which can fulfil man's highest aspirations, bring consolation
to his heart, and also be justified at the bar of intellect.   By its revelation of the living Light which the great Founder brought to men
nearly 2,000 years ago, Christianity does contain that philosophy
and can make that greatly needed contribution.   Despite the changes
and accretions of the intervening centuries, that Light still shines.
Men and women of every walk of life, humble and exalted, have
borne witness to its shining and to their direct interior awareness
of the Divine Presence and Power.   Spiritual light is not dependent
for its illuminating power upon knowledge and acceptance of the
changing dogmas of any particular period or denomination.   Perception of spiritual truth calls for no blind obedience, no enslavement
of the reasoning mind.   Rather does it demand for its reception
a free, unfettered, active but reverent mind, and an awakened intuition; for there, *within* the highest parts of man's nature, the existence
of the Divine in all creation, and therefore within every man, may be
directly realised and known.

THE MYSTIC QUEST

How is this interior illumination to be obtained? Not by blind
faith, but by the free use of the reasoning faculty and the regular
practice of prayer, meditation and contemplation, the last being
defined as scientific prayer.   In his book of that title, prayer is defined
by Dr. Alexis Carrel in these words: " A serene contemplation of
the immanent and transcendent principle of all things.   An uplifting
of the soul to God.   An act of love and adoration towards Him from
Whom comes the wonder which is life.   The effort of man to communicate with an invisible Being.   A mystic state when the
consciousness is absorbed in God."

" Prayer ", Dr. Carrel continues, " finds its highest expression
in a soaring of love through the obscure night of the intelligence.
Prayer leaves the domain of the intellectual in order to reach that

[1] *Jn.* 1: 9.

of immediate feeling. To pray it is only necessary to make an effort of reaching out to God. The best way of communicating with God is without doubt fully to accomplish His will."

The method by which an individual can attain direct spiritual awareness, God-consciousness, will be peculiar to himself, though certain general, age-old rules have been enunciated. The Psalmist said: " Be still, and know that I am God." [1]

Ritualists say that through participation in Sacraments man may enter into conscious unity with the living Christ. Through loving service he may also learn to know, to love and to serve the God in All: through beauty he may perceive, worship, portray and discover God as " the principle of beauty in all things " (Keats). Through sacred chanting, as also through silent contemplation, *excluding every other thought*, he may find and know the God within, the Inner Ruler Immortal " seated in the heart of all beings." [2]

The two stories which follow serve to illustrate the theme that direct spiritual realisation is attainable, and when attained can both transform and illumine:-

An old peasant was sitting alone in the back pew of an empty Church. " What are you waiting for? ", he was asked. " I am looking at Him," he answered, " and He is looking at me."

A group of students in a Theological College asked a very learned Professor to read the Shepherd's Psalm.[3] He read it with great feeling and beautiful emphasis. Then someone called for a retired Minister to come up and repeat the 23rd Psalm. His sweet face shone with an inner light as he said the same words with reverence and meaning. When he had finished, there was not a dry eye in the room. Afterwards one of the students asked the Professor why he, with his great learning, could not produce that profound effect. The Professor was honest and humble in his reply: " Well," he said to the young man, " I have studied the Bible and I know all about the Shepherd but, you see, our friend *knows the Shepherd*."

There, I suggest, is the heart of the problem of religion; to know, by direct experience, the Power and the Presence of God and of

[1] *Ps.* 46:10.
[2] *Bhagavad Gita.*
[3] *Ps.* 23.

His Son, Christ our Lord. A Greek word for such direct interior spiritual knowledge is " gnosis ", and at the time of the foundation of Christianity those who possessed it were known as Gnostics. Tragically, because of the apparent errors of some Gnostics, these were proscribed and persecuted as heretics. The contribution of religion to the cure for man's present ills is *spiritual knowledge based upon interior experience.* Simply put, Christians need both to *know about* the Shepherd and to *know* the Shepherd. As the numbers of illumined and inspired men and women increase, there is reason to believe, so will Christianity become a greater power than at present for world peace and progress.

If the Christian religion can again become a centre and source of spiritual light born of direct knowledge, and so give truly spiritual teaching concerning man's intimate relationship with God and how that relationship may be realised; if it can restore the lost knowledge of the purpose for man's existence; if it can establish that reason and strict justice for man form part of its teaching, and provide the means of their intelligent application in the attainment of human happiness and the solution of life's problems; if it can give to humanity sure *and safe* guidance in the search for interior knowledge of God and in the quest for conscious union with God: if Christianity can truly illumine human minds then, it is submitted, it could lead humanity out of its present militancy into world peace, and out of its divided-ness into unity of action for the welfare of all mankind.

CHAPTER II

THE SYMBOLICAL LANGUAGE

SOME GENERAL PRINCIPLES

THE Christian Bible, as also the Scriptures of other Faiths, have from remote times been regarded as belonging to a special, even unique, category of literature. Exponents of Oriental religious writings, the early Kabbalists, the disciples of Ammonius Saccus, other neo-platonists of Alexandria known as " Analogeticists ", and their successors down to modern times—all these have regarded world Scriptures as being largely, but not entirely, allegorical. They looked upon them as being constructed of symbols, analogies and parables. As previously stated—and this is the main theme of this work—these allegories are said to preserve for posterity, to reveal and yet to conceal, profound spiritual and therefore power-bestowing truths.

REASONS FOR SECRECY

This method of writing is referred to as the Sacred or Mystery Language, and is said to have been invented and used by Sages of old in order both to reveal to those who would be helped, and to conceal from those who might be harmed thereby, a deep spiritual wisdom which can bestow theurgic powers upon its possessors. The necessity for this reservation becomes clear when the use to which modern man puts scientific discoveries is observed. One example of the misuse of knowledge is the release, as the explosive agent in atomic bombs, of the energy derived from nuclear fission and fusion.

Recognising that their discoveries belonged to the race, the philosophers and scientists of former days knew that such knowledge placed in general hands, and particularly in the hands of disruptive

elements in society, could be extremely dangerous. They therefore constructed the cryptic language in which the inspired Scriptures
and Mythologies of the world have been written. Although founded
in general upon historical events, these narratives have under-
meanings and in some cases even a sevenfold significance. Whilst
apparently historical, each story also has an inner purport and
contains within itself layer upon layer of hidden knowledge.

TEACHING BY PARABLES

Our Lord made use of this method of teaching. When addressing
His disciples He spoke openly of spiritual truths, but to non-disciples
He spoke in parables. Indeed, He used the words: " Give not that
which is holy unto the dogs, neither cast ye your pearls before swine,
lest they trample them under their feet, and turn again and rend
you." [1] He also said to them: " It is given unto you to know the
mysteries of the kingdom of heaven, but to them that are without
in parables." [2]

One reason for this differentiation is not far to seek. Knowledge
can bestow power, and the writers of the Sacred Language were in
the same position in which a small group of modern scientists would
find themselves after having first discovered atomic energy. They
would not dare immediately to make their discovery universally
available. Similarly the wise men of old, having investigated the
structure of matter and discovered the force locked up within it,
would feel a tremendous sense of responsibility. They had both
to prevent the misuse of their knowledge and to ensure its preservation for the future benefit of mankind.

Actually, in the case of knowledge of the superphysical and
spiritual worlds, their structure, their natural forces and the Intelligences associated with them, and their correspondences with the
superphysical vehicles and powers of man, the need for secrecy is
far greater. In wrong hands, the power which such knowledge
puts at man's disposal is far more dangerous than physical atomic
energy. The products of nuclear fission and fusion can only wreck
physical objects. Occult knowledge and the power associated with

[1] *Matt.* 7: 6.
[2] *Matt.* 13: 11.

it, if misused, can destroy the integrity, harden and warp the nature and in consequence seriously retard the evolution, of the transgressors and those under their malign influence. The ancient seers therefore devised not the algebraical symbols and formulae of the modern scientist, but a cryptic language in which some of the words retain their normal meaning, whilst others are cryptograms or hierograms for spiritual and occult truths. In doing this, the writers of old knew that only those who possessed the keys of interpretation would be able to discover the truths which the Sacred Language both reveals and conceals. The secret is rendered still safer by the fact that, in order successfully to use the keys, one must have developed the intuitive faculty and be imbued with a strong sense of moral responsibility.

Such, briefly and but partially described, are the origin and the purposes of the Sacred Language in which the Scriptures and Mythologies of ancient peoples were written.

CHAPTER III

PROBLEMS ARISING FROM A LITERAL READING OF THE BIBLE AND SOME SOLUTIONS

SINCE comprehension and appreciation of the esoteric teachings contained in the Bible depend upon a knowledge of the Sacred Language, a fuller and more detailed exposition of this particular category of literature must now be given. At the outset of this task it is recognised that to those who have hitherto regarded the Bible solely as a record of historical events, the idea that it was written in allegory and symbol in order to transmit universal truths to mankind may seem strange, and even incredible.

PREPARATION

The subject is profound; impartial examination and progressive study are essential to its comprehension. Apart from the parables of Jesus, the language of analogy, dramatic allegory and symbol is for many people a little known art form. Vocabulary, grammar and composition must, in consequence, be carefully studied before the transmitted ideas can be perceived and grasped. Time, too, is always required to become accustomed to a new method of presentation and a new aspect of truth.

In art, some training in appreciation is necessary in order to enjoy and understand a great picture and receive the artist's message. Preparation and experience are needed in order to open the eyes and prepare the mind. This is true also of music. With the exception of those passages—perhaps the slow movements—which can be readily enjoyed, a great symphony can at first hearing be difficult to comprehend. As one perceives its significance and understands its method and form, however, the whole work takes on a

new meaning and evokes a new delight.   To a child a wonderful
jewel is but a glittering toy.   He will choose just as readily any shining
thing, however tawdry and cheap.   A connoisseur in precious stones,
on the other hand, sees in them depths of beauty hidden from others,
comprehends and appreciates both the stones themselves and the
craftmanship of the jeweller.

The foregoing applies equally in gaining appreciation and comprehension of those symbols which are universally used in the Scriptures
and Mythologies of ancient peoples; otherwise allegories and symbols
may be wrongly regarded as unnecessary obstructions and their
interpretations as arbitrary, and at best far-fetched.   Due preparation
is required before one may receive the benefits to be derived from a
study of the Sacred Language.   Since profound truths are conveyed
and spiritual experience, knowledge and power can be obtained by
the successful interpretation of the Bible, the student's preparations
must in their turn be not only intellectual, but spiritual as well.
Indeed, such preparations assume the character of a vigil.

THE VEIL OF ALLEGORY

Whilst many of the incidents in the Bible are doubtless founded
upon historical fact, great wisdom and light are to be discovered
within the Scriptural record of historical and pseudo-historical events.
When, however, statements are made which could not possibly be
true, three courses of action present themselves to the reader.   He
can accept them unthinkingly in blind faith; he may discard them
as unworthy of serious consideration; or he may study them carefully
in search of possible under-meanings and revelations of hitherto
hidden truths.   Incidents such as the passage of three days and nights
and the appearance on Earth of vegetation before the creation of
the sun,[1] and the action of Joshua in making the sun and moon stand
still,[2] simply cannot be true in their literal reading.   As has been
said, here and in so many other places the Bible " piles the incredible
upon the impossible ".   If, however, the intention was not to record
either astronomical or historical facts and events alone, but also to
reveal abstract, universal and mystical truths and to give guidance

[1] *Gen.* 1: 13-16.
[2] *Joshua* 10:12-14.   q.v. p. 29 and Part One, ch. V.

in finding and treading "The Way of Holiness";[1] and if, further-more, night, sun and moon are but concrete symbols of abstract ideas, then the outwardly meaningless narrative may reveal inward truth and light. Before the truth and the light can be perceived, however, the veil of allegory must be lifted and the symbols inter-preted; for, as said, the Teachers of ancient days, in order to safeguard and yet reveal the truth when the time should be ripe, deliberately concealed within allegory and symbol the deep, hidden wisdom of which they had become possessed.

TIME AS MIRROR OF ETERNITY

The authors of the Scriptures saw eternal truths mirrored in events in time. For them, illumined as they were, every material happening was alight with spiritual significance. They knew the outer world for what it was—the shadow of a great reality. They could say with Browning: "Earth's crammed with heaven and every common bush afire with God", and with him would add "but only he who sees takes off his shoes." Their records of the history of the Universe and of the Earth—the Scriptures of the world—portray far more than events in time; they reveal eternal truth, ultimate reality, universal occurrences. Sometimes the real was more visible to them than the shadow, whereupon history took second place. At other times the record of physical events predominated. This is advanced as the key to the mystical study of the Bible, the clue to the discovery of the inexhaustible treasures of wisdom and truth concealed within the casket of exoteric Scriptures.

The spiritual teachers of long ago, by using historical events as well as allegories and symbols, proved themselves able to overcome the limitations of time. They recorded history in such a way as to reveal to readers of both their own and of later times the deeper truths of life. Even thousands of years after their death such teachers are able to give to men of every age both guidance along the pathway of spiritual illumination, and the solutions to their personal problems. Concealment from the profane of truths which they desired to impart to the worthy, and to the worthy alone, is admitted; the motive being to safeguard both the individual and the Race from the dangers

[1] *Is.* 35: 8.

of premature discovery and possible misuse of knowledge which could bestow theurgic and thaumaturgic powers.   Thus came into existence the legends, the Mythologies and the Scriptures of the world, many of them being pregnant with spiritual and occult ideas.

DIFFICULTIES OF A LITERAL READING OF THE BIBLE

In addition to its value as a vehicle for hidden wisdom, the Sacred Language can prove helpful in solving otherwise insoluble Biblical problems.   Whilst belief or faith in the possibility of supernatural intervention makes some Scriptural statements credible, physical laws and astronomical facts cannot be changed.   Admittedly some miracles strain almost beyond reasonable limits one's power to believe them.   The hydrostatic pressure exerted in dividing and holding back on either side of a dry bed the waters of the Red Sea [1] and the river Jordan [2] must have involved the use of almost incalculable energy.   Nevertheless, if direct divine theurgic action is presumed to have occurred, then these " miracles " would not have been impossible.

The heliocentric system, however, cannot be altered.   The sun is at the centre of our Solar System, for which it is the source of light.   Planets revolve on their axes throughout their orbital motion round the sun, without which there could be neither day nor night. Yet in *Genesis*, chapter one, it is plainly stated that there were three days and three nights before the sun, moon and stars were created. This is an astronomical impossibility.

The rotation of the Earth causes night and day.   The sun does not move round the Earth, and cannot by any humanly conceivable means be made to do so, yet Joshua is said to have lengthened the day by making both the sun and the moon stand still.[3]   The prolongation of either day or night by the arrest of the motion of either sun or Earth (the moon would not be directly concerned in such a procedure) is a total impossibility; for if the Earth had suddenly stopped turning, no human being would have lived to record the event.   Every movable object on Earth, including the oceans and

[1] *Ex.* 14 : 21-31.
[2] *Joshua* 3 : 14-17.
[3] *Joshua* 10 : 12-14. q.v. Part One, ch. V.

the atmosphere, would have continued the normally rotating movement and thus travelled towards the East faster than the speed of sound.

The story of Noah and his Ark also provides a grave stumbling block. It would have been extremely difficult, if not impossible, to collect pairs of animals from the four quarters of the Earth; the sloth, for instance, which travels with extreme slowness, would have needed to start its journey very much before the onset of the Flood to reach the Ark in time. The problem of housing and feeding so large a number of animals throughout forty days and forty nights would have been extremely difficult, if not insurmountable.

The literal reading of the story of the tower of Babel, and especially of verses 6, 7, 8 and 9 of the Eleventh chapter of the Book of *Genesis*, affirms that the Supreme Deity is deliberately and callously responsible for the major self-produced sufferings of mankind. According to the text, every evil work by man upon man, including individual and organised crime and the waging of innumerable wars, arose and still arises from the two supposed actions of a personal Deity, first in confounding human language so that men can no longer understand one another's speech, and second in scattering humanity abroad upon the face of the Earth.

Such supposed Divine actions can, indeed, legitimately be regarded as having been major causes of human errors, born of individualism, and their grievous effects. This attribution to the Supreme Deity of motive and conduct so detrimental to humanity as to remove for long ages all possibility of harmonious human relationships on Earth, is totally unacceptable to any thoughtful and reverent mind.

The study and acceptance of the Bible less as literal history and far more as a revelation of fundamental truths by means of allegories, thus receives strong support from the story of the tower of Babel.

In the case of Jonah, the digestive secretions and processes occurring in the stomach of a large mammal like a whale would have rendered it extremely unlikely that he could have remained alive and unaffected after three days and three nights of subjection to such disintegrating forces.

Incredibility apart, the obscenity, such as the drunkenness of Lot and his incest with his two daughters; [1] the sensuality; the brutality; the attribution to the Supreme Deity of the human weaknesses of anger, jealousy, bloodthirstiness, and His encouragement of the Israelites to attack and massacre the animals, men, women and children of other tribes—these are all Biblical incongruities which thoughtful and sensitive people must find repellent.   Orthodox opinion is divided concerning the desirability of including such portions of the Scriptures in Sunday School and University curricula.

BIOLOGY, NOMENCLATURE AND THE LIMITATIONS OF TIME

In the New Testament, also, difficulties are met if a literal reading of certain passages is accepted.   In the case of Jesus, some of the Evangelists affirm an immaculate conception and a virgin birth [2]—regarded as a virtual impossibility—and others do not.   The genealogies of Jesus as given in the Gospels of St. Matthew and St. Luke are totally different and can hardly apply to the same person. St. Matthew traces His descent through Joseph, which is entirely meaningless in the case of a virgin birth.   St. Luke, however, traces the genealogy through Mary.   Furthermore, the events of the night before the Crucifixion of Jesus are too numerous to have occurred within the prescribed time.   Here is a list of them: the Last Supper; the agony in the Garden; the betrayal by Judas; the hailing and the questioning, first before Caiaphas, secondly before the Sanhedrin and then before Pilate; the questioning in the Hall of Judgment (regardless of the fact that Courts to try malefactors did not sit in the middle of the night) [3]; the visit of Herod (recorded by St. Luke); the return to Pilate; Pilate's speeches and his washing of his hands; the scourging, the mocking and the arraying of Jesus in a purple robe; the long and painful bearing of the Cross to Golgotha—all these events could not possibly have occurred in so short a time.

Although a number of Christian denominations proclaim the Bible to be the verbally inspired word of God some churchmen frankly

---

[1] *Gen.* 19: 30-38.

[2] *Matt.* 1: 18, *Lk.* 1: 34, 35 and 41.

[3] The possibility that the urgency of the case could have made immediate action imperative has not been overlooked.

recognise the above-mentioned difficulties. Canon T. P. Stevens, Vicar of St. Paul's Church, Wimbledon, when explaining his reasons for banning the teaching of certain Old Testament stories in his Sunday Schools, said:

" No matter how many say the Bible should be taught in full, I am not going to do it. Men like Bernard Shaw, Arnold Bennett and H. G. Wells, all turned against the Church through wrongful teaching, when they could have been a powerful force to us . . . .

" It takes a man of considerable intelligence to understand the whole of the Bible. Some of the stories are helpful, interesting and lovely, but quite often they deal with rape, murder, lies and brutality, exaggerated nationalism and war. What purpose is to be served by teaching all these unpleasant stories to the young? If they are intelligent they will get the strangest ideas of God.

" I believe the Christian religion is in a state of decline partly because so many people cannot make head or tail of it. Unfortunately the whole Christian Church is against me. I am the odd man out over this question." [1]

A new dark age is seen by Dean Inge, as reported in *The New Zealand Herald*, 8-6-50: " Dean Inge, ' The Gloomy Dean ', is aged 90 today (June 6th). . . On the eve of his birthday, the Dean declared: We seem to be on the threshold of another dark age. . . The first thing ought to be to get rid of a good deal of the Old Testament. We are living in an age different from the days when I had a fashionable West End Church, where ladies dripping with pearls and furs would sing the Magnificat with more fervour than a Communist ever sang the Red Flag."

Most, if not all, of these difficulties disappear when once it is assumed that the authors' intention was less to record history alone than also to reveal cosmogonical, solar, planetary and racial ideas and to describe mystical and psychological conditions and experiences of man. Incredibilities and impossibilities in both the Old and the New Testaments are referred to later on in this and successive volumes of this work, where explanations and interpretations of some of them are offered.

[1] q.v. *The N.Z. Herald*, 2-5-50.

THE SOLUTION OF THE PROBLEM

One explanation given of these incongruities is that they were not contained in the original writings. Later interpreters, editors and translators are, by some Biblical scholars, held responsible for them. Belief in the literal verbal inspiration of the Bible has been applied, it is said, to these altered and translated versions, and not to the original texts. Whilst doubtless there is some truth in this view, many of the criticisms can successfully be met and most of the problems solved if once the existence of the Sacred Language be accepted and applied in interpretation of the Scriptures. Sheer ignorance, deliberate interference with original texts, deletions, interpolations, successive editings and translations, have undoubtedly been responsible for some at least of the confusion. The repellent passages, the many mis-statements of fact, and the attribution to the Supreme Deity of the characteristics of a bloodthirsty, tribal fetish, make the literal reading of many portions of the Old Testament entirely unacceptable.

Nevertheless, in those books which bear the imprint of inspiration, in conformity with the allegorical method of writing, the statement of impossibilities is, it is submitted, part of a carefully constructed cover or blind, a veil of incredibility, incongruity, absurdity, inconsequence, fantasy, and even horror, as in the case of the glyph of Satan as Beelzebub. A famous Rabbi, Moses Maimonedes, Jewish theologian and historian, wrote: " Every time you find in our books a tale, the reality of which seems impossible, a story which is repugnant to both reason and common sense, then be sure that the tale contains a profound allegory veiling a deeply mysterious truth; and the greater the absurdity of the letter, the deeper the wisdom of the spirit."

THE TESTIMONY OF EARLY AUTHORITIES

The secret meaning of the Scriptures is again openly confessed by Clement when he says that the Mysteries of the Faith are not to be divulged to all. " But ", he says, " since this tradition is not published alone for him who perceives the magnificence of the word; it is requisite, therefore, to hide in a Mystery the wisdom spoken, which the Son of God taught." [1]

[1] *Clement of Alexandria*, Vol. 1, *Stromata*, Ch. xxi, p. 388.

Not less explicit is Origen with regard to the Bible and its symbolical fables. "If we hold to the letter", he exclaims, "and must understand what stands written in the law after the manner of the Jews and common people, then I should blush to confess aloud that it is God who has given these laws; then the laws of men appear more excellent and reasonable." [1]

"What man of sense", he writes, "will agree with the statement that the first, second and third days in which the *evening* is named and the *morning*, were without sun, moon and the stars, and the first day without a heaven? What man is found such an idiot as to suppose that God planted trees in Paradise, in Eden, like a husbandman, etc.? I believe that every man must hold these things for images, under which hidden sense lies concealed." [2]

When, in addition, we read Paul's unequivocal statements that the story of Abraham and his two sons is all "an allegory" and that "Agar is Mount Sinai" [3]—then, indeed, little blame can be attached to either Christian or heathen who declines to accept the *Bible* in any other light than that of a very ingenious allegory.

"Rabbi Simeon Ben-Jochai, the compiler of the *Zohar*, never imparted the most important points of his doctrine otherwise than orally, and to a very limited number of disciples. Therefore, without the final initiation into the *Mercavah*, the study of the *Kabbalah* will be ever incomplete, and the *Mercavah* can be taught only ' in darkness, in a deserted place, and after many and terrific trials ' [the preparation, in those days, of Candidates for Initiation [4]]. Since the death of that great Jewish Initiate this hidden doctrine has remained, for the outside world, an inviolate secret ",[5] and this despite the publication of the *Zohar* with its profound if allegorical revelation of parts of the esoteric Kabbalah.

"Among the venerable sect of the Tanaim, or rather the Tanaim, the wise men, there were those who taught the secrets practically and initiated some disciples into the grand and final Mystery.

---

[1] See *Homilies* 7, in *Levit.*, quoted in *The Source of Measures*, pp. 306-7.

[2] Origen: Huet., *Origeniana*, 167; Franck, p. 142.

[3] *Gal.* 4: 22-26.

[4] Initiation.   For a description of this process, see Part six, Ch. I.

[5] *The Secret Doctrine*, H. P. Blavatsky, V, 67.

But the Mishna Hagiga, Second Section, say that the table of contents of the *Mercavah* must only be delivered to wise old ones. The *Gemara* is still more dogmatic. The more important secrets of the Mysteries were not revealed even to all priests. The Initiates alone had them divulged. And so we find the same great secrecy prevalent in every ancient religion." [1]

"What says the *Kabbalah* itself? Its great Rabbis actually threaten him who accepts their sayings *verbatim*. We read in the *Zohar*: [2] 'Woe . . . . to the man who sees in the Thorah, i.e., Law, only simple recitals and ordinary words! Because if in truth it only contained these, we would even today be able to compose a Thorah much more worthy of admiration. For if we find only the simple words, we would not only have to address ourselves to the legislators of the earth, to those in whom we most frequently meet the most grandeur; it would be sufficient to imitate them, and make a Thorah after their words and example. But it is not so; each word of the Thorah contains an elevated meaning and a sublime mystery . . . . The recitals of the Thorah are the vestments of the Thorah. Woe to him who takes this garment for the Thorah itself . . . . The simple take notice only of the garments or recitals of the Thorah, they know no other thing, they see not that which is concealed under the vestment. The more instructed men do not pay attention to the vestment, but to the body which it envelops.' " [3]

AN ILLUSTRATION

The story of the cursing of the fig tree [4] may here be taken as an example of an account of somewhat unlikely event which, when interpreted as an allegory, becomes not only acceptable but a source of illumination. It seems un-Christlike to curse the fig tree, and still more so when we realise that the act was performed in the very early Spring before the Passover. The tree would not be likely to have had any figs upon it at such a time, for it was out of

---

[1] *Isis Unveiled*, Vol. II, p. 350.

[2] *Zohar*, Vol. iii, fol. 1526.

[3] Quoted from *The Secret Doctrine*, Adyar Edition, Vol. V, pp. 66-68.

[4] *Matt.* 21:19.

season. Thus the story could be regarded as self-contradictory, even absurd. In that very absurdity, however, is said to be both a clue to the meaning and an encouragement to look for the wisdom concealed within the supposed narrative of events. Indeed, as is so often the case, the world's allegories are less records of events in time and place than enunciations of eternal and universal laws. Here, omitting details and interpretations (given later in this work) of the many symbols employed—such as the Deity, Christ His Son, the disciples, the people, the soil, the fig tree, fruitlessness and stagnation—the story may be understood as a statement of fundamental law. Simply put, this law is that if all living things and beings, including races, nations and men, do not share the fruits of their lives, they will wither away and die. He who seeks to have, to hold and to hoard for himself alone the fruits of his life, his outer possessions, his discovered wisdom, truth and power, giving nothing to others, that man will inevitably find that his own life, outer and inner, stagnates and withers away.

SELFLESS GIVING—A FUNDAMENTAL LAW

Attention is thus drawn to a great and mysterious principle—it might be called " the law of flow "—which is: give to live, share to enjoy, serve to unfold. This is the ideal of selfless giving, in obedience to which there is not loss but gain, not death but more abundant life. Disobedience of this law, motived by desire for exclusively personal possessions and powers, brings not gain but loss, not life but death. This has been demonstrated throughout the history of both nations and individuals.

This law is rightly described as fundamental, for it is the law by which the Universe subsists. The Logos Itself nourishes and sustains the Solar System by the perpetual outpouring, self-giving, " self-emptying " (kenosis) of Its own life. This kenosis, this self-emptying attitude of mind and mode of life, is a key-word in the Christian religion. It is applied to the life of the disciple by Our Lord in His words: " . . . he that hateth his life in this world shall keep it unto life eternal ",[1] and " except a corn of wheat fall into the ground and die, it abideth alone: but if it die, it bringeth forth much

---

[1] *Jn.* 12 : 25.

fruit." [1]   The neophyte must become " the wheat of Christ ", as a Christian mystic has said.

The poverty of the Nativity of Jesus, the surrender to Pilate, to the Jews and to Crucifixion, the Sacred Heart, the open wounds and the piercing of the skin, are all symbols of this attitude of uttermost selflessness towards life. Such self-emptying, such entirely self-forgetting love, such figurative death is necessary, it is said, for the attainment of more abundant life.   To die, in the sense of separated individuality, egoism and possessiveness, is to live unto life eternal, and this is thought by mystics to be one of the greatest truths ever uttered.

Apparently we are in the presence of a strange law.   In order to live the larger life in imitation of the Great Exemplar, the Lord of Love, we must die to self-desire: we must pour ourselves out in selfless sacrifice and service: we must surrender self for love's sake. Universal love is the only true way to eternal life, because it involves " self-emptying " of self.   Self-forgetfulness is the basis of all spirituality.   Every sincere esotericist is faced with this truth.   The renunciation seems always to be of that which we held most dear.   These words " self-emptying " and " dying ", applied to the Logos, are not to be taken as wholly expressing the truth; for, of course, the Logos does not ever become empty, nor does " He " [2] ever really die.

What is, in fact, the result of such a figurative death? The question leads one's thought to the strange spiritual law under which self-surrender brings not loss, but renewal.   The Logos is ever Self-renewed from a higher dimension.   The sun does not exhaust itself despite its immeasurable outpouring, for proportionate inpouring occurs.   The spiritually minded man recognises that selflessness does not bring loss but gain, and even abundance.   This is true in every walk of life, whether secular or spiritual.

In relating the incident of the withered fig tree, the author of the Gospel according to St. Matthew enunciated this law in the form of a story describing an action of the Lord of Love which brought about a cessation of life of a fruitless tree. [3]   A profound spiritual truth of the greatest significance to every neophyte of every age who seeks to

[1] *Jn.* 12 : 24.
[2] See footnote 2, p. 69.
[3] *Matt.* 21:19

discover the " strait gate " and enter upon " the narrow way ", is portrayed by means of a miniature drama, an allegory concealing the all-important law that life is not lost, but fulfilled by renunciation. The positive aspect of this natural law is represented by the presence of the Christ Himself, Whose whole life was lived in obedience to it. This reading is supported by the fact that, after the incident, Our Lord went on to refer to the nature and range of the tremendous powers attainable by those who enter upon the Path of Discipleship and Initiation:

" Jesus answered and said unto them, Verily I say unto you, If ye have faith, and doubt not, ye shall not only do this which is done to the fig tree, but also if ye shall say unto this mountain, Be thou removed, and be thou cast into the sea; it shall be done.

" And all things, whatsoever ye shall ask in prayer, believing, ye shall receive." [1]

The entry of Jesus into Jerusalem and the acclamation by the crowd, commemorated by the Church as Palm Sunday, which immediately preceded the withering of the fig tree, indicated that a certain spiritual advance had been made, a triumph of the spirit over the flesh, of the Christ-power within over the lower quaternary (the docile ass) and the multitude of habits, desires and appetites (the responsive crowd) inherent in the substance of the physical and super-physical bodies. Jerusalem is a symbol of universalised consciousness as an immortal, spiritual being. Entry into Jerusalem portrays realisation of the Self as divine, eternal, indestructible and universal. The heavenly city, " the city of the living God " [2] is a symbol of the *Augoeides*,[3] the *karana sharira*,[4] the Robe of Glory, the Causal Body [5] in which the self-radiant divine fragment, the Monad-Ego, abides and is self-manifest at the level of the abstract intelligence.

LITERAL OR SYMBOLICAL?

If it be objected that all this is too much to deduce from so simple and so briefly described an incident as the withering of the fig tree,

---

[1] *Matt.* 21: 21, 22.

[2] *Heb.* 12 : 22.

[3] *Gr.*

[4] *Sk.*

[5] All these titles are names for the same principle of man—the vehicle of the reincarnating Ego at the formless levels of the mental plane.

it can be answered first, that a literal reading presents one with an unacceptable attribute in the character of the Christ, Who said: ". I am come that they might have life, and that they might have it more abundantly ";[1] and second, that in its literal meaning the incident introduces a meaningless and somewhat repellent exercise of thaumaturgic power such as has been displayed, for example, by the medicine men of primitive peoples, and by the *Tohungas* of the Maoris.

Whilst it is admitted that the fact that one idea is preferable to another is no proof of its verity, the cumulative evidence obtained by similar interpretations of a very great number of Bible stories is so strong as to amount to proof. When to this is added the avowed intention of ancient writers, and the strongly worded command of Christ to conceal from the profane, and yet reveal to the worthy, power-bestowing knowledge and the mysteries of the kingdom (pearls), which could be dangerous in the wrong hands (swine), then the case for the existence and use of the Sacred Language would seem to be unassailable.

[1] *Jn.* 10 : 10.

CHAPTER IV

EXAMPLES OF THE INTERPRETATION
OF ALLEGORIES

TIMES change and part of the esotericism of one age becomes the exotericism of its successor. The heliocentric system, the electro-atomic structure of matter, the transmutation of electrical energy into heat, light and other radiations, the manufacture of explosives, psycho-somatic medicine and demonstrations of human powers of extra-sensory perception—this carefully concealed knowledge of the Mystery Schools of old has now become well-known. The upper layers, at least, of the ancient scriptural allegories and myths have now been uncovered. Deeper layers yet remain and these, in their turn, will be revealed as humanity evolves and the keys of interpretation continue to be discovered and employed.

THE SEED IS THE WORD OF GOD

One of these keys was given to His disciples by Our Lord. His explanation of the Parable of the Sower shows that the seed was a symbol for the Word of God, and the differing conditions of the ground—rocky, thorny and fertile—were descriptive of states of the human mind and brain at differing phases of evolutionary development. The publication of *The Secret Doctrine* [1] revealed other keys, bestowed a wealth of knowledge upon mankind, and initiated a new cycle of occult research.

EATING FLESH AND DRINKING BLOOD

An example of a vivid use of the symbolical language is found in the words of Jesus: " Verily, verily, I say unto you, Except ye eat

[1] H. P. Blavatsky.

the flesh of the Son of man, and drink his blood, ye have no life in you. Who so eateth my flesh, and drinketh my blood, hath eternal life. . . "[1] Clearly Our Lord must here be making use of the words " flesh ", " blood ", " eateth " and " drinketh " in a metaphorical sense. One simplified interpretation of this passage, here offered in advance of the fuller and more detailed expositions to follow,[2] is that the flesh of Christ represents spiritual knowledge. When the human intellect has absorbed and become illumined by divine truth and is inspired by interior revelation, this experience is symbolically described as the eating of the flesh of the Deity. The blood of God, or Christ, is the ever-outpoured divine life by which the Universe is sustained, without which it cannot live. When a spiritually illumined man, having become aware of this universal life in all beings, becomes consciously identified with it, he is said in the symbolical language to drink of the blood of God, or Christ. An enriching mento-spiritual experience is described in terms of physical nourishment. Indeed, as Our Lord said, these two attainments bring a realisation of immortality or entry into eternal life.

PEACE BE STILL

The story of the stilling of the tempest[3] is another example of an inspired allegory. In a human and psychological interpretation, the ship may be regarded as a symbol of the body of man, which conveys the soul with its various attributes over the waters of life. The disciples are regarded as personifications of human qualities and tendencies, such as: the impulsiveness of Peter; the possible simplicity of James and John, sons of Zebedee, who were fishermen; the business capacities of Matthew; and the deep and faithful love of John, the only disciple who was present both in the courtroom and at the foot of the cross. Judas, who betrayed his Master, is also present in each one of us as the tendency to fall below, and even betray, our highest principles for material gain. Happily the divine Presence also exists in each one of us, even if asleep for a time, just as Our Lord slept when the voyage began. A great storm arose,

[1] *Jn.* 6 : 53-54.
[2] q.v. Part Two, ch. II.
[3] *Mk.* 4 : 36-41.

however, and in their anxiety the disciples awoke the sleeping Passenger, the Lord Christ. He, in His majesty and might, stilled by a word the raging storm.

Interpreting and applying this story to the storms of human life (especially of emotion, as is indicated by placing the incident upon water), when assailed by temptation, driven by desire or wishing to eradicate an unwanted habit, we are advised to withdraw our thoughts from the difficulty, concentrate powerfully upon our divine nature and, *to the exclusion of every other thought*, affirm its irresistible power. Then the darkness of the undesirable state of mind will disappear in the great light shining out from the God within. Symbolically, the awakened Christ will still the tempest.

Thus, in its purely human application the story shows us that when we are threatened by the storms of life, the gusts of passion, anger and hatred, the cravings of sensual desire, which threaten the success and even the safety of our lives, we should awaken the sleeping, divine power within us and call upon its aid. Thus exalted and empowered, we shall find ourselves able to say to the tempestuous aspects of human nature with certainty of obedience—" Peace, be still." The importance of the trials and stresses of life is also indicated in this wonderful story; for had it not been for the storm on Galilee the Christ might not have been awakened. So, also, the struggles and storms of our lives. These can prove to be the means of the awakening of our higher, more spiritual powers.

THE MIRACLES OF HEALING

The story of the woman healed after twelve years of incurable sickness [1] is also capable of a symbolical interpretation, as are all the accounts of miraculous healing by the Christ. A deep faith awoke in this woman, so that she set forth to find the great Teacher and Healer Who was in her land. Despite her weakness she found Him, but was unable to come near on account of the throng of people in the way. Her faith was great, however; she stretched forth her hand and touched, not His person, but the hem of His garment and straightway she was whole.

---

[1] *Matt.* 9 : 20-22, *Mk.* 5 : 25-34, *Lk.* 8 : 43-48.

" EVERY ONE THAT IS OF THE TRUTH HEARETH MY VOICE " [1]

The Christ undoubtedly possessed and exercised superior knowledge and power which enabled Him to perform seeming miracles. The historicity of the accounts of them is not here in question. The narrative method does, however, suggest that universal applications of the events are also being revealed; for all who are spiritually imperfect, and so " sick ", will become whole if they but seek within and there discover the divine Principle, the Christ Presence, the " Christ in you " referred to by the Apostle Paul.[2] The throng in the way symbolises all the un-Christlike attributes of mankind; impurity, cruelty, unkindness, sefishness and self-indulgences which come between us and our highest nature. Eventually these must go, but in the meantime if, full of faith, we reach upwards with our aspiring thought and prayer, we may touch the fringe of the divine consciousness within us, as symbolised by the hem of His garment. Those who have passed through this experience will know that when once the consciousness of the divine Self within has been found and entered, floods of inspiration and healing grace descend upon both soul and body. Indeed, thereafter, straightway one is whole.

MYSTICAL WOUNDS

In the Initiatory sense sickness, suffering, limitations and wounds all refer to the mystic ill-health inseparable from the transformation of a man into a Superman and an Initiate into an Adept. The Apostle Paul thus had his thorn in the flesh; he was said to suffer from epilepsy. St. Francis of Assisi, St. Catherine of Siena and St. Theresa of Avila all bore testimony to the receipt of inner wounds, mystical sufferings endured in addition to their physical sicknesses. All of these wounds refer in part to the forceful breaking down and the dissolution of the illusion of self-separateness, and to the transcendence of the limitations of matter and the material vehicles.

INTERIOR HEALING GRACE

The " heal " for every wound is, as an old English medical maxim says, " within the wound ". It consists of the Christ Principle,

[1] *Jn.* 18 : 37.
[2] *Col.* 1 : 27.

Power and Life which form the Second Aspect of the threefold, Spiritual Soul of every man; for each Soul is a reproduction of the Universal Soul, the Triune Godhead, the Blessed Trinity. When once this redemptive healing, this Christlike power, is aroused into activity and the outer man [1] becomes aware of that power and surrenders to it then, as if by a miracle, a mystical transformation occurs. Integration, wholeness, relative perfection, are attained. Mystically, the Master within draws the disciple into union with Himself. This process is assisted by the external Master Who increases the idealism, the power and the aspiration of the outer man so that he becomes responsive to the Master, the Christ, within.

WHIP, NAILS, THORNS AND SPEAR

The weapons by which these wounds are made symbolise the dangers through which knowledge of the Mysteries may alone be approached, and by which those Mysteries are guarded. The crown of thorns portrays the true royalty of Spirit and indicates that sovereignty is only attained by suffering. The thorns, nevertheless, symbolise the possibility, which is almost a certainty, that suffering will result from the wrongful use of the separative and analytical attributes of the formal mind, especially in the early stages of its development. These mental characteristics inevitably cause pain and sorrow (the pricks of the thorns), and since the head is the physical centre of mental life the thorns are placed upon it as a crown. Before perfection the two aspects of the mind in man—the higher and the lower (the two thieves crucified with Christ)—strive continually for mastery, and the pains and wounds of that mystical conflict are also symbolised by the thorns, the whip, the nails, the spear, and the pain they produce. The true meaning of the crown of thorns is ever unperceived, is indeed unrecognisible, by unillumined man (the throng demanding and watching the Crucifixion). By them it is thought to be a crown of thorns, a mockery of royalty, since the suffering only and not the triumph and the mystical coronation are seen.

THE ROSE AND THE CROSS

In one aspect the opened rose upon the cross, in Rosicrucian symbolism, also represents perfected manhood. The rose is a symbol

[1] The sick woman who finds the Christ.

of the Higher Self of perfected man in its body of light, from which universal love, wisdom and blessing flow out upon the world, as represented both by the special fragrance of the flower and by the water and the blood flowing from the wounds of the crucified Christ.

The cross is generally interpreted as the symbol of self-sacrifice, immortality and holiness. Esoterically, however, the cross describes the whole mystery of creation. Creative Spirit as the positive, masculine creative potency, the Great Breath or " Word " (the vertical arm), descends into and penetrates matter as Space, the feminine creative potency, the Great Deep (the horizontal arm). The point of intersection is the critical centre at which the process of creation occurs and from which the product, the manifested Cosmos, arises. In this sense the rose upon the cross symbolises the newly-formed Universe. The descent of Spirit into matter (the vertical into the horizontal arms of the cross), and the subsequent attainment of self-conscious and perfected life (the rose), also suggests the processes of involution and evolution, of forthgoing and return, depicted in the Parable of the Prodigal Son.[1]

CRUCIFORM MAN

Man himself is perfectly symbolised by the cross, the vertical arm representing the Spirit in him and the horizontal the material entered, impregnated and supported by the former. Man's physical body is cruciform in a number of ways. The spinal column, for instance, is a vertical support from which, at right angles, the ribs[2] extend horizontally. The spinal cord is the major electro-magnetic " cable " of the body, and from it at right angles and horizontally large numbers of afferent and efferent nerves carry the nerve fluid and nerve impulses throughout the body. With arms outstretched in love and sacrifice, man's whole body makes a perfect cross. He only assumes this posture however when, rose-like, his heart is open in love and compassion for the world. Thus the rose upon the cross is both a beautiful and a dynamic symbol and an ideal to which to aspire, despite the inevitable pricks of the thorns.

[1] q.v. Part Four of this Volume.

[2] The rib is horizontal to the spine and so Eve, the feminine creative potency, is formed from Adam's rib.

UPON THE MOUNT

The mount is frequently used as a symbol of exalted states of consciousness. Many of the great events recorded in the Bible, occurred on mountain tops. Elijah, for example, had need of the counsel of the Lord and a voice said: " Go forth, and stand upon the mount before the LORD." [1] This is interpreted as an exhortation to elevate the centre of human awareness from the physical to the inner spiritual nature of man.

EARTHQUAKE, WIND AND FIRE

In the story of Elijah, illumination was preceded by an earthquake, rushing wind and fire. The earthquake is a symbol of the purely physical state of consciousness and of the instability and impermanence of the physical world, also symbolised by the sand upon which a house must not be built. The rushing wind refers to the disturbed state of the emotions, whilst the fire, in one meaning, represents the restless and disruptive activity of the critical, analytical and prideful mind. The Lord was not in any of these three phenomena, but after they had passed a great peace descended upon Elijah.. His soul was steeped in silence and in that stillness " the voice of the silence ", the " still small voice " of God, was heard. The story may now be seen as a manual of meditation, a description of the means whereby self-illumination may be obtained. The centre of self-awareness must be dissociated from the physical body (earthquake), from the emotional body (rushing wind), from the mind (fire), and established on those still higher levels wherein the Spiritual Self of man perpetually abides. Thereafter a great stillness descends upon the devotee, and in that profound quietude of heart and mind self-identification is attained with the God-Self, the Christ within. Thereafter illumination, comprehension, knowledge, are communicated to the mind and brain of the outer man.

In this preliminary chapter single interpretations, applying to psycho-spiritual human experience only, are given as illustrations of the theme of this book. Other keys of interpretation, Macrocosmic and microcosmic, are described and the results of their application offered in later Chapters of this Volume, and also in those

[1] 1 *Kings* 19 : 11.

Volumes in which certain of the Books of the Bible are interpreted verse by verse. The incident of Elijah and the " still small voice " will, for instance, be fully considered in the Volume dealing with the First Book of Kings.

THE LOGOS OF THE SOUL

As stated elsewhere, one of several possible methods of interpretation is that in which each story is regarded as descriptive of an interior, subjective experience, as if all happened within the soul of every man. The Apostle Paul evidently took this view. For him the nativity of Christ, for example, was a condition of the soul of man, for he said: ". . . I travail in birth again until Christ be formed in you." [1] Even the physical presence on Earth of the historical Christ, Whom Paul never met, is regarded by him as a mystical experience rather than an external visitation. The interior, rather than the historical, Christ was apparently of more importance to Paul, who said: ". . . Christ in you, the hope of glory " [2] and " . . . work out your own salvation with fear and trembling. For it is God which worketh in you . . . ".[3]

The German mystic of the Middle Ages, Scheffler,[4] who wrote as Angelus Silesius, expressed in the following words the necessity for translating into interior experience certain episodes in the life of Christ:

" Though Christ a thousand times in Bethlehem be born
And not within thyself, thy soul will be forlorn.
The Cross on Golgotha thou lookest to in vain
Unless, within thyself, it be set up again."

Herein lies the heart of true religion, which is less of theology, creed, blind faith and outer observances than of deep interior experience. The inspired authors of many Biblical narratives were well aware of this fact, and had themselves attained to profound

[1] *Gal.* 4 : 19.

[2] *Col.* 1: 27.

[3] *Phil.* 2:12 & 13.

[4] Scheffler (1624-1677) of Breslau, Silesia, Germany. Studied medicine in Strassburg (1643) and in Leyden (1644-46); contacted Jacob Boehme in Padua, Italy (1649-52); became a Franciscan monk and Priest (1661); died in the monastery of St. Matthias, Breslau (July 9, 1677). Books: *Cherubinischer Wandersmann* (1657) and *Geistliche Hirtenlieder.*

mystical illumination. They knew that realisation of the Presence and activity of the God within the Soul of every man bestowed spiritual, intellectual and occult powers which could, in truth, be grievously misused. Serious injury could be caused, both to those who prematurely discovered these interior powers and to all others who came within the range of their influence. Hence the safeguard of the symbolical language.

CHAPTER V

THE SUN STANDS STILL UPON GIBEON

THE INVISIBLE SUN WITHIN MAN

THE student of the Wisdom Religion is confronted with the statement that the whole Universe, physical and metaphysical, is reproduced or recorded in man and his physical and superphysical vehicles of self-expression: that sun, planets, satellites, their Regents, powers, beings, kingdoms of Nature and orders of life are all represented by a system of mutual resonances in every human being. Man is, in fact, described as an epitome of the whole Universe, a reproduction in miniature of all Nature, visible and invisible.[1]

This fundamental concept was known by ancient philosophers as the theory of the Macrocosm or " Great World " and the microcosm or " little world ". In the reflection of the Macrocosm (God and the Universe) in the microcosm (man) was said to lie the key to all knowledge; for through the part the whole may be perceived: through knowledge of the individual the universal may be comprehended. Hence the words carved over the doors of the Mystery Temples of old: " Man, Know Thyself."

" Man ", says the Ancient Wisdom, " is that being in whom highest spirit and lowest matter are united by intellect." Man is an epitome of the Cosmos, a microcosm in which the Macrocosm exists potentially.

If, as was taught and believed in the ancient Schools, all Nature exists potentially in man, then a clue may be discovered to a mystical meaning of the words of the title of this Chapter. The reference may be not to the external physical sun at all, but to a solar power and light indwelling within both Nature and man. " Life is a pure flame " says Sir Thomas Browne, the English mystic, " and we are lit by an invisible sun within us."

[1] q.v. Introduction, *Occult Powers in Nature and in Man*, Geoffrey Hodson.

4

In the sixtieth Chapter of the Book of *Isaiah*, which reads like a charge to an Initiate, there is also a suggestion that, at a certain stage of evolution, a sunlike source of light is revealed or self-declared within the spiritually awakened individual. He discovers an interior light and thereafter is no longer mentally and spiritually subjected to the alternations of night and day. The sun within him becomes his light for evermore. The Chapter begins with the words: " Arise, shine; for thy light is come, and the glory of the LORD is risen upon thee." Later verses read:

" *The sun shall be no more thy light by day; neither for brightness shall the moon give light unto thee: but the LORD shall be unto thee an ever-lasting light, and thy God thy glory.*"

" *Thy sun shall no more go down; neither shall thy moon withdraw itself: for the LORD shall be thine everlasting light, and the days of thy mourning shall be ended.*" [1]

There is evidence here that neither the physical sun nor the physical moon are referred to. It is apparent that some other non-physical, source of illumination is denoted.

A further interesting reference from the Bible, which supports this concept of the sun, is contained in the story of Joshua and his power to cause the sun and moon to stand still. Joshua had gone from Gilgal to relieve the besieged city of Gibeon, in answer to a call from its citizens. After the victory an extraordinary, not to say impossible, event is said to have occurred:

" *Then spake Joshua to the LORD in the day when the LORD delivered up the Amorites before the children of Israel, and he said in the sight of Israel, Sun, stand thou still upon Gibeon; and thou, Moon, in the valley of Ajalon.*

" *And the sun stood still, and the moon stayed, until the people had avenged themselves upon their enemies. Is not this written in the Book of Jasher? So the sun stood still in the midst of heaven, and hasted not to go down about a whole day.*

" *And there was no day like that before it or after it, that the LORD hearkened unto the voice of a man: for the LORD fought for Israel.*" [2]

Here, again, it seems clear that the reference is neither to the physical sun nor to the physical moon; for if the verses are taken

[1] *Is.* 60 : 19, 20.

[2] *Joshua* 10 : 12-14.

literally the astronomical knowledge of the authors is seen to be seriously at fault. As previously stated, it is the Earth which moves, not the sun, and if the Earth's rotation were suddenly arrested it would probably disintegrate. Moreover, if the sun had remained in the midst of the heavens there would have been neither need for nor value in a similar arrest of the movement of the moon.

JOSHUA MAKES THE SUN STAND STILL

What, then, is mystically implied by Joshua's action in keeping the sun " in the midst of heaven "? What is the significance of the statement, made both in the account of this incident and also in certain rituals of Initiation, that the sun can be held still at its meridian? In occult philosophy, the sun within man is his highest Spiritual Self, the Monad, centre and source in him of that divine Fire and Light of which, in their essence, both Macrocosm and microcosm consist. The moon, on the other hand, is used as a symbol of mortal man, who derives his light from the Spiritual Self or sun within, and with varying degrees of perfection and in different phases reflects that solar light.

The sun and the moon may therefore be taken to represent immortal and mortal aspects of human nature, the Spirit and the flesh of man. If one accepts this interpretation, Joshua is revealed as a highly developed man, an Initiate of the Greater Mysteries or School of the Prophets, perhaps, who, before he can pass to the next phase of his unfoldment, must have brought the highest (sun) and the lowest (moon) aspects of his nature under his control and placed them in harmonious relationship. In his outer life he must also have acquired the power to maintain the spiritual sun within him always at its meridian or position of maximum power. In terms of physical life and conduct, this may be taken to imply attainments of the power to rule all outer activities by spiritual will and according to spiritual laws. Since this power is dangerous, the way to its attainment is concealed, even while revealed, under a veil of symbology, and, indeed, of absurdity.

In terms of the seven principles [1] of man, Joshua represents the mind. Up to a certain stage of unfoldment the mind imprisons,

[1] q.v. p. 62.

distorts and, in consequence, frequently loses the light of the interior sun, the divine Self within.   Intellectually, man is subject to night and day, or to alternating periods of spiritual and intellectual light and darkness.   When, however, symbolically the battle of Gibeon has been successfully fought as by Joshua, then victory has been attained by the mind over both sun and moon and mastery achieved of interior spiritual power and light and of their material expression.

THE MYSTICAL BATTLE OF GIBEON

The description of the battle of Gibeon, like many others in world Scriptures, may be thus regarded as an allegory of the universal and perpetual Armageddon for which the whole of Nature, and so man himself, is the field.   It is the universal and individual conflict between Spirit and matter, life and form, consciousness and vehicle of expression.   Joshua personifies the man in whom that battle has been won, as Gibeon was won, by the aid of the Lord, the divine in man.   Victory was attained, because the forces of both sun and moon, or his spiritual and material natures, were under his control.   He, himself, had placed his sun at its meridian or position of maximum power.   Never again could the lower quaternary, the fourfold personality, obscure the rays of the threefold spiritual sun, the divine Self within.

The peace after the conflict may be taken to refer to that stillness of mind in which alone the direct rays of the spiritual sun can shine down into the mortal personality and illumine it.   Thus, the astronomically absurd standing still of both sun and moon can provide an important and even deliberate clue to the inner meaning of the allegory, as also a valuable guide to the attainment of self-illumination. By an effort of will and thought, Spiritual Self, mind and bodily consciousness can be brought into perfect " vertical " alignment and held there, always " on the plumb ".[1]

THE ANCIENT WISDOM AS SUN

Stillness of mind has ever been recognised as essential to self-illumination.   Elijah heard the divine Voice not in earthquake,

[1] Vertical.

wind or fire, but in the silence which followed after they had passed. The Psalmist enunciates this law in the words: " Be still, and know that I am God." [1]

The Ancient Wisdom itself is also regarded by many as the source of both the body of ideas common to World Faiths and the spiritual light received by man; for just as the physical sun brings light and life to the evolving forms of Nature, so the Ancient Wisdom is as a sun which brings illumination to the unfolding minds of men. Ideally orthodox religion should perform the two important functions of revealing to mankind this light of the Ancient Wisdom and providing the means whereby that light directly reaches the brain-mind of man. This the Greater Mysteries have done, for when a person is admitted to a valid occult Order he receives that light. In addition the act of consecration and the training which precede and follow it help to open his consciousness to its rays. Successive Initiations are recognitions of successive ascents into higher states of consciousness. Each ascent both draws the Initiate nearer to the Source, the spiritual sun, and by stimulation of appropriate physical and superphysical sense-organs increases his ability to perceive its light. Symbolically, the sun is first placed at its meridian or place of maximum power and, thereafter, is maintained in that position. Symbolically, for the successful Initiate, personified by Joshua, the sun stands still.

THE SOLAR FIRE

One condition of the descent of the solar fire from the spiritual sun, through the Monad or human, microcosmic sun, through the intellect and into the brain, is a complementary ascent from the centre of the planet of the fire, sometimes referred to as lunar, resident there. In occultly trained and developed man this force flows up into the spinal cord, to be concentrated at a force-centre at the base of the spine. Thence, when fully aroused, this fire rises in serpentine motion [2] within the spinal cord into the middle of the head, the Sanctuary or " East " in the Temple of the body. This extremely occult, potent power-bestowing and " dangerous " energy is universally

[1] *Ps.* 46 : 10.

[2] One of its names is the " serpent fire ". q.v. pp. 65, 83, and Part 3, Ch. I, ref. " Serpents ".

symbolised by dragons and serpents in various forms in one of their hidden meanings.

Egyptian religious art portrays portions of ceremonies of Initiation, and in most of the sculptures, relics, murals and papyri Candidates wear a triangular apron. This symbol also has many meanings. In one it represents the protective action of the will, which prevents this power from flowing forward into and through the physical creative organs and directs it upwards along the spinal cord into the head. There it is met by and united with the descending solar fire. This union is sometimes symbolised by marriage and even illicit unions. This flow and union of the two fires opens the doorway at the crown of the head (rolls away the stone of the sepulchre), and the consciousness of the Initiate is thereafter immortal, free (resurrected) from the separative tendency of the mind and the mortality of the body, from both of which it has now arisen.

The genuine secrets of the Mysteries then discovered consist less of expositions of facts, of intellectual concepts concerning life, than of direct, living experience of the divinity and universality of life and its mode of manifestation. The result is ever a secret, and always incommunicable to those who have not entered into the experience.

THE MOUNTAIN TOP AND SUN-CONSCIOUSNESS

The tables of the law were not so much deliberately broken by Moses as by the operation of certain laws of Nature revealed in the allegory. Only on the mountain-top—symbol of the higher consciousness, of spiritual exaltation—can illumination be gained. The resultant power, wisdom and knowledge are always marred, if not lost, as consciousness descends to lower levels. According to the Biblical allegory the tables of the law are broken, or spiritual light is darkened for those who as yet remain in the vale of exclusively mundane awareness, worshipping the golden calf of materialism and material power. For such men substituted secrets, in the form of allegories, parables, symbols, and the theology, creeds and observances of exoteric religion, will always be necessary and, indeed, all that is available to them. The genuine secrets can be known only by him who ascends regularly by the practice of meditation into the illumined state of his own Sun-self,[1] and through that into the Sun-Self of the Universe. By maintaining himself in that condition, he symbolically causes the sun to stand still.

The inner purpose of religion is thus to lift its followers on to the mountain-top of full spiritual awareness. There, as depicted by the story of Elijah and the " still small voice ",[2] communion with God, the divine Principle *within*, is attainable. On the mountain-top Moses inwardly perceived, rather than received from without, the laws of existence and their application to human conduct. On the mount Christ preached His greatest sermon,[3] and was transfigured.[4] So also every aspirant to light must symbolically ascend and there-after remain upon the mount, elevated mentally towards the sun within man.

THE OMNIPRESENT SUN

As in the many solar allegories in scripture and myth the physical sun is used as a symbol for both the all-pervading, omnipresent spiritual sun and its consequent presence in man, so may that luminary also be used in meditation as a gateway leading to spiritual illumination. When successful, meditation on the fiery orb leads the aspirant into its heart, in which the fire and the force aspects of the Solar System begin to be perceived. From this point of view the Universe is all sun. The globe of fire disappears, giving place to all-pervading sun-power, sun-life and sun-fire.

This is the universal Triplicity, the Trinity, reflected microcos-mically in man as his threefold Spiritual Self. In the exaltation of sun-consciousness all beings are recognised as part of the sun. The devotee knows himself as a manifestation of universal sun-fire and sun-force. For him, thus exalted, all objects glow and shine with the solar fire indwelling in every atom and every cell. The Earth itself is alight with a fiery glow. The subtler vesture of the Soul of the devotee shines uplifted. His consciousness is ablaze with sun-light and sun-fire. In ecstasy he knows himself as one with the sun, not

[1] " Life is a pure flame, and we are lit by an invisible sun within us." Sir Thomas Browne.
[2] 1 *Kings* 19 : 12.
[3] *Matt.* Chs. 5, 6 & 7.
[4] *Matt.* 17 : 1 & 2.

in duality but in unity and identity. The Solar System is known as a single sun, within which the thought of duality cannot arise. Sun-ness becomes the totality of existence. The sun is everything: everything is the sun.

The would-be Initiate must command this spiritual sun within him, his very Self, to stand still. This sun he must maintain at its maximum power, or in the perfect relation to his own life and consciousness indicated in the phrases " at its meridian " and " in the midst of heaven ". A similar symbolical reference to the sun occurs in the passage from *Isaiah*, Chapter sixty, verses nineteen and twenty, quoted earlier in this Chapter.

CHAPTER VI

THE AGELESS WISDOM

ANCIENT SOURCES OF KNOWLEDGE

WHENCE came the knowledge which is thus both revealed and concealed beneath the veil of allegory and symbol in the Scriptures of the world? Throughout the ages there have been aspiring men and women who have sought to solve the mysteries of life and death. There have also been illumined men and women who, having solved those mysteries, have given their solutions to certain carefully selected disciples.[1] These disciples in their turn have delivered a portion of this knowledge to the world.[2] In the east it is called *Brahma Vidya*, the Wisdom of *Brahma*, the Supreme Deity. Greek philosophers of the neo-Platonic Schools, notably Ammonius Saccus and his disciples,[3] referred to this knowledge as *Theosophia*, Divine Wisdom. It was also known as gnosis, meaning directly perceived spiritual knowledge, and those who had entered into first-hand experience of it were known as gnostics or knowers. In English it is severally termed Theosophy, the Ancient Wisdom, the Ageless Wisdom and the Wisdom Religion of the planet Earth.

Certain power-bestowing teachings, it is here repeated, were regarded as potentially dangerous and were, therefore, either withheld or veiled. As general knowledge has since advanced, some of these teachings have become public knowledge. Nevertheless direct experience of them still remains an interior secret, an esotericism, which can be personally realised but never fully conveyed to others. The way to such knowledge is also both revealed and concealed in

---

[1] The Lord Christ followed this practice, saying to His disciples: "Unto you it is given to know the mystery of the kingdom of God: but unto them that are without, all these things are done in parables." (*Mk.* 4: 11).

[2] "But we speak the wisdom of God in a mystery, even the hidden wisdom, which God ordained before the world unto our glory." (1 *Cor.* 2: 7).

[3] *Neo-Platonism and Alchemy*, by Professor Alex. Wilder, M.D.

the Scriptures and Mythologies of mankind. This "narrow way" has from the earliest period of man's occupation of the Earth been followed by a small number of spiritually awakened human beings. Guidance concerning this spiritual way of life, and descriptions of experiences through which the soul [1] passes and of the tests, ordeals and triumphs of the neophyte, run like a silver thread through the tapestry woven by the inspired authors of the Scriptures and Mythologies of ancient peoples. In one interpretation of them—the Initiatory—the great figures, heroes, Prophets, Apostles, Saviours and their adversaries, represent followers of the Ancient Way at various stages of attainment or failure. The accounts of the lives of such people as Jacob and his twelve [2] sons, the twelve tribes of Israel, the twelve disciples of Christ, and Hercules and his twelve labours, have proved extremely instructive to those who can pierce the veil of allegory beneath which the secrets of discipleship and Initiation are concealed.

The teachings of the Ageless Wisdom are thus to be found at the heart of the great World Faiths as a group of central doctrines common to them all. The Ancient Wisdom is indeed the oldest of all religions, having from the first included the highest and noblest conceptions of the soul of man which have ever been presented to or recognised by the human mind, and knowledge of the nature of the divinity within him. *Theosophia* is the Wisdom of Divine Beings, and carries with it the idea that Divine Wisdom has been and can be attained by man as the natural and legitimate goal of his evolution.

This universality is revealed by an examination of the sacred books of various religions and the original sayings of the world's greatest Teachers, for a singular uniformity is found in them all. One might readily suspect that this uniformity is something more than a coincidence, apart even from the consideration that there can only be one truth. The highest and best teaching must always

---

[1] *Soul.* Throughout this work, in order to reduce ambiguity concerning the meaning of this term to a minimum, a capital initial is used when the unfolding, immortal, spiritual principle of man is meant, e.g. Spiritual Soul. The term " Ego " is also used to denote this centre of the sense of individuality in man. A small " s " is used when the *psyche*, the mental and emotional aspects of the mortal personality, are referred to—e.g. soul.

[2] *Twelve.* This number has its own mystical meanings, referring partly to the powers in man corresponding to the Signs of the Zodiac, and also to states, qualities and degrees of development of the human soul. Twelve is regarded as symbolic of spiritual perfection and completion.

approximate to this, and therefore present a considerable amount of similarity when we strip it of all merely fortuitous differences in the modes of its presentation. The Ancient Wisdom provides an actual basis for this parallelism by disclosing the existence of a Hierarchy of Initiates and Adepts, Who preserve from age to age the esoteric teachings which otherwise might have been entirely lost.

THE KEEPERS OF THE SACRED LIGHT

There are several considerations which would point to the existence of such a Hierarchy as the original source from which all great Teachers have derived their knowledge. The theory that there does exist a unifying truth, an esoteric knowledge or *Theosophia*, within the reach of every member of the human Race, its attainment being the natural goal of his development, carries with it the idea that such relatively secret knowledge must have its living representatives.

"The Secret Doctrine (or Theosophy) is the accumulated Wisdom of the Ages and its cosmogony alone is the most stupendous and elaborate of all systems . . . the facts which have actually occupied countless generations of initiated seers and prophets to marshall, set down and explain—are all recorded on a few pages of geometrical signs and glyphs. The flashing gaze of those seers has penetrated to the very kernel of matter, and recorded the soul of things there, where an ordinary profane observer, however learned, would have perceived but the external work of form . . . . The Secret Doctrine is an uninterrupted record, covering thousands of generations of seers, whose respective experiences were made to test and verify the traditions, passed on orally by one early race to another, of the teachings of higher and exalted Beings who watched over the childhood of Humanity . . . They did this by checking, testing and verifying, in every department of Nature, the traditions of old, by the independent visions of great Adepts; that is to say, men who have developed and perfected their physical, mental, psychic and spiritual organisations to the utmost possible degree. No vision of one Adept was accepted till it was checked and confirmed by the visions—so obtained as to stand as independent evidence—of other Adepts, and by centuries of experience." [1]

[1] *The Secret Doctrine*, H. P. Blavatsky.   (Vol. 1, Adyar Ed., p. 316).

THE DANGERS OF MISAPPLIED KNOWLEDGE

Before some of the chief tenets of the Ageless Wisdom are presented, the theme of this work may usefully be enlarged upon. This theme, as previously stated, is that certain of these teachings, if thoroughly grasped, can prove to be sources of magical power. To preserve and convey this power-giving knowledge a peculiar language was invented by its discoverers. By means of pseudo-history, allegory and symbol this information is at the same time both revealed and concealed. Man's unawareness of spiritual and occult teachings is due, however, not only to their protective concealment within Scripture and Mythology, but also to his lack of interest in them. Humanity at this phase of its evolution is, not unnaturally, more interested in the material world, its pleasures and rewards, than in the quest for interior enlightenment, the attainment of which, it may be added, demands a measure of renunciation. Blood sports, racing, gambling, indulgence in alcohol and sex, and the attainment of money and power, tend to absorb man's interest, inevitably leaving little room in his mind for the higher culture and for aspiration to spiritual unfoldment.

When, however, a person seriously turns from worldly things to a real quest for knowledge, that knowledge is always to be found. Even then, full perception cannot be reached without due preparation. Just as one cannot take electricity out of the air and immediately use it, so spiritual enlightenment demands self-education and training before it can be discovered, harnessed and used. Whilst certain aspects of occult lore are admittedly reserved because they are a source of great power which could be harmfully employed, the majority of men remain uninformed because they have neither seriously sought spiritual understanding nor proved ready to undergo the training necessary for its attainment.

In order more fully to understand the reasons for the universal practice of veiling certain ideas in allegory and symbol, it is necessary to know both the true nature of man and his capabilities. Concerning human nature, the apostle Paul's definition conforms to the most ancient teachings: " Know ye not that ye are the temple of God, and that the Spirit of God dwelleth in you? " [1] and ". . . ye are the

---

[1] 1 *Cor.* 3: 16.

temple of the living God. . ." [1] The living God, the pure Spirit in man, is not a separate individuality but a Ray of the one infinite ocean of Light, the Universal Godhead. This knowledge places great power within reach of its possessor, for if the divine Ray within man becomes an active influence in his physical individuality, it endows him with God-like powers.[2] "The highest revelation", declares Emerson, "is that God is in every man." Such, briefly, is man—pure Spirit enshrined in a physical body and operating through a human mind. "The first man is of the earth, earthy; the second man is the Lord from heaven. . . . Behold, I show you a mystery. . ." [3]

Man's capabilities include the ability to bring about the manifestation in his outer self of the purely spiritual aspect of his nature. He then becomes endowed with superhuman powers, including those of almost irresistible will, supersensory faculties and supernormal physical capacities. Used for the benefit of his fellow-men, these can be of value. Misused for personal or national gain at the cost of others, they can be extremely harmful. A wonderful possibility and a very grave danger are, however, associated with these enhanced powers. The possibility is that man may use them to gain still greater knowledge which can be placed at the service of his fellow-men. The danger is that, blinded by egoism and a passion for domination, he may be tempted to use his increased faculties for destructive purposes. In order that the danger may be reduced to a minimum and the power-giving knowledge be preserved and made available to mankind, it is formulated and delivered in a very ancient language composed of allegory, parable, imagery and symbol.

TEACHINGS CONCERNING MAN

What, then, was discovered and taught direct to disciples and in parables to non-disciples? What is the "mystery of the kingdom of God",[4] ultimately to be known direct by the sincere seeker? The answer can be offered here only in the merest outline; a digest, as it

[1] 2 *Cor.* 6 : 16.
[2] *Gen.* 3: 5.
[3] I *Cor.* 15: 47-51.
[4] *Mk.* 4: 11.

were, of certain central ideas to be found in world religions, philosophies and Mythologies, however deeply veiled. *Theosophia* is all-inclusive and some of its more universal ideas are presented later in this work, more particularly in the Chapter on the Parable of the Prodigal Son. Full knowledge of man himself, his complete anatomy, is contained within the age-old teachings, together with a very practical philosophy of life consistent with the scientific method of thought and—all-important—a description of the means whereby that knowledge may become direct, personal experience.

The ancient sages taught, and their successors still teach, that man is sevenfold in his make-up, being a threefold immortal, spiritual being incarnated in four mortal, material bodies. The three parts of man's spiritual nature are reproductions or reflections in him of the Will, the Wisdom and the Intelligence of the Supreme Deity. In their vesture of light these three Aspects of the Divine in man are called severally his individuality, his Inner Self or Spiritual Soul and, more technically, the Ego [1] in the Causal Body. The pertinent teaching concerning both the Deity and man is that they are threefold. God the Trinity reproduces Himself as the threefold Spiritual Self or Soul of every human being.

The Apostle Paul states this truth more plainly, perhaps, than any other Biblical writer in such utterances as: ". . . ye are the temple of the living God; as God hath said, I will dwell in them, and walk in them, and I will be their God . . ." [2] and ". . . know ye not that your body is the temple of the Holy Ghost which is in you, which ye have of God, and ye are not your own? . . . therefore glorify God in your body, and in your spirit, which are God's." [3] Directly stated, Man-Spirit and God-Spirit are one Spirit.

When once this knowledge becomes personal experience, it provides a key to almost unlimited power. Cosmic forces and Intelligences are then contacted, and can be invoked and employed mentally and physically in any manner that may be decided upon. As has already been stated, since this tremendous power is susceptible

---

[1] *Ego:* Used throughout the work to denote the unfolding Spiritual Self of man in which the attribute of individuality inheres. The adjective " Egoic " refers to the Ego in this meaning.

[2] *2 Cor.* 6 : 16.

[3] *1 Cor.* 6 : 19-20.

of misuse the true and full significance of such statements was veiled by the ancient writers. One outstanding example is the story of the stilling of the tempest by the hitherto sleeping Jesus Christ, Who personifies God's Spirit and Presence within man.[1]

In this spiritual aspect of his nature man—sometimes called the microcosm—is regarded as one with the Divine, the Macrocosm. That Supreme Spirit, Who is the "immortal and eternal God Who forever reigneth serene above the water floods", and the Spirit of man are one Spirit. In Hinduism, because of its paramount importance, this truth is referred to as the sovereign secret, or the royal secret. The Deity is neither external to nor different from man. God and man are one and indivisible throughout all eternity. This is the supreme truth taught directly in all Mystery Schools and in the esoteric aspects of all religions. In Hinduism the Spirit in man is described as "the Inner Ruler Immortal seated in the heart of all beings", "the one Godhead hidden in all creatures, the inmost soul of all." In Christianity the Deity in man is the "Christ in you, the hope of glory",[2] the "God that worketh in you",[3] the living God for which the body is a temple.

The stories of Adam, Eve, the tempting serpent and the tree of knowledge of good and evil in the Garden of Eden; Abraham ready to sacrifice his son, Isaac, on a mountain; Elijah and the still small voice; Moses on Mount Sinai receiving the Ten Commandments; Joshua making the sun and moon stand still; Jonah in the belly of the whale; the Nativity of the Lord Christ in a stable; His withering of the fig tree; His stilling of the tempest; His healings and raising of people from the dead; His Resurrection and His Ascension—these all reveal in allegory the secret of power. This aspect of the universal Wisdom is also revealed in such non-Biblical stories as those relating the labours of Hercules; the voyage of the Argonauts to gain the serpent-guarded Golden Fleece at Colchis; Osiris slain and Osiris risen; and the birth in prison of the Lord Shri Krishna and His victory over many evil beings, including the black serpent Kaliya.

[1] q.v. Part One, Ch. IV.
[2] *Col.* 1: 27.
[3] *Phil.* 2 : 13.

The distinction between the Logos of a Universe and the Deity in man lies neither in Their location nor in Their essential nature, but only in the degree in which Their triune powers are made manifest. In God these are manifested fully, but in man in a gradually increasing degree of fulness as his evolution proceeds. Ultimately the inherent divine powers will be fully expressed by the Spiritual Self of every man, as they are now by the Deity. In this teaching the destiny of man is revealed: he is a God-in-the-becoming, a pilgrim God. Both the Lord Christ and the Apostle Paul affirmed this fact in such words as: " Ye shall be perfect, even as your Father which is in heaven is perfect " [1] and " Till we all come in the unity of the faith, and of the knowledge of the Son of God, unto a perfect man, unto the measure of the stature of the fulness of Christ." [2] Such, as revealed in the Ageless Wisdom, is the threefold, immortal, Spiritual Self of man, sometimes referred to as the Higher Triad, and such is the sublime purpose of man's existence.

Man's four more densely material vehicles—sometimes referred to as the lower quaternary—in the order of their deepening density are the mental, the emotional, the etheric and the physical bodies. The mental body, the most tenuous of the four, is composed of mental matter or mind-stuff and this is his vehicle of analytical, logical thought. The emotional body, man's vehicle of feeling and desire, is composed of material which is denser than mind-stuff but finer than the physical ether. The vital or etheric body is composed of etheric substance which is finer than the gaseous, and functions as the conserving principle of his bodily vital forces and the connecting link between the superphysical and physical bodies. The corporeal body is composed of solid, liquid and gaseous materials and is his vehicle of self-expression in the physical world, his densest, heaviest instrument of awareness and action. Man's seven bodies, comprising the Higher Triad and the lower quaternary, all occupy the same space, the finer interpenetrating and extending as an aura beyond the denser.

Knowledge of this sevenfold nature of man can be a key with which to unlock powers within man and the Universe around him,

[1] *Matt.* 5 : 48 (R.V.).
[2] *Eph.* 4 : 13.

which is also sevenfold. Each of man's seven bodies is in mutual resonance with forces and Intelligences in the corresponding seven parts of the Cosmos. The powers and Intelligences associated with the seven planes of Nature, the planets and the twelve Signs of the Zodiac, can be evoked and employed for constructive or destructive purposes by the man who possesses this key of the septenary constitution of Universe and man. For this and other reasons such power-bestowing knowledge, though partly conveyed, is heavily veiled in world Scriptures and Mythologies. In many of them the seven principles of man are personified by *dramatis personae* who display their typical attributes, as is indicated later in the present and also in succeeding volumes of this work.

SPIRITUAL KNOWLEDGE LOST AND REGAINED

When man's consciousness is limited to the fourfold mortal aspect of himself, he is temporarily unconscious of both his divine nature and his unity with God. When limited to brain consciousness, he may be said to suffer from spiritual " amnesia ". This forgetfulness can be overcome by arousing into activity and directing into the brain a certain electro-vital power resident in the physical body of man. This tremendous force is already partly active, being the source of nerve energy and of the procreative impulse and power. When more fully aroused, sublimated and directed into the heart and the head, it greatly heightens the speed of the vibratory frequency of the cells and the organs of the brain—electrifies them, in fact. Thereafter, the man thus sensitised becomes aware that he is a spiritual being endowed with divine powers. Because this force follows undulating pathways in its ascent along the spinal cord from the sacrum to the brain, it is sometimes referred to as " the Serpent Fire". Its potency is so great, however, that in many ancient Scriptures it is only referred to under a protective veil of such symbols as serpents, dragons, hydras and other dangerous reptiles. For the same reason, knowledge of the method of its premature awakening is also protectively concealed in allegories of the conquest of serpents by Saviours and heroes.

As man's evolution proceeds the Serpent Fire is naturally awakened, thereby assisting him to recover the lost knowledge of his

5

own divinity and his unity with God. This is the ultimate object of all spiritual endeavours. Especially is it the goal of all who seek the way of mystical illumination. The Lord Christ described this experience in His words: " I and my Father are one " [1] and " I am in my Father, and ye in me, and I in you." [2] Alexander Pope states: " All are but parts of one stupendous whole." An American poet has recently written of " The burning oneness binding everything." [3] Oneness with God, and through Him with all that lives, is the supreme truth and its full and continuous realisation is the highest attainment of man.

In a Hindu Scripture, the *Bhagavad Gita* (*The Lord's Song*), the Lord *Vishnu* as the Second Aspect of the Trinity, says: " He who seeth Me in everything and seeth everything in Me, of him will I never lose hold, and he shall never lose hold of Me." [4]

In *Passport*, Angela Morgan writes:

" Hurl thou thy cry at Heaven's gate,
God must admit thee soon or late.
Thy passport? Saints could ask no more,
His image at thy very core."

The true salvation of man, following his " Fall ", is an ascent into full experience of this fact of oneness with God, implying ascension into conscious union with the Deity.

THE PURPOSE OF MAN'S EXISTENCE

Why, then, does the human Spirit become incarnate in a physical body with the consequent loss, however temporary, of knowledge of its divinity and unity with God? The purpose of man's existence is spiritual, intellectual, cultural and physical evolution. This is a dual process, consisting on the one hand of the gradual unfoldment from latency to full potency of man's threefold spiritual attributes, and on the other of the evolution of his four material vehicles to a condition in which they perfectly make manifest the developed powers of the human Spirit. Life in a physical body is essential to this attainment.

---

[1] *Jn.* 10: 30.
[2] *Jn.* 14: 20.
[3] *There is a Spirit*, Kenneth Boulding, Sonnet 1.
[4] 6th *Discourse*, 30. Translated by Annie Besant.

The Spiritual Self of man is like a seed, in that it contains the potentiality of the parent plant, which is God. This seed is " sown " or born on Earth, puts forth shoots, stems and leaves, and eventually it flowers. The resultant human individuality in its four vehicles is strengthened by the winds of adversity, purified and refined by the rain of sorrow, beautified and expanded by the sunshine of happiness and love, and ultimately reaches the fully flowered state. Just as in seeds all parental powers are inherent, so in the Monads of men all divine powers are potentially present from the beginning. The experiences of life, combined with the interior evolutionary impulse, bring these inherent powers to increasing fulness and perfection of expression. All experience is valuable; nothing is wasted. Life is truly educative. Egoic unfoldment and bodily development proceed simultaneously, inner evolution being accompanied by the outer development of the four mortal bodies. Here theosophical teaching becomes eminently practical, for when this all-important knowledge of the purpose of human life is gained and accepted the intelligent man co-operates, and in such co-operation with the divine plan resides the whole secret of human happiness.

To what heights, then, does humanity ultimately attain? The goal of human evolution is the standard of perfection described in Christianity as " the measure of the stature of the fulness of Christ." [1] This implies the attainment of a divine state of perfected (only as far as human evolution is concerned) and resistless will, perfected and all-embracing wisdom and love, and perfected and all-inclusive knowledge.

The Ageless Wisdom affirms that the attainment of this culmination of human development is absolutely certain for every man. The command: " Be ye therefore perfect, even as your Father which is in Heaven is perfect ",[2] will be literally obeyed by the Spiritual Self of all human beings. *A lost Spiritual Soul is an impossibility in Nature*, for the true Self of man is immortal, eternal and indestructible. Indeed, there is nothing to be saved from, nowhere to be lost, for God as the enfolding and indwelling life of the Universe is omnipresent. Man needs only to be on guard against the defects

[1] *Eph.* 4 : 13.
[2] *Matt.* 5 : 48.

of his own character and the transgressions to which they lead, for all his sufferings arise (karmically) [1]—educatively moreover—from such transgressions.

The evolutionary process is itself everlasting, being without conceivable beginning or imaginable end. Beyond human perfection is a still higher attainment reached during passage through the super-human kingdoms of Nature, followed by a general ascent towards the spiritual stature of the Logos of a Universe. Beyond that again progress continues towards the highest possible degree of unfoldment attainable at the end of a major cosmic period of manifestation. Even then, at the succeeding re-emergence of Cosmos from chaos, of activity from quiescence, development will continue from the point previously attained and proceed to still greater heights. Perfection is thus hardly the best word, since it suggests finality. Actually it is only attained in a relative sense, for it must give room to still further perfection, according to a higher standard of excellence in the following period of activity—just as a perfect flower must cease to be a perfect flower and die in order to grow into a perfect fruit, if such a mode of expression may be permitted.[2] Man is an evolving spiritual being and will one day become as God now is. Man is a God-in-the-becoming, a pilgrim God.

THE NATURE OF DIVINITY

What is meant by the term " God "? The Ageless Wisdom affirms the existence of one transcendent, self-existent life, eternal, all-pervading, all-sustaining, whence, whereby and wherein all things which exist live and move and have their being. This life is immanent in our Solar System and world as the Logos, the " Word ", worshipped under different names in different religions but recognised as the one Creator, Preserver and Regenerator. The Solar System is directed and guided by the Solar Logos through a Hierarchy of highly evolved Beings, the " Mighty Spirits before the Throne ". On Earth this direction and guidance are carried out by a Hierarchy of Perfected Men, referred to as *Rishis*, sages, Adepts, Saints. The Divine, Absolute Principle reveals Itself in a universal process of perpetual unfoldment

---

[1] *Karma (Sk.)*   The law of cause and effect.
[2] *The Secret Doctrine*, Adyar Ed., Vol. 1, p. 115.

of potentialities. Although this is fulfilled according to eternal law it is not mechanical, being directed and aided by the Solar Logos through His Ministers. God is thus presented as both Transcendent and Immanent, as the Creator,[1] Sustainer and Transformer of all worlds and the spiritual Source of all beings within His Solar System.

These definitions of Deity do not harmonise with the idea of God generally accepted in Christianity. In the Ageless Wisdom God is not presented as an anthropomorphic figure, an Almighty Being in human form and with human tendencies combined with divine powers. He[2] is not regarded as susceptible of propitiation, but rather as an embodiment of eternal law. He does not bestow favours on some and withhold them from others, all His children being regarded equally. He is not distant in a far-off Heaven, but actually present as the divine life in Nature and the divine Presence in man, the " God which worketh in you. . ."[3]

The Solar Logos is, however, said not to be so impersonal and impartial as to be unmindful of the aspirations and vicissitudes of human beings. On the contrary, He may be thought of as responding to sincere and selfless aspiration to increasing wisdom and power to serve. Within the law of justice, or cause and effect, nations and individuals receive divine aid both directly and through the mediation of Representatives. Divine Grace is regarded as a reality which may descend upon man, either directly from the Solar Logos or from the innermost Divine Self. A wealth of testimony is provided by those who have experienced unexpected exaltation, inspiring enhancement of their will-power and intellectual grasp. Seemingly miraculous upliftment of Spirit and the healing of disease are similarly affirmed.

At this point the student of the Ageless Wisdom meets with a statement concerning Deity which, though inevitable in logic, may at first be unacceptable, and even repugnant. It is that God, as the divine Principle in Nature and in man, is evolving together with the whole Universe and all which it contains towards a goal which

---

[1] Emanator is philosophically a more acceptable term, the Universe being regarded as an emanation from the Absolute and under the direction of the Logos, or " God ".

[2] The masculine is used for convenience only, the divine Principle being regarded as equally masculine, feminine and androgyne.

[3] *Phil.* 2 : 13.

is beyond the comprehension of mortal man. This unfoldment to ever greater heights is the ultimate destiny of man, " the one far-off divine event, to which the whole creation moves."[1] Since the Spiritual Self of man is a God-in-the-becoming, his future splendour, wisdom and power are entirely without limit.

THE JUST MEN MADE PERFECT

The goal of human perfection has already been reached, such perfected men being known as World Saviours, *Mahātmas*,[2] *Rishis*, Adepts and, when They take pupils, Masters of the Wisdom. These superhuman Beings constitute the Inner Government of the World, and are the true spiritual Teachers and Inspirers of mankind. Each member of this Adept Fraternity would seem to be referred to in the Bible as having been " made an high priest for ever after the order of Melchisedec."[3] The Apostle Paul may have wished to indicate them by his phrase " just men made perfect ".[4] This august assembly is also known as " The Great White Brotherhood of Adepts ", the Adept Hierarchy, the *Sangha* of Buddhism, and the " Seven *Rishis* and Their Successors " of Hinduism. Nietsche expressed this idea of man as an evolving being in his words:

" Man is something to be surpassed."
" Man is a bridge and not a goal."
" Man is a rope stretched over the abyss
    between the animal and the super-man."

How is this state of Adeptship attained? It is a natural result of evolutionary progress and is achieved by means of successive incarnations in material vehicles, newly-formed during the pre-natal period of each succeeding life. Repeated reincarnations in physical bodies provide the necessary time and opportunity for such attainment. The multifarious experiences thus passed through draw out the latent powers of the evolving Spiritual Soul, which is the true man. Every experience has its value in terms of an increase of innate Egoic power, wisdom and knowledge. At the near approach to perfection, however,

[1] *In Memoriam*, Tennyson, St. 36.
[2] *Mahātma*, (*Sk.*) Great Spirit.
[3] *Heb.* 6: 20.
[4] *Heb.* 12: 23.

rebirth is no longer a necessity. All further progress can then be achieved in the superphysical worlds. This is stated in the Book of *Revelation* in the following words: " Him that overcometh will I make a pillar in the temple of my God, and he shall go no more out. . ." [1]

" WHATSOEVER A MAN SOWETH, THAT SHALL HE ALSO REAP " [2]

All reincarnations are connected with each other by the operation of the law of cause and effect. Under this law all actions, feelings and thoughts produce their own natural and perfectly appropriate reactions, which may follow the causative actions immediately, later in the same life, or in succeeding incarnations. It is referred to in many places in the Bible, Paul's statement being: " God is not mocked; for whatsoever a man soweth, that shall he also reap." The Sanskrit word *karma* (action) is used to designate this law, its operation and the effects it produces. Under its working, actions motivated by love, service and unselfishness produce pleasure and a growing freedom of self-expression, which encourage the actor to repeat them. On the other hand actions motivated by dislike, greed and selfishness produce pain and an increasing limitation of self-expression, which discourage the actor from repeating them. Furthermore, the intensity of pleasure or pain is governed by the degree in which unselfish and selfish motives find expression in action. This balanced compensation is affirmed in the words of the Lord Christ: " Judge not, that ye be not judged. For with what judgment ye judge, ye shall be judged; and with what measure ye mete, it shall be measured to you again." [3]

Human suffering is thus seen to be neither a retribution imposed by the Deity, a punishment inflicted from above, nor an unjust, accidental adversity. On the contrary all pain is self-inflicted, and therefore justly received. It is, moreover, designed to apprise the actor of his transgression. Suffering is thus seen to be both just and truly beneficent, because educative in its ultimate effect. Recognition of the law of action and reaction solves the problem of justice for man. All human conditions—suffering, disease, happiness and health—are

[1] *Rev.* 3 : 12.
[2] *Gal.* 6 : 7.
[3] *Matt.* 7: 1-2.

self-created under law.   The problem presented by the birth of babies which are malformed or diseased is solved when the sequence of cause and effect is recognised as operating throughout a series of lives. Whilst such afflictions seem on the surface to be completely unjust because unearned, and so undeserved, they are not really so.   They are, in fact, *the strictly appropriate effects of causes generated by the same Ego in former lives*.   Without this explanation life is, indeed, a hopeless riddle defying solution.   The twin doctrines of reincarnation and *karma* throw a flood of light upon human life, revealing the existence of justice, purpose, and an assured goal for all men.

MAN CAN MASTER CIRCUMSTANCES

The principle needs to be advanced here of the modification of *karma* by intervening actions performed before causes have had time to produce their full effects.   Whatever one's actions in the past— good or bad in varying degress—the reactions which they produce are not to be regarded as an inescapable fate, or as a dead weight from which there is no relief.   Both individuals and nations by their subsequent actions are constantly modifying the operation of the law upon themselves.   Thus, neither individuals nor nations are paralysed by their past actions.   Everything is not irretrievably fated. Man can master circumstances and make of each experience an opportunity for a fresh beginning, however heavily the past may weigh upon him.   He can pass from the grip of the law by learning to work with it.

Civil law is an enemy to the criminal because it restrains him, restricting the expression of his criminal tendencies.   To the good citizen, however, the same law is an assurance of security; it is not an enemy but a friend, not a source of restriction but a preserver of freedom.   This is also true of the universal law of cause and effect. To selfish, lawless and cruel people it brings nemesis, retribution in the form of a reaction appropriate to every pain-producing action. To unselfish, law-abiding, kindly people the law brings health, happiness and freedom.[1]   Furthermore, every such helpful action *performed before the effects have had time to be precipitated* reduces, and may even

---

[1] For a fuller exposition of this subject and for further Biblical texts, see *Reincarnation, Fact or Fallacy?*, Geoffrey Hodson.

neutralise, oncoming adversities. Such, briefly, is the principle of the modification of human *karma*. There is thus a spiritual alchemy by means of which adversity resulting from actions motivated by selfishness can be diminished, or even nullified. This is achieved by self-purification, self-discipline, and the enactment of deeds motivated by universal, non-possessive love.

THE PATHWAY TO PEACE

Such a mode of life partly constitutes " The way of Holiness " and the " narrow way " of Christianity, the " Noble Eightfold Path " of Buddhism and the " Razor-edged Path " of Hinduism. The Christ said: " Enter ye in at the strait gate: for wide is the gate, and broad is the way, that leadeth to destruction, and many there be which go in thereat: Because strait is the gate, and narrow is the way, which leadeth unto life, and few there be that find it." [1] This way of life leads to a quickening of evolutionary progress and the development in advance of the normal time of supernormal faculties, including spiritual intuitiveness and thamaturgic powers. It also leads to discipleship of an Adept Teacher, and thence through successive Initiations to Salvation or Perfection, *Nirvana*, *Moksha* or Liberation. [2]

The lives of Christ and His Disciples, as well as of other great Teachers, may be regarded as dramatic representations of the experiences of the soul on this Path. The teachings of the Lord Christ, particularly those in the Sermon on the Mount, of the Lord Buddha concerning the Noble Eightfold Path and its applications to the spiritual life, and of the Lord Shri Krishna as recorded in the *Bhagavad Gita*, indicate the motives and the conduct necessary for this attainment.

The Noble Eightfold Path was defined by the Lord Buddha as consisting of: " Right Belief, Right Thought, Right Speech, Right Action, Right Means of Livelihood, Right Exertion, Right Remembrance, Right Meditation or Rapture." This path—noble indeed— He summed up in these words: " To cease from sin, to acquire virtue, to purify the heart, to serve the world." " The way of Holiness ",

[1] *Matt.* 7: 13-14.

[2] Since this esoteric aspect of religion is referred to under a veil of symbolism in the Scriptures of the world, and especially in the Bible, it is more fully expounded in Part Six of this Volume.

leading to hastened progress and rapid development of spiritual powers, is open today as of old. Success in finding and treading it demands purity of life, selfless service and an unconquerable will.

This group of ideas may briefly be summed up as follows:—

Man is essentially a spiritual being, his mind and his body being only temporary means of self-expression and self-unfoldment. When this true Self is discovered and becomes the directing power, there is permanent peace for the individual and for the Race. Without that discovery peace is impossible. The search for and the discovery of the Self is therefore of supreme importance.

The evolution of the Spiritual Self to perfection through successive lives on Earth is the true purpose of human existence.

Man's experiences are decided by the operation of the Law of Cause and Effect. Cruelty brings war to Nations and pain and disease to individuals. There is no possible escape from this sequence.

Inversely, kindness brings happiness and health. Until this Law is recognised and accepted as a rule of life, there will continue to be both war and disease.

The Spirit within all men is one Spirit. Each man belongs to one spiritual Race, which is without divisions of any kind.

Experience of this unity, and its application to human life, constitute the only possible means whereby lasting peace can be established on Earth and assured health and happiness be attained by every human being.

Such, in part, are the teachings of the Wisdom of the Ages concerning man. Such is the pathway to health, happiness, perfection and eternal peace. As already stated, whilst making the less dangerous aspects of *Theosophia* available to mankind, the great Teachers of the Race concealed the more dangerous, power-bestowing knowledge beneath the allegories and symbols of which the Sacred Language consists. In Their compassion They have also provided the keys whereby layer after layer of truth may be unveiled. Some of these keys and the fruits of their application are presented in succeeding Chapters and Volumes of this work. Since, however, one of these keys (the Initiatory) is concerned with the interpretation of certain passages as revealing knowledge of this Path, Chapter I of Part Six of this Volume is devoted to an exposition of this ancient ideal.

PART TWO

THE MYSTERIES OF THE KINGDOM

CHAPTER I

SOME KEYS OF INTERPRETATION

WHILE the preceding Chapters contain introductory examples of the use of the symbolical language and methods of interpretation, in this Chapter a fuller exposition is offered. This is very necessary, for those who would discover the truths concealed within the Scriptures of the world should first acquaint themselves with the various keys to the symbolical writings. Then, reading each story very carefully, giving special attention to the symbols employed, they should dwell in concentrated thought upon its various parts, meditatively seeking the reality behind the shadow, the eternal truth within the story in time; for successful interpretation is primarily an experience in consciousness.

Certain age-old symbols serve as signposts on the way, each with its meaning constant throughout all time, as the doctrine everywhere revealed is constant also. The Hierophants [1] of Egypt, Chaldea, Assyria and Greece, the sages of the Eastern worlds and the inspired authors of the Bible all made use of these symbols as living, time-free ideographs which questing men of every age might comprehend. Nations, civilisations and religions rise and fall, but these earthly symbols of spiritual truths are ageless and unchanging. By their use an Egyptian Hierophant, a Jewish Prophet, an Essene monk, an Eastern sage, may speak direct from the remote past to the mind of modern man.

The authors who wrote in this allegorical manner wished to reveal Macrocosmic and microcosmic truths, to describe supersensuous conditions of consciousness. They used history only as weft and warp on which to weave a representation of everlasting verities, the esoteric wisdom of all ages, the deeply occult knowledge of the Initiates of the Mystery Schools of both ancient and more modern days. Time

[1] Hierophant. See Part 6, Ch. I.

and the world of time were of far less importance to these inspired authors than eternity and the eternal truths of which they wrote.

When we open our Bible, then, we should remember that we are reading a special category of literature, foreign to us at first. In order to discover the intention of the authors we need to learn the meaning of the words, to understand the method of writing and to possess the keys of interpretation.   We must, indeed, find a Rosetta stone. Then, as we learn to lift the veil of allegory, symbol, imagery, and even incongruity, the light of truth will illumine our minds.

THE THEME OF CYCLIC FORTHGOING AND RETURN

The Bible is found to be capable of many interpretations, wisdom being concealed within it layer upon layer.   The outer layer is pseudo-history, local and temporal.   The inner layers consist of universal, eternal truths.   Among the earliest Races there moved men and women who were not less informed than ourselves con- cerning the mysteries of life, but more so.   They had been drawn near to the Adept Teachers of the Race and had been received by Them as Initiates of the Greater Mysteries.   These are the inspired authors of the world's Scriptures, cosmogonical and occult legends, and myths. They saw outer, temporal events, beings and things as mirrors of eternal verities.   Egyptian practice may provide us with an illustration.   In that country the scarab beetle[1] was inti- mately associated with the Creative Deity, one of whose titles was Khepera.   Why this association of a lowly insect with the Creative Lord of All? The life habits of the scarab suggest an answer.   This beetle encloses its egg, its seed of life, in a ball of mud, rolls the ball to a sunny spot and leaves it to the warming, hatching influence of the sun.   Ultimately the egg hatches and brings forth a larva, which finds itself surrounded by its necessary food.   Consuming this, it passes through its transformations and ultimately emerges as the winged scarab, to become in its turn a parent of further eggs.

The Creative Logos produces from within Himself the seed- thought of the Universe-to-be.   This is sometimes described as the golden egg, or the egg of *Brahma*.   This dynamic, Archetypal idea is brought into association with pre-cosmic matter, or the virgin

---

[1] It was also a symbol of resurrection and reincarnation.

sea of peace, just as the scarab's egg is deposited in the mud. The next step in the creative process is the operation of cyclic law. The major cycle of forthgoing and return, with its innumerable sub-cycles, is not inaptly represented by the scarab's action of forming the ball of mud and rolling it to a sunny spot. As the larva finds itself surrounded with the essential sources of nutrition, so are all living beings provided at all levels with both interior sustaining life and the external food which Nature supplies. Similarly, as the larva passes through its metamorphosis to become winged and free of the limitations of its ball of mud, so does the Soul of man become gradually transformed from the matter-blinded state to the spiritually illumined one. The physical body entombs him no more. He can leave and return to it at will without a break in consciousness. He is winged, free. Observing the natural habits of the scarab beetle, the Ancient Egyptians saw in them a physical example of both immortality, or resurrection, and the universal law of cyclic progression. In the same manner as the newly formed scarab becomes, in its turn, a parent setting in motion the same cyclic procedure, so does the Soul of man descend again and again into incarnation, become born in a physical body, shake off that chrysalis at death and withdraw to his Source. Thus, indeed, the scarab beetle does display the attributes and actions of both the Supreme Creative Cause and the Spiritual Soul of man.

Innumerable natural objects and things were similarly incorporated by the inspired authors of the past into their supposed historical accounts of local, planetary and celestial events. The Sacred Language was thus used to write history, allegory and myth in such a way that eternal truth was both concealed and revealed.

BONDAGE AND EXODUS

What is the central idea, the one plot, of the same great story which is at the heart of every inspired allegory? It is the story of manifested life (the Macrocosmic Prodigal Son), of its emanation from its spiritual Source (the Father's home), and of its forthgoing or descent on its involutionary journey deeper and deeper into the material, evolutionary field, where it becomes clothed, imprisoned, entombed, in vehicles of increasing density until the densest level (eating of the husks which the swine did eat) is reached. In our Solar System, as far as we know, the densest matter is that of the mineral kingdom of Nature (the pit in the earth into which Joseph was lowered, bondage in Egypt, and the rock tomb of the Christ). After burial there for a time, life wins free from its densest encasement and thereafter gradually ascends on the evolutionary pathway back to its Source ("I will arise", the raising of Joseph, the Exodus, and the Resurrection of Christ). The result of this cyclic pilgrimage, with its innumerable, component sub-cycles, is the germination of the seeds of the deific potencies locked up in the units of universal Spirit-Life known as the Monads, the Immortal Germs.

COMPONENT CYCLES

The major cycle of forthgoing and return is comprised of innumerable minor cycles of decreasing dimension, as if wire were twisted round a spirally arranged wire, the surrounding wire being in its turn surrounded by other spiral coils, and so on almost *ad infinitum*. Every component round of a spiral repeats in miniature the processes, procedures, difficulties and attainments typical of cycles of larger dimensions. Periodically a number of cycles and sub-cycles—or arcs of cycles and sub-cycles—converge and culminate together. Major historical events frequently occur at such convergences. Crises in the lives of individuals are often precipitated at the time of such coincidences of cycles and sub-cycles. The predictions of advanced occultists are based upon knowledge of this phenomena. The microcosm is ever a reproduction, and repetition in miniature, of the Macrocosm. The spinning of the Earth on its axis in its orbit round the sun is a useful analogy.

The human Egoic cycle of pre-natal descent, incarnation in a physical body, the restricted life therein, death, escape into the super-physical worlds and reabsorption into the Egoic Source, reproduces all major cycles of which the grand cycle is composed. So also all other lives, including those of the minutest insects and infusoria.

THE PRODIGAL'S RETURN

In horticulture, just as the gardener must plant his seeds in the darkness below the surface of the earth, so the divine Gardener, "plants" His seeds in the darkness, spiritual and intellectual, produced by incarnation in the densest matter of His Universe—His physical garden. In the same manner as plant seeds in due course germinate and push up shoots which develop into stems, leaves, flowers, fruit and further seeds, so the seed-like Monadic powers germinate and develop to reach their full fruition at the close of the upward cycle, or pathway of return. The result of pilgrimage through the great cycle is the awakening from latency to potency of the once embryonic parental powers locked up in the seeds.

This cyclic progression is the central theme of all stories, the one great plot upon which all other plots, secular and sacred, are based. In the world's allegories, life is personified by the heroes, whether single persons—human, semi-human or wholly divine— or families, groups, tribes or nations. Resistant matter is personified by enemies, whether human or satanic. Battles between these two inevitable opponents portray in allegory the conflict between Spirit and matter, life and form, consciousness and its vehicles of self-expression. This is the eternal Armageddon, the *Kurukshetra* [1] of the Soul, whether of Universes, planets, Races or individual men. The whole Bible is a great allegory of this pilgrimage of fall and redemption, forthgoing and return. The Parable of the Prodigal Son is, perhaps, the most direct Christian enunciation of this theme of themes, this master plot of all sacred Scriptures, traditional histories, inspired allegories, myths, legends and fairy tales.

THE RAPE AND REDEMPTION OF PERSEPHONE

From Greek Mythology, the story of Persephone may perhaps be usefully considered at this point, if only in one of its more simplified versions, and one possible interpretation offered in outline only.

Lord Leighton's well-known picture, "The Return of Persephone", portrays the reunion of mother and child. The entrance to the Underworld is shown as a cave. The god Hermes, with his caduceus or staff formed of a central rod and two intertwined serpents,

---

[1] " The field of the Kurus ", a plain near Delhi where the battle between the Kauravas and Pandavas was said to be fought. The scene of the receipt by Arjuna of the teaching from Shri Krishna recorded in the *Bhagavad Gita*. The Hindu Armageddon or great battlefield, typifying the area of conflict between Spirit and its material encasement, particularly in man.

is bearing Persephone to the upper air from below. At the entrance to the cave is her mother, Ceres, into whose arms he will deliver her daughter.

This allegory has numerous meanings. In one interpretation Ceres is the goddess of Nature and Agriculture and Persephone is the plant life, or product of Nature, which sleeps below the ground during the Winter. In Spring the resurgent life-force—Persephone and Hermes together—brings forth and gives vitality to the new vegetation. This grows and its fruits ripen throughout the Summer, after which activity in the plant kingdom begins to die down, ceasing almost completely at the onset of Winter. Allegorically, Persephone descends to the Underworld to become the enforced bride of Pluto, King of Hades—the personification of matter, the physical world and body and life therein, and the dark period of any cycle.

The story goes on to say that Pluto agreed to give Persephone up, and Zeus agreed that she should be completely freed and returned to her mother, but only on condition that she had not eaten any food whilst in the Underworld. Unfortunately she had eaten some pomegranate seeds, an action which made her subject to Nature and to the earth. It was therefore decided that she should spend one-quarter of each year in the Underworld as the bride of Pluto, and that for the rest of the time she would be reunited with her mother. Such is one interpretation in which the story is regarded as an allegory of Nature's processes, Persephone representing the life-force in Nature, Hermes the power of reproduction and growth, Ceres the source of that life, and Zeus the Lord of the Universe.

A solar allegory is also unfolded, the period spent underground in Hades being the Wintertime in the Northern Hemisphere, when the sun lacks power for some three to four months of the year, thereafter rising to shine in the midst of the heavens.

Applied to the Cosmos as a whole, Divine Consciousness descends from its lofty spiritual state deeper and deeper into matter, until at last the deepest depths are reached—the mineral kingdom—symbolised by the Underworld. Then, in the course of evolution, Spirit and consciousness begin to win free from the domination of matter and to shake off the shackles of materiality, ultimately to become spiritualised. At the close of the cycle that which had been embodied and imprisoned has been freed and returns to its Source—Persephone is reunited with her mother.

Cycles follow cycles, however, and in the case of man always in an ascending spiral. Persephone must therefore go down into the Underworld again and again. By other symbols, such as those of the serpent which regularly sloughs its skin and the scarab which rolls over and over its ball of mud containing its eggs, recurrent cycles of generation and regeneration are also portrayed.

In the microcosmic or human interpretation of the myth, the Ego of man is Ceres, the mother. Before birth the Ego sends a ray of part of its life—Persephone—down from the Causal world through the realms of mind and emotion, the upper air, into the physical world—Hades—to be born on Earth. Pluto personifies the elemental desires. Every time a Soul is born to live in this darkened, material, physical body and world, Persephone, who personates that Soul or Ego, has returned to the Underworld. You and I are all Persephones in Hades at the present moment. At death we shall be freed, returning eventually back to the Source from which we came, which is the Ego in the Causal Body—Ceres.

Finally, an occult interpretation is possible. The Spiritual Soul of man, the essential Self behind the bodily veil, can prematurely win freedom from almost total imprisonment in the physical body if, symbolically, it can find Hermes, the rescuer or redeemer, and his staff. The nature of this staff gives the key to the process of the liberation of consciousness from the physical body and its deadening, blinding influence; for in one interpretation—the human—the caduceus represents very accurately the oppositely polarised, serpentine, triple creative power in man. When no more used for procreation, this power is transmuted or turned upwards until the two serpents' heads, or two serpentine currents of creative fire, enter the head and illumine and enfire the brain, there to free the Soul from the limitations of the body. Hermes with his staff has then allegorically liberated Persephone from the Underworld. At the command of Zeus (the Monad) and with the submission of Pluto (the now-disciplined body elemental consciousness), Persephone (the personal Ego) is restored by Hermes (the Serpent Fire) to her mother (the Spiritual Self) on Olympus (Causal Consciousness).

Such are some of the possible meanings of the story from the Eleusinian Mysteries, of which many of those who now find themselves deeply interested in Occult Science may have been members; for, in their outer garb, the Eleusinia were public spectacles and a distinguished citizen of Athens could become an Initiate of these Outer or Lesser Mysteries. At first members merely received and enacted the symbolic glyph. As they passed from the Outer or Lesser to the Inner or Greater Mysteries, allegory gave way to reality. The forces symbolised by the caduceus began to awaken, as the Hierophant touched the Initiate with the great Wand of Power, the Thyrsus. This culminated in his being freed from the body which, becoming unconscious and entranced, was placed in the care of the Priests. The freed Initiate Soul, symbolised by Persephone, could then ascend to the state of Egoic consciousness or become one with Ceres, its goddess mother.

The caduceus has another meaning. That already given is its possible dynamic significance, but in addition it has a kind of moral meaning, as have all symbols. The two serpents represent also the pairs of opposites, such as success and failure, heat and cold, pleasure and pain, happiness and despair, love and hate, health and disease, presence and absence, activity and inertia. Before the Soul can be perfected and fully liberated, it must have become equipoised in consciousness between all the pairs, being equally indifferent to either of their components. This attainment is called in Hindu philosophy *Upeksha*, a Sanskrit word meaning the poise of indifference, the dynamic balance between all pairs of opposites. This attainment implies that the whole nature has been brought into perfect equipoise, dynamic equilibrium, and in consequence has become immovable, stable like the gyroscope. Then, as it were, the Soul (Persephone) is no longer a prisoner of Pluto, but by the staff of Hermes is liberated, free. Such, in outline only, is a portion of the mystery of the caduceus, such the story of Persephone.

CHAPTER II

FOUR MAJOR KEYS

ALL HAPPENS WITHIN

THE foregoing enunciation of the main theme of all allegories may now be followed by the statement and application *to man* of four of the seven possible main interpretations of the allegories and symbols of the world.

The *First Key* is that all the recorded, external, supposedly historical events also occur interiorly. All happens within every Race, nation and individual. Each recorded event is descriptive of a subjective experience of man. This application is essentially twofold, referring both to the experiences and attainments of Races and individuals advancing by the normal, gradual, evolutionary method, and to individuals who are treading " The way of Holiness ".

The need for the veiling in allegory and symbol of magical and occult knowledge is especially great in the latter of these two applications; for quite early in the approach to and entry upon the Path of Swift Unfoldment an enhancement of the will power, and of the mental and psychic faculties, begins to be apparent. Premature discovery of these supernormal faculties, and their employment for purely personal and destructive purposes, could prove extremely harmful both to those who misuse them and to their fellow men.

The Apostle Paul would seem to have accepted this first, mystical interpretation; for him the Nativity of Christ, for example, was not only a particular event which occurred at a certain time in Bethlehem. The narratives of the Annunciation, the Immaculate Conception and the Nativity of Christ also describe allegorically the gradual awakening into conscious activity within the Soul of advanced man of Christlike powers of perception, action and attainment. The very presence of the Christ on Earth, as well as His activities, were for Paul but mirrors of the interior awakening, activity and perfecting

of the inherent, redemptive Christ-power and nature within man—
the Logos of the Soul. Thus he wrote: ". . . I travail in birth
again until Christ be formed in you " [1] and " To whom God would
make known what is the riches of the glory of this mystery among
the Gentiles; which is Christ in you, the hope of glory." [2]

As the student of the Bible reads the great narratives with this
key in his hand, as it were, he can consciously share in the recorded
experiences. He can ascend the mount with Abraham, Moses,
Elijah and Jesus and, in however slight a measure at first, begin to
share in their illumination. With the two dejected disciples he can
walk the road to Emmaus, and hear the wise words of their temporarily unknown companion. With them, at the breaking of the
bread, he can experience that inner light which came when " their
eyes were opened, and they knew him. . . " [3] Such, indeed, is
part of the intention of the inspired authors, but as one studies the
Scriptures of the world one must read intuitively, sensitively, with
one's mind open and responsive to that vaster consciousness which so
often seems waiting to burst through.

PEOPLE PERSONIFY HUMAN QUALITIES

The *Second Key* is that each of the persons introduced into the
stories represents a condition of consciousness and a quality of character. All the actors are personifications of aspects of human nature,
of attributes, principles, powers, faculties, limitations, weaknesses
and errors of man. When, however, purely human beings are the
heroes, the life of a person at the normal stage of development for the
time is being described. When the hero is semi-divine, the accent
is upon the progress of the divine Self in man after it has begun to
assume preponderant power. When the central figure is an *Avatar*
or " descent " of an Aspect of Deity, His experiences narrate those of
the Spiritual Self during the later phases of the evolution of the divine
in man to the stature of perfected manhood. Such is the general
purpose, and such the method, of the ancient writers of the world's
immortal stories.

[1] *Gal.* 4 : 19.
[2] *Col.* 1 : 27.
[3] *Lk.* 24 : 16-31.

The Deity, or Father, generally refers to the highest spiritual Essence in man, the Divine Spark, the Immortal Germ, the Logos of the Soul, the Dweller in the Innermost, the Monad. This is especially true where the Supreme and Eternal Deity in Its universal character of Solar Logos is implied. A tragic, mind-darkening degradation of the " I AM THAT I AM ",[1] Jehovah, to the stature of the deity of a single tribe, sometimes bloodthirsty, wrathful and jealous, is thought by some authorities to have been made in the days of the restoration by Ezra of the destroyed books of the Israelites. The Supreme Emanator, referred to as " God " and " the Spirit of God ",[2] is above all things universal and divine. The limitation of the One Uncreate to become the personal God of a single tribe has led to much confusion and an appalling degradation of the idea of the Supreme Deity.

Whenever this Eternal One is introduced into the narratives, It is susceptible of interpretation as a personification of the Monad of man, as also of the Oversoul of the Race. The bosom of Abraham refers to the state of consciousness in which the Monad of man perpetually abides and to which the Spiritual Soul or Immortal Ego can, and eventually does naturally, attain. Those following the Initiatory Path seek to hasten this attainment of realisation in waking brain-consciousness, first of their divine, immortal nature, and thereafter of their unbroken unity with the Supreme Lord of All. The full recognition of man's unity with God, of the oneness of man-Spirit with God-Spirit, is the ultimate goal of all who seek " the strait gate " and enter upon " the narrow way ". In Hinduism, this state is called *Moksha* or Liberation; in Buddhism, *Nirvana* or conscious absorption; and in Christianity, Salvation, Ascension, Christhood, and being " carried by the angels into Abraham's bosom ".[3] The symbol of the disciple John leaning on the bosom of Jesus [4] is susceptible of a similar interpretation. Thus Abraham, as also many other people in the Bible, personates both a principle of man and a state of consciousness.

[1] *Ex.* 3 : 14.
[2] *Gen.* 1 : 1-2.
[3] *Lk.* 16 : 22.
[4] *Jn.* 13 : 23.

In this method of Biblical study the characters, divine, semi-divine, patriarchal and human, are regarded as personifications of principles and powers of Nature as the Macrocosm, and of man as the microcosm. This reading is supported by Paul, who writes: ". . . all these things happened unto them for ensamples "[1] and ". . . it is written, that Abraham had two sons, the one by a bond-maid, the other by a free woman . . . which things are an allegory . . ."[2] It is not unreasonable to assume that such a theory may also be true of many other portions of the Bible. One may even go further than this and assert that the practice of studying the Scriptures of the world in their literal meaning, and as records of actual historical events alone, can lead to confusion of mind.

Three other errors in modern Christianity urgently need to be corrected, I submit. These are: the degradation already mentioned to the level of a tribal god[3] of the concept of Deity as Emanator of the Universe and Embodiment of impersonal life, law and intelligence; insistence upon full reliance on an external (instead of an interior) redemptive power; and the erection of an edifice founded upon incredible theological dogmas. The author of *Proverbs*, who writes: " As a thorn goeth up into the hand of a drunkard, so is a parable in the mouth of fools ",[4] would seem to have been expressing a somewhat similar view.

These difficulties are all avoided and profound inspiration consistent with reason is gained by the recognition of underlying mystical intent and meaning of the Scriptures. Thus the humility, the devotion and the selfless love of Mary, the Mother of Jesus; the human frailty and the inherent sainthood of a Magdalene and a Peter; Martha the active, and Mary the far more valuable, spiritual, contemplative aspects of human nature and modes of human life—all these attributes (or people) are in every man and the conditions of life draw out now one, now another. The twelve disciples of Jesus personify them in their twelvefold classification as microcosmic manifestations of the

----

[1] 1 *Cor.* 10 : 11.

[2] *Gal.* 4 : 22-24.

[3] Exoteric Hebraism alone presents this view of Jehovah. Kabbalism, the Theosophy of the Hebrews, their esoteric wisdom, proclaims the unnamed Deity as the self-existent, impersonal Emanator under law of Cosmos and all that it contains.

[4] *Prov.* 26: 9.

attributes of the zodiacal Signs. Discipleship, or nearness to the Teacher, indicates that their perfecting had reached an advanced stage. Allegorically, they were supposedly purified and refined to become co-workers with Jesus, Who represents Macrocosmically the sun and microcosmically the Monad. Ultimately, all will be fully developed as powers of heart and mind and Spirit. Only as the twelve zodiacal qualities in man are " discipled ", or disciplined and refined, is he able to respond to the inner will and to comprehend pure wisdom as represented by the Master.

In his remarkable book, *Dictionary of the Sacred Language of all Scriptures and Myths*,[1] strongly recommended to every student of this subject, G. A. Gaskell gives not the zodiacal classification preferred by some students, but the following list of the twelve disciplining qualities:—

The analytical lower mind	—	Peter
Faith and enquiry	—	Andrew
Hope and progressiveness	—	James
Love and philosophy	—	John
Courage and forcefulness	—	Philip
Perseverance	—	Bartholomew
Intellectual truth-seeking	—	Thomas
Modesty and receptiveness	—	James Alphaeus
Gentleness and attentiveness	—	Simon Zelotes
Broadmindedness	—	Judas, brother of James
Critical deliberation	—	Matthew
Prudence	—	Judas

The Christ-Presence and Power, whether asleep, awakening or being " born ", or fully grown to " the measure of the stature of the fulness of Christ ",[2] must be added to these to complete the full description of man. The interaction between these various aspects of human nature, the effects they produce upon one another, the waxing or waning of one or more of them at different times and in different lives, and the gradual, triumphant emergence and predominance of the royal Spiritual Self, the Immortal King within, the Hero of every saga—all this is portrayed by the Initiated authors of the Scriptures of the world. Thus, the narratives themselves

[1] Geo. Allan & Unwin Ltd., London.
[2] *Eph.* 4: 13.

describe the experiences—particularly the tests, ordeals, defeats and victories—of one person, who is man himself. Successful exploits describe interior achievements, while partial and complete failures, defeats and surrenders are allegories of temporary victories of the purely human over the divine in man, conquests of matter over Spirit. In the main, the manifold experiences of the immortal Self of man in its journey towards perfection are narrated as adventures of numbers of persons in the one story. The labours of Hercules, the voyage of the Argonauts, the journeys and experiences of the Israelites, the lives of the Lord Shri Krishna and of the Lord Christ, amongst many others, are all descriptive in the symbolic manner of the journey of the Soul and the psychological, intellectual and spiritual experiences passed through on that journey.

STORIES DRAMATISE PHASES OF HUMAN EVOLUTION

The *Third Key* is that each story is thus regarded as a graphic description of the experiences of the human soul as it passes through the various phases of its evolutionary journey to the Promised Land, or cosmic consciousness—the goal and summit of human attainment. Inspired allegories are always distinguishable from mere novels and biographies by several characteristics, one of which is the intrusion of the supernatural and the inclusion of angelic and divine beings, even Deity Itself, in the story. When these are found, the existence of a hidden revelation may always be suspected. The reader possessed of the keys may then penetrate the veil of symbolism to find aspects of the hidden wisdom revealed. One of the keys thus to be employed is that the different people figuring prominently in such a story represent powers, qualities and particular characteristics of every human being, as has already been said. Sometimes such qualities are absent, sometimes they are awakening, being born or healed, and sometimes they are dominant, according to the temperament and degree of development of the person being described.

In this third interpretation, also, each story may be studied from at least two points of view. The first is that of normal evolutionary experience and natural mental and emotional states, and the second is that which regards the sacred allegories as descriptive more especially of the experiences of those who enter in at the " strait gate " and pursue " the narrow way ",[1] which leads swiftly first to the " birth " in man, and later to full unfoldment, of the Christ-consciousness and Power.

In the Parable of the Sower,[2] the different conditions of the ground represent various evolutionary phases and states of spiritual receptiveness of the Race and the individual, from complete unresponsiveness (rocky ground) to full perception and ratification (fertile ground). In the Parable of the Ten Virgins,[3] the foolish ones may be regarded as those who are not as yet sufficiently evolved to be able to respond to impulses descending from their Higher Self (the bridegroom). The wise virgins, on the other hand, may be interpreted as personifying all those in whom the Spiritual Self has attained to a considerable degree of evolutionary unfoldment and the outer, physical nature is sufficiently developed to be aware of this fact and to give expression, in the conduct of daily life, to the higher idealism and the fruits of spiritual experiences. This is followed by the progressive illumination of the mind-brain by the Ego (betrothal), leading to the fusion of the immortal and mortal natures (marriage).

The incidents of the marriage feast of Cana [4] may thus be taken to refer to this interior union achieved by those who have awakened the power of the Christ-Presence within them (the Presence of the Master). The all-essential blending or " heavenly marriage " of the outer mortal and the inner immortal natures has occurred in them. The presence of the Christ in the story indicates that spiritual wisdom, spiritual intuitiveness and a Christlike love and compassion were already well developed. Under such conditions the " water " of the desireful aspects of the emotions automatically becomes transmuted into the " wine " of spiritual wisdom and will. This is not a miracle, but a natural process which occurs when a steadfast aspirant ascends " the narrow way," as thus described in allegory and symbol. The grape and the vine also symbolise knowledge, wisdom and comprehension of the spirit of things. As fermentation gives a certain " strength " to wine, so the action of the intellect upon accummulated

---

[1] *Matt.* 7: 13-14.
[2] *Matt.* 13: 1-9.
[3] *Matt.* 25: 1-13.
[4] *Jn.* 2: 1-11.

esoteric knowledge turns it into the power of pure wisdom, implicit insight and deeply penetrative intuitiveness.

THE SYMBOLISM OF LANGUAGE

The *Fourth Key* is that all objects, as also certain words, have each their own special symbolic meaning. The Sacred Language of the Initiates of the Mystery Schools is formed of hierograms and symbols rather than of words alone, their meaning being ever constant, as constant also is the doctrine which this language everywhere reveals.

Certain words are used as keys with which to unlock the inner meaning and these keys, being turned seven times, will reveal seven layers of sacred wisdom. This fact is allegorically referred to on many occasions, as when the fiery furnace had to be heated " seven times more than it was wont to be heated " [1] before the three men— Shadrach, Meshach and A-bed-ne-go—become fused into the form of the fourth, " like the Son of God ".[2] Similarly, the walls of Jericho had to be circumambulated seven times before they fell down.[3]

The idea thus emerges that in order to discover the Sacred Wisdom of the Christian Scriptures we must divest ourselves of the idea that they were conceived and written entirely as chronologically and historically accurate accounts of actual events alone. The Gospel narrative, for example, describes the progress of an advanced and elevated Soul through the final ascending phases of evolution until the highest, the Ascension, is attained. The great drama, to be fully appreciated, must be transferred from the material to the psychological, intellectual and spiritual realms and levels of human experience. An interpretation of the Gospel narrative from this point of view is suggested in Part Five of this volume

The disciples, then, are personifications of the noblest attributes of man. Though still imperfect, they are becoming increasingly spiritualised, or brought into the presence of their Master, Who personates the Dweller in the Innermost, the God-Self of man. The disciples are not yet equal to the Christ, being younger in evolution and, in consequence, still under the delusion of self-separateness.

---

[1] *Dan.* 3: 19.
[2] *Dan.* 3: 25.
[3] *Joshua* 6: 1-20.

This is shown by their question as to who will be greatest in the kingdom of heaven [1]. They are still tainted by grosser material attributes, hence the symbolical washing of their feet by their Master.[2] A traitor still lurks in their midst, who must be self-revealed and self-slain before the great Ascension can occur. The Master admonishes, rebukes and warns them, indicating the spiritualising activity of the Divine Presence within.

All of the recorded—and miscalled—miracles could have been performed by an Adept, or even by an Initiate of lesser degree, by the exercise of theurgic powers. But they also illustrate the processes of the arousing into activity (healing, restoring sight and awakening from the dead) of the spiritual powers and perceptions stirring in the outer, aspiring personality.

The Gospel story, indeed all the inspired portions of the Bible, are addressed less to the reasoning mind, which they frequently affront, than to the intuition, which can perceive in them the story of the Spiritual Soul of humanity whose deific powers and possibilities, and the process of their development and active use, are portrayed by symbols and illustrated by dramatic allegories. This mystical view, it may be repeated, does not totally deny the presence of history. The kernel of tradition within the stories can still be a record of real events, however much the illumined records lift them out of time and space by the use of the Sacred Language.

INCONGRUITIES AS CLUES TO DEEPER MEANINGS

The student of the allegorical language is nearly always given a clue—one, moreover, which at first sight is very strange. This clue consists of an additional veil, cover or blind which tends to increase confusion, and to repel one who approaches with purely literal or profane mind the Sanctuary wherein divine knowledge is enshrined. One should guard carefully against this repulsion, whether due to a statement which is incongruous, incredible, impossible, or to a story which offends logic and the sense of justice, or even of decency and morality. So many people are turned away from the Scriptures, and even from religion itself, by the discovery of these

[1] *Matt.* 18: 1.
[2] *Jn.* 13: 3-17.

characteristics of the Bible. The subject is therefore of great importance, both for this reason and because the incongruities themselves may be regarded as deliberate in certain cases, in order to conceal power-giving knowledge and to draw attention dramatically to a deeper wisdom. An apparent digression is here made, therefore, to examine certain of them and to suggest possible resolutions of the problems which they admittedly present. The statement concerning them given in Part One, Chapter III, is here repeated and they are further considered.

Certain admittedly difficult Biblical passages are:

(a) Three days and nights of creation pass before the sun is created.[1]

Here creative epochs are implied rather than planetary alternations.

(b) Deity enjoins aggression, massacre and extermination.[2]

Enemies of the soul are personified by enemies of Israel.

(c) Noah collects pairs of every living creature from all parts of the Earth—arctic, temperate and tropical—and keeps them alive in the Ark for forty days.[3]

The seeds of all living things are preserved from one creative epoch to its successor. The fruits of each human rebirth are preserved between successive lives, the Ark being the symbol of the conserving vehicle, cosmic or human.

(d) The sins of the fathers shall be visited upon the children unto the third and fourth generation.[4]

Each human life is the " father " of those which follow, they being referred to as its children. Sowing and reaping occur from life to life (karma).

(e) Jericho is brought down by the sound of trumpets, horns and shouting.[5]

The Logos Doctrine of the formation and the dissolution of Universes by the Voice of God, the occult potencies of sound, and their use in

[1] *Gen.* 1: 1-16.
[2] *Gen.* 7: 4 & 23, 18: 13, 19: 24-25; *Ex.* 22: 20.
[3] *Gen.* 7: 2-4.
[4] *Ex.* 20: 5.
[5] *Joshua* 6: 1-20.

chanting to break down limitations of consciousness (walls) and to purify its vehicles, are all implied. (*Mantra Yoga*).

(*f*) Joshua makes the sun and moon stand still to prolong the day.[1]

The source of spiritual power and light (the sun) is brought to maximum power (the midst of the heavens) over the mortal man, enabling him to overcome the enemies of the soul (Gibeonites) and attain serenity.

(*g*) The defeat of Samson by cutting off his hair, and his destruction of the temple by leaning his weight on the pillars.[2]

Hair is the symbol of the effective relationship between the Spiritual Soul and the mind-brain. When this is severed, the power and the guidance of the inner Self are lost to the outer man, who becomes a slave to matter and sense (Delilah). cf. Nazarenes.

When man attains to equilibrium bettween the pairs of opposites (the pillars), limitations (the temple) upon consciousness are dissipated and undesired qualities (the Philistines) are destroyed.

(*h*) Elijah goes to heaven in a chariot of fire.[3]

The sublimation of the fiery, creative force in man enables him to ascend to spiritual states of consciousness (heaven).

(*i*) Jonah enters the belly of a great fish and remains unharmed for three days and three nights.[4]

At Initiation the Candidate is withdrawn from his body (the ship), enters the Underworld (the sea), and is then elevated into full spiritual awareness (the fish) or attains to Christ-consciousness. After the passage of sufficient time (generally three days and three nights), he returns to his body (is delivered to dry land).

(*j*) Tribute money is found inside a particular fish.[5]

All the necessities (the tribute money) for spiritual, intellectual, and even physical, living are to be found in the divine aspects of human

[1] *Joshua* 10: 12-14.
[2] *Judges* 16: 17-30.
[3] 2 *Kings* 2: 11.
[4] *Jonah* 1: 17.
[5] *Matt.* 17: 27.

nature (the fish). Man should learn to draw upon the Christ-power within him.

(k) A fig tree is withered for not bearing fruit in early spring.[1]

Unless a man gives freely of the fruits of his life, they will wither away and be lost. The text is the enunciation of a law, rather than the description of an act.

(l) Lazarus is raised after being dead for four days.[2]

Death symbolises total spiritual unawareness, and miraculous restoration to life its recovery by virtue of the action of the interior divine Power and Presence (the Christ). The period of death refers to the time during which the body of the Candidate is unconscious (figurative death) while Initiation is being conferred.

(m) The flesh of Christ is meat and the blood of Christ is drink.[3]

Our Lord insists that the consumption of His flesh and blood is essential to salvation. The " flesh " of a Divine Being is a symbol for spiritual truth and law. Eating such flesh implies full comprehension of eternal verities. Blood symbolises the ever-outpoured divine life by which the Universe and man are spiritually sustained. Drinking such blood implies conscious absorption in the one life of the Universe, and the realisation of unity with its Source.

(n) The events of the night before the Crucifixion are too numerous to have all occurred in one night.[4]

Amongst them are:

The Last Supper.
The agony in the Garden.
The betrayal by Judas.
The hailing before Caiaphas and the questioning.
The hailing before the Sanhedrin and the questioning.
The hailing before Pilate and the questioning in the Hall of
    Judgment. (Courts to try malefactors did not sit in the
    middle of the night).

[1] *Matt.* 21: 19.
[2] *Jn.* 11: 39-44.
[3] *Jn.* 6: 50-58.
[4] *Lk.* Chs. 22 & 23.

The visit of Herod, told of by St. Luke.
The return of Pilate.
Pilate's speeches and the washing of hands.
The scourging, mocking and arraying of Jesus in purple robes.
The long and painful journey to Golgotha.

The whole experience is interior, the account of each event describing attainments and changes of consciousness as the threshold of perfection is approached.

Whilst interpretations of these and a great many other incongruous statements in the Bible will be offered in their due place in later volumes, fuller explanations of two or three of the more perplexing texts may, perhaps, usefully be added here.

With regard to (a), the days and nights of creation refer to alternations of creative activity or " day ", and creative quiescence or " night ". These are later referred to in the text of this book by their Sanskrit names of *Manvantara* and *Pralaya* respectively.

With reference to (f), Joshua personifies the Initiate who has brought his Monadic will, symbolised by the sun, to its position of maximum power (the midst of the heavens). In consequence, he prevents the oncoming of night (mental darkness) and maintains his personal nature (the battlefield of Gibeon) in that condition of prolonged illumination (day) which ensures victory in the battle between the Spirit (the Israelites) and the matter (their enemies) in him. This wonderful allegory has been more fully considered in Part One, Chapter V. Even from this brief interpretation, however, the element of impossibility is seen both as a hint or clue, and as an indication of a profound occult idea.

With regard to (m), quite clearly Our Lord was not exhorting mankind to consume human flesh and blood when He said: " Whoso eateth my flesh, and drinketh my blood, hath eternal life; and I will raise him up at the last day. For my flesh, is meat indeed, and my blood is drink indeed. He that eateth my flesh, and drinketh my blood, dwelleth in me, and I in him. As the living Father hath sent me, and I live by the Father: so he that eateth me, even he shall live by me." [1] The words " flesh ", " blood ", " eateth " and " drinketh "

---

[1] *Jn.* 6 : 54-57.

7

are not used in the usual sense. They are symbolical, metaphorical, and they convey a hidden under-meaning.

What, then, do those four words—" flesh ", " blood ", " eateth " and " drinketh " mean? The flesh of Christ may be interpreted as divine truths, spiritual laws, or that in which He is clothed, by which He is covered, and through which He is made manifest. The time comes, and is also hastened as " The way of Holiness " is entered upon, when the human intellect becomes illumined with divine knowledge, inspired by the interior discovery and revelation of spiritual truths. This experience in consciousness is symbolised as the eating of Christ's flesh. Bread is also used to describe this knowledge of divine laws, processes, purposes. Eating consecrated bread is an allegory for the reception, absorption and application to life of that knowledge, gnosis, *sophia*, esoteric wisdom. Bread is also a symbol of the cyclic regeneration of life after each return to the seed state.

The blood of God, or Christ, is the ever-outpoured divine life by which the Universe is sustained, and without which it could not live. The life-force does, indeed, perform a function for the Universe and all it contains which closely resembles the life-sustaining office which human blood performs for the physical body. Normally man is unaware either of the outpouring and omnipresence of this divine life, or of the fact that it is the spiritually sustaining life within him.

At a certain stage of the evolution of the human intellectual principle, this fact is intuitively perceived. By spiritual practices, meditation and prayer, and aided by his Master and the Hierophant and other Officiants in the Sacred Initiatory Rites of the Temples of the Greater Mysteries, this realisation by the aspirant can be hastened. Ultimately the full knowledge may be gained both of the outpouring of the Christ-life into the Universe and man, and of man's identity with that life and its divine Source. This attainment is described symbolically as drinking Christ's blood. Our Lord was referring to a state of consciousness of unity with the Cosmic Christ and His outpoured life, and not to a physical action.

Once this symbolical eating and drinking, this spiritual *agape*, has occurred, then the process can be initiated in others who in their turn, starving for truth, can be fed in vast multitudes. As the incident of feeding the five thousand [1] allegorically tells, in this ministration there is and can be no loss.   On the contrary, there is more of spiritual wisdom, knowledge and upwelling life afterwards than before.

Thus, in the fourth interpretation, all objects, as also many words, have each their own special meaning.   The symbols employed in the Sacred Language are associated with one or more of the four elements of earth, water, air and fire.

[1] *Matt.* 14 : 15-21.

PART THREE

AN ALPHABET OF THE SACRED LANGUAGE

CHAPTER I

AN ALPHABET OF THE SACRED LANGUAGE

THE reader who accepts the approach made in the preceding Chapter is now offered an extension of the *Fourth Key* in the form of certain interpretations, arranged in alphabetical order, of universally used symbols.

ABLUTIONS, bathings, cleansings, refer to self-purification, the washing off of material accretions from the physical body, the elimination of selfishness and sensuality from the emotions, and of pride and possessiveness from the mind. In the case of the washing of the disciples' feet by Our Lord, thoroughness (down to the feet) of purification by the action of the spiritual upon the material nature is indicated, for the feet symbolise the lowest (the physical) manifestation of the spiritual Self of man. The ancient writers do not appear to have scorned the use of the pun: the washing of the disciples' feet by the Master also implies a clarification of the mind, and so of the " under-standing "!

ACHES and pains are symbolical of disorders of the soul, of disharmony and disease resulting from errors of conduct and phases of spiritual aridity.

AETHER, as the basic elemental substance out of which the Universe was formed, represents the highest spiritual nature of man, the divine *Ātman*.[1] The aetherial worlds of the Gods symbolise the highest levels of consciousness in the Universe, those realms of Spirit from which the lower worlds proceed, from which they are modelled and to which they ultimately return.

AIR would seem to refer chiefly to the activities of the abstract mind and the intuition. Clouds, in one interpretation, represent a

[1] *Ātma* (or *Ātman*) (Sk.). The Universal Spirit, the divine Monad, the seventh Principle in the septenary constitution of man. Macrocosmically, the Supreme Soul.

veiling of clear perception, or the clouding of the lower mind from the illumination or " sunlight " of the higher. Clouds have still other and varied significations. A white cloud symbolises the vehicle of the Christ-consciousness, particularly in its aspect of intuitional illuminant to the human mind. When aspiring thought and meditation are directed towards the divinest aspects of man's nature, the realm and the vehicle of intuition are penetrated, as it were, to produce a downflow of spiritual rain, meaning intuitive perception of truth, wisdom in the conduct of affairs, and benefits derived from spiritual sources. This vehicle of intuition in itself is a sheath for the manifestation and expression at lower levels of the spiritual will, the kingly Self of man. When consciousness is exalted to the level of pure wisdom, spiritual intuitiveness and full realisation of unity, sometimes symbolised by a white cloud, then the almost omnipotent power of the Will-Self of man may be discerned. Thus the author of the Book of *Revelation* wrote: " And I looked, and behold a white cloud, and upon the cloud one sat like unto the Son of man, having on his head a golden crown, and in his hand a sharp sickle." [1]

Since, however, clouds shut out the light of the sun, they are, as also suggested above, symbols of that obscurity with which the higher nature of man is regarded by the analytical mind-brain. Elemental storms generally refer to disturbed mental and emotional conditions. Still air represents both the higher emotions and the intuition, whilst rushing winds sometimes refer to disturbed mento-emotional states. In another meaning the cloud represents that effect upon the lower vehicles produced by a special descent and manifestation of the light of the higher, which has the appearance of a luminous mist. Therefore God frequently appears in a cloud.[2]

ALTARS symbolise the physical body with its emotional and mental attributes, wherein the divine Self is enshrined. Sometimes the heart is referred to as the altar at which worship of the Divine should be performed. Altars ideally perform a dual function. They are centres from which aspiration and prayer rise from the lower to the higher, and to which spiritual benediction and power descend in response.

[1] *Rev.* 14: 14.
[2] *Ex.* 19: 9, 24: 15-16, 34: 5.

ANCESTORS, or progenitors, are symbols of preceding cycles—solar, planetary, racial—and of previous human incarnations; for all of these are the parents of the present dispensation, manifestation, individuality and personality. In this sense the visitation of the sins of the fathers (preceding lives) upon the children (later lives) does not appear to be cruelly unjust, as it certainly does if the fifth verse of Chapter Twenty of *Exodus* is taken literally.

ANGELS, when not referring directly to members of the Angelic Hosts, as is often the case, refer to the highest spiritual Principle of man, the *Ātma*, and sometimes to the Monad itself. The Monad is forever at one with the Logos, and it is therefore true of all men that ". . . their angels do aways behold the face of my Father which is in heaven." [1] This indicates the truth that the Monad is ever in the presence of the Spiritual Source, the Supreme Lord.

ANIMALS, when predatory, refer to the desires and passions of the flesh. Their taming, or destruction, symbolises mastery over the lower nature. This must be done by each individual for, and largely by, himself alone. Therefore, in allegories of lion killing, weapons—being external instruments—do not suffice. When honey was extracted from the carcase of a lion by Samson,[2] the sublimation of the creative force was indicated.

Ants have been used as symbols of the spiritual Monad and of that power of cosmic electricity (known in Tibetan as *Fohat*[3]) which, by " digging holes in space " or initiating the atom-forming process, prepares the matter of space for divine husbandry. Flying insects, particularly butterflies and small birds, sometimes figuratively connote the Angelic Hosts.

In many World Scriptures kine are used as symbols for divine fertility, reproductive capacity and boundless supply. Oxen add the quality of service, whilst bulls accentuate that of masculine virility and creative capacity. Both are seen as manifestations of those God-like attributes in both Nature and man. The uninitiated, ignorant of these inner meanings, worship the symbol—an all too

---

[1] *Matt.* 18: 10.

[2] *Judges* 14: 8-9.

[3] *Fohat* (Tn.). The constructive force of cosmic electricity, polarised into positive and negative electricity; the ever-present electrical energy; the Universal, propelling, vital force.

common example of the degeneration of sublime truth into crude superstition. The wise, on the other hand, recognising the aptness of the symbology, reverence the divine power which it represents and see in such living creatures manifestations of that power.

ANOINTINGS, symbolise the receipt by the presonality of spiritual wisdom, love, life and consecration. The various parts of the body have each their special meaning, which will be suggested at the appropriate places. Anointing the head with oil, for example, means that the mind is illumined with intuition and that the Christ life, bliss, harmony, have been brought to manifestation in and through the personal life, now wholly sanctified. Oil is derived from trees in the same way that the Christlike attributes are derived from the spiritual Tree of Life, which is God.

BARRENNESS is used in the Sacred Language as a symbol of a spiritually unfruitful condition of human consciousness, of the unresponsiveness of the mind (the wife) to the fructifying rays from the spiritual triad (the husband) and, more especially, to the descent of the Monadic ray.[1] Similarly, fruitfulness represents the evolutionary stage at which this has been remedied, the outer personality being thereafter illumined by the light of the imperishable Self. In consequence, a son (spiritual intuitiveness) is said to be conceived and born in the supposed old age (advanced evolutionary stature) of a hitherto barren (pre-Initiate) wife.[2]

BATTLES are symbols of the conflict between Spirit and matter, between the involutionary and the evolutionary impulses and processes, between will and desire, between " good " and " bad " in humanity —racial and individual. In the symbolical language all wars refer, microcosmically, to some phase or phases of the conflict between the Monad-Ego of man and his mortal vehicles, between the ascending Self and the descending, ensouling life of the matter of which those vehicles are formed. The so-called enemies of the hero, or chosen people, are the appetites, desires, resistances and inertia of matter

---

[1] Occult philosophy includes the idea that all people are susceptible of classification into seven major types or basic temperaments, called in occult philosophy " Rays ". Over each of these an Adept Official is said to preside, partly to assist the evolution of those evolving on His Ray. q. v. *The Seven Human Temperaments*, Geoffrey Hodson, T. P. H., Adyar, Madras, India.

[2] *Lk.* 1: 24.

itself, ever in opposition to Spirit. As the Old Testament shows they must be slain, extirpated, root and branch. Thus viewed, the brutality and bloodlust displayed by Jehovah are seen as symbols of the relentlessness with which spiritually inspired man roots out the undesirable tendencies in his lower nature. Indeed, the Old Testament is cleansed of its objectionable characteristics when it is realised that in many cases its authors were not recounting pure history; they were revealing the laws and principles of the occult aspects of Nature, and the occult life of neophytes and Initiates of the Hebrew Schools of the Prophets [1] and the corresponding Mystery Centres of other nations.

BIRDS represent the spiritual Self, whether of Universe or man. This is not infrequently symbolised by an aquatic bird such as the swan or pelican, which lives upon and flies above the water (of space). The glyph of the pelican tearing open its own breast to feed its seven young symbolises first the Logos of the Solar System in the perpetual act of pouring out His inexhaustible life-force that the sevenfold Planetary Schemes, with their many septenary divisions, may be vivified, and second the Monad of man which ensouls and vivifies spiritually its seven Principles or vehicles. The bird-shaped head-dress indicates both the union of the brain-mind with the spiritual intellect and the mastery and protection of the lower self by the higher. Interpretations of other bird symbols will be found in their alphabetical sequence.

BURNT OFFERINGS are a symbol of self-purification. All coarse, animalistic emotions and sensual desires are renounced on the spiritual path, and the energy normally expressed through them is transmuted into spiritual power. When animal desire is thus sublimated it is, as it were, consumed, whilst the force put into its indulgence " ascends " as a fragrance to be received by the God within man, and to find expression through the higher aspects of human nature and as the nobler activities of the earthly man. Again, the repulsion aroused by the concept of a Deity, which would welcome and encourage the slaughter and burning of animals as part of ceremonial worship disappears when the symbolical intention of the authors is understood.

[1] 2 *Kings* 2 : 5, 4 : 38.

CANDLESTICK. The *Menorah* or seven-stemmed golden candle-stick was said to have been constructed in accordance with divine guidance received by Moses on the Mount.[1] Its decreed position in the Hebrew Sanctuary suggests that it was not meant to serve as an illumination, since only the central candle was kept burning during the day. The other six candles were lighted from it, referring perhaps to the existence of that One Light from which all other lights proceed. Since, furthermore, the original Sanctuary in the desert was dark, having no windows, even seven candles could not have provided the necessary illumination. Clearly, then, the golden candlestick was intended to be both an embellishment and a profoundly philosophical symbol, representing all septenates in Nature and in man. Unlighted it symbolises the concealed Wisdom, whilst lighted it typifies Wisdom revealed. The Kabbalistic Tree of Life, with its threefold supernal Sephiras and its sevenfold manifested Macrocosmic and microcosmic connotations and almost infinite number of correspondences, may also be presumed to be referred to by the symbol of the seven-stemmed golden candlestick.

CHARIOTS represent the whole personality within the enclosing aura at the superphysical levels, and within the skin of the physical body (the sides and floor of the chariot). The wheels typify the mobile power, the capacity to respond in relatively free motion to the impulses of the life-force. The pole of the chariot by which the horses are harnessed, and along which their strength is conveyed to the vehicle, might perhaps be regarded as the etheric double, the storehouse and conveyor of vital energy.

A fuller and more complete interpretation is to be found in the *Kathopanishad*[2] as follows:

" Know the Self as the lord of the chariot and the body as, verily, the chariot, know the intellect as the charioteer and the mind as, verily, the reins.

" The senses, they say, are the horses; the objects of sense the paths (they range over); (the self) associated with the body, the senses and the mind—wise men declare—is the enjoyer.

---

[1] *Ex.* 25: 31-40.

[2] *Kathopanishad* 1-3-3 to 1-3-9, Dr. Radhakrishnan's translation from his *The Principal Upanishads*.

" He who has no understanding, whose mind is always un-restrained, his senses are out of control, as wicked horses are for a charioteer.

" He, however, who has understanding, whose mind is always restrained, his senses are under control, as good horses are for a charioteer.

" He, however, who has no understanding, who has no control over his mind (and is) ever impure, reaches not that goal but comes back into mundane life.

" He, however, who has understanding, who has control over his mind and (is) ever pure, reaches that goal from which he is not born again.

" He who has the understanding for the driver of the chariot and controls the rein of his mind, he reaches the end of the journey, that supreme abode of the all-pervading."

CORN symbolises matter that is the product of the action of the creative Father-Mother, and which gestates within and is born from the womb of the latter. Creative action under law uses this " corn ", or direct product of the universal matrix, to form Universes, suns and planets, and these are represented as the loaves of bread. Before such utilisation can occur the secondary substance must become charged with electric, creative energy, or be " leavened ". In terms of human consciousness corn is the symbol of will-mind, the germ representing the will, the protoplasm ·the mind and the enclosing membrane the *ahamkaric* sense or individualising, enclosing, separating agent, while the husk is the formal mind of each life cycle.

A grain of corn is also a symbol of the human Ego, the immortal, evolving principle of man. The germ thereof is the Monad-Ātma, the chemical constituents are the inherent qualities and powers, the epidermis is the auric envelope, particularly of the *Augoeides*,[1] and the husk (which later must die) is the mental attribute of accentuated self-personality. In order to develop, the Ego must be incarnated in mortal bodies, even as the grain must be planted if it is to bear fruit. The husk must have been removed and the enclosing skin must decay before the fructified germ can produce the shoot and stem

---

[1] *Augoeides* (Gr.) : " the self-radiant divine fragment " the Robe of Glory of the Gnostics and the *Kārana-sharira*, " Causal Body ", of Hinduism.

upon which a whole ear of corn can grow, and the one bring forth many.

To become fruitful with developed Egoic powers (the grains of corn in the ear), man must use those powers in the material worlds. He must further permit the husk and skin to lose power to limit the inner development. Symbolically, the husk must be removed and the epidermis must decay, meaning that dependence upon the separative, self-enclosing illusion of I-ness must cease; for then alone can full fruitfulness in the evolutionary sense be achieved, and full nutriment of the lower man by the higher occur. Again, as in the miracle of the loaves and fishes, it is the intuition with its universalising action and revelation of unity (the Christos) which makes possible this process. Symbolically, the Christ feeds the multitudes with bread and fishes.

THE CROWN is the symbol of supremacy or kingship over the lower nature, and of enthroned royalty officiating from the summit of power. In occult terminology, the Monadic Ātma rules the whole nature of man. Philosophically the crown is the highest of all Principles, the One Source both unmanifest and manifest, the apex of the spiritual triangle, the One Alone. It is also the highest and most secret Wisdom, the very heart of truth.

The crown of Lower Egypt was formed like an open mouth with a projecting tongue, curled at the end. This may symbolise the Word of Power metaphorically uttered by the kingly Logos to create the Universe, and by the royal Monad of man to illumine and direct the individuality. The triple uraeus (serpent band of gold worn by Egyptian royalty), formed of three coiled snakes, was often associated with the Egyptian crown, symbolising both the threefold Wisdom of the three Aspects of Deity and the three currents—positive, negative and neutral—of the creative Serpent Fire occultly aroused, sublimated and directed into the head of the initiated Pharoah. An ancient tradition existed that the Monarch of a people was a manifestation of a god, and from this has come down to recent times the idea of the divine right of Kings. Occult science indicates that the earliest High Priests, Hierophants and Rulers of nations of old were either Adepts or highly initiated Members of the Occult Hierarchy of this planet. This tradition would seem to be remembered in the triple uraeus of the Egyptian Kings, since in all such highly evolved men and women the Serpent Fire or *kundalini* would have been fully aroused.[1]

The crown is also used as a symbol in the Book of *Revelation* in which " a woman clothed with the sun " is described as wearing a crown of twelve stars,[2] indicating that the spiritual powers of the twelve Zodiacal Signs were all developed and were shining as jewels in the perfected Higher Self.   The clouds of glory in which the Christ was said to ascend [3] refer to the radiant aura, the *Augoiedes*,[4] of the Adept, the splendour of the Causal Body, symbolised also by the light and beauty of the Sanctuary of a Temple of the Greater Mysteries.

The crown aptly represents the actual appearance of the upper portion of the illumined aura of a highly evolved man.   The up-rushing individual aspiration is met by the downrushing divine response.   The flow of power from below and above forms a crown-like radiance, which also is a characteristic of certain Orders of *Devas*,[5] called in Hinduism " Bright Crested Ones ".

DECAPITATION. Beheading is frequently used in Scriptural allegories, one interpretation being more especially applicable to the Initiatory Path and referring to the necessary " cutting off " of the power of the critical mind (head) to prevent the illumination which is only attainable by means of spiritual intuitiveness.   In Hinduism it is said: " The mind is the great slayer of the real.   Let the disciple slay the slayer." [6] This does not mean that the mind is not a valuable instrument and that the analytical faculty should never be used; for as St. Paul wrote, one should " Prove all things; hold fast that which is good." [7]

[1] Serpent Fire or *Kundalini Shakti* (Sk.); the power of life; one of the forces of Nature; the seven-layered power in the base of the spine of man.   It has three currents which flow along three canals in the spinal cord, named *Ida* (negative), *Pingala* (positive) and *Sushumna* (neutral).   These names are sometimes also applied to the currents of force which flow in these canals.   This occult electricity is intimately associated with Azoth of the Alchemists, the creative principle in Nature, and *Akasa* (Sk.), the subtle, supersensuous, spiritual essence which pervades all space.   See also Glossary—*Kundalini* and *Kundalini Shakti*.

[2] *Rev.* 12: 1.

[3] *Acts.* 1: 9.

[4] *Augoeides*—see Glossary.

[5] *Devas*—Angelic Hosts. See Glossary, also *The Kingdom of the Gods*, Geoffrey Hodson.

[6] q. v. *The Voice of the Silence*, Fragment 1, from *The Book of the Golden Precepts*, translated and annotated by H. P. Blavatsky.

[7] *Thess.* 5: 21.

Thomas, " the doubter ", was allowed, even encouraged, to touch the wounds of the risen Christ in order to be utterly sure of His identity, and was not rebuked for his request for permission to do this.[1]   Moses asked God for proof of His divine powers to deliver the Israelites from bondage in Egypt, and such proof was given by the turning of his rod into a serpent, and later by the making of his hand " leprous as snow " and then restoring it to normal.[2]   It is legitimate, therefore, for the student of metaphysics to apply the intellect in constructive search, analysis and experiment in order to pierce illusion and discover truth.   The use of the mind for this purpose must nevertheless be carefully directed, lest its analytical faculty and the humiliation of possible failure should turn the student away from his quest for truth and blind him to the light of intuition.   In this sense only—of control and direction—must the mind be " slain ".   Sometimes, however, it must be rendered temporarily quiescent and receptive, listening, as it were, to the Voice of the God within which is revealing truth from supra-mental levels and permitting intuitional preception to bestow enlightenment.   When, later, the process of generalisation has been completed and the principles involved have become clear, the formal mind may be used, Thomas-like, to interpret the metaphysical idea and to indicate its logical expression in thought, word and conduct.

Decapitation is a symbol for this stilling of the mind, this procedure of robbing it of its power to kill intuition.   Thus in the conflict between David and Goliath [3] the two armies, Philistine and Israelite, were drawn up against each other for a war—another portrayal of Kurukshetra or Armageddon.   The Philistines were numerically the stronger and the Israelites under King Saul the weaker.   There emerged from the ranks of the Philistines a giant called Goliath, clad in armour.   He walked up and down between the two armies with great arrogance, challenging an Israelite to personal combat. There then appeared a young shepherd boy, David, armed with the sling which shepherds used to drive predatory birds and animals away from their flocks.   Although unprotected by armour, David

[1] *Jn.* 20: 25-28.
[2] *Ex.* 4: 1-7.
[3] I *Sam.* 17.

offered to fight Goliath. His offer was laughed at, and even King Saul tried to dissuade him. Nevertheless he persisted, and having taken five smooth stones from the brook placed one in his sling, approached the giant and slung the stone into his forehead, thereafter killing him by cutting off his head. The Philistine army immediately fled, leaving the Israelites victorious.

In the human interpretation of this Biblical story the enemies of Israel are the undesirable attributes of the lower nature, including in this case arrogance. The mental qualities of pride and rigidity (the armour) are specially indicated. The Israelites, on the other hand, represent the Ego within the personality travelling on its journey to perfection and on its way passing through many obstacles, interior and external (enemy tribes). David is the young Initiate, all shepherds personifying Adepts and Initiates. The fact that he took his stones from a stream indicates Initiateship, meaning that he had "entered the stream" and become consciously one with the river of divine life. The smooth stone taken from the stream and slung into the brain of Goliath represents the faculty of Intuition which found entrance into the concrete mind and thereby overrode excessively (gigantic) egoistic tendencies, as personified by Goliath. The light of intuition must pierce the head, as did the stone, and enter both the pineal and pituitary glands [1] (the forehead), symbolically killing the over-argumentative, prideful, destructive attributes of the lower mind (Goliath).

John the Baptist, also decapitated, represents the Ego preparing the personality for Initiation, as his mission, his message and his way of life allegorically indicate. He was captured by Herod—who, in his turn, personifies the arrogant, acquisitive, aggressive mind—and thus became the victim of the dancing girl Salome, who personifies sensuality. She demanded and received his head "in a charger" [2] (sensual passion "cuts off" the controlling action of the mind). Thus beheading generally refers to the "slaying" of the lower Self, particularly the formal mind, by the successful Candidate for Initiation, as also by all who would become illumined by the light of intuition.

[1] q. v. *The Secret Doctrine*, Vol. V, pp. 480-482, H. P. Blavatsky.
[2] *Matt.* 14 : 10, 11.

8

The human Race as a whole is at present largely—but certainly not entirely—at the Goliath stage. Its enemies are those countries and their leaders who, like the Philistines, Goliath, Herod and King Kamsa,[1] seek to prevent unification, to pervert loyalty and to enslave weaker peoples. They will not always succeed, however. David, as intuitive perception, is being " born " in man and will grow up and eventually " slay " the would-be " slayer "; for mankind evolves and in the process unfolds new faculties, including that of the intuitive perception of the unity of all life, and so of the brotherhood of all men. In due course humanity will reach the stage at which wars, oppression, crime and vice will quite naturally die out as a result of man's development, and his resultant larger view of the true relationship between human beings, as also of the real purpose for their existence. The " escape " of Shri Krishna, the success of David and the birth of the Christ child all allegorically refer to this future of the Race.

Doves, with their soft beauty of colouring and their harmonious, cooing voices, aptly symbolise that purest wisdom which, descending into the lower nature, " mightily and sweetly ordereth all things ". The sellers of doves who were driven out of the temple and their tables overthrown by Jesus[2] are those who, having attained to a measure of wisdom and occult knowledge, commercialise their newfound powers. In so doing they pretend to spirituality, but are in reality debasing the sacred science for personal gain. The Hierophants expel these from the Sanctuary. Eventually the awakened Christ-power within them purifies the temple of the lower nature of these undesirable characteristics.

The Eagle. This royal bird of prey flies nearest to the sun and is of keen vision. It abides in a lofty, remote eyrie, from which it descends to earth, catches quadrupeds, and then ascends to the greatest height to which any bird can attain. Macrocosmically, the eagle symbolises the highest spiritual Principle existing in Creation —the kingly aspect of the Divine. Microcosmically, it stands for the triple, kingly Ego which is able to contact the Monad (the sun), and is able also to descend into the personality (a quaternary or

---

[1] Kamsa, the uncle and enemy of Shri Krishna.
[2] *Jn.* 2: 14-15.

" quadruped "), seize its consciousness and elevate it near to the Monad. The eagle is the swiftest, strongest and noblest of all birds and therefore an apt symbol for the Highest in Universe and man. Interestingly, it is used in many Christian Churches as decorative support for the lectern upon which the Bible rests and from which the Scriptures are read.

EARTH and all physical, solid objects refer, in the main, to the physical body of man and to human states of waking consciousness. The four elements of earth, water, air and fire apply, in general, to interior experiences, activities and states of consciousness at the levels of physical nature, the emotions, the mind and the inner Spirit of man respectively.

THE EGG is a universal symbol for the origin and secret of all that exists. We may perhaps imagine early man watching the gradual development of the germ within the closed shell which—without any apparent outward interference or force—produced an offspring needing naught save heat. When the chick or reptile had gradually evolved into a living creature, it broke its shell and appeared to the senses of the onlooker as a self-generated and self-created being.

The Initiate writers used this phenomenon to portray in comprehensive form the abstract principles of emanation and evolution. The First Cause was pictured to early man by his teachers as an ever invisible, mysterious " bird " that dropped an " egg " into chaos, which egg became the Universe. Hence *Brahma* was called *Kalahamsa*, the swan in space, time and eternity. At the beginning of each *Mahā-Manvantara* [1] *Brahma* is said to lay a Golden Egg, which typifies the great circle, itself a symbol of the Universe and its spherical bodies with their aerial and orbital motions.

THE FATTED CALF, which formed part of the feast provided for the Prodigal Son on his return, symbolises fullness of faculties, richness of powers and attainments typical of the " returned ", liberated, ascended Adept. Implicit insight into first causes, infallible spiritual intuitiveness and discernment are among these developed powers or " riches ". The molten calf which the Israelites worshipped at the foot of Mount Sinai symbolises the grossly material expression

[1] *Mahā*-Manvantara—see Glossary.

of submission to the force of desire, and so the negation of intuitive wisdom; and also the dead-letter reading of the Scriptures and sub-servience to the outer forms and ceremonies of religion, divorced from true spirituality.

FIGURATIVE DEATH. The law that form must die before life may be free is enunciated in the famous words of the Christ: ". . . Except a corn of wheat fall into the ground and die, it abideth alone: but if it die, it bringeth forth much fruit." [1] The dying of the grain is that self-same death of the Christ upon the Cross, and of the Logos of a Universe or the " Lamb slain from the foundation of the world." [2] The tenth plague and the Passover allegorically and dramatically reveal this same process and this law.

The seven days during which the Israelites were bidden by the Lord, through Moses, to eat unleavened bread [3] refer to the seven sub-cycles of the last evolutionary major cycle. In Cosmoi, this is the last completed cycle of the existence of Solar Systems. In Planetary Schemes, Chains and Rounds [4] the last complete phase consists of seven stages, in each of which universalisation of conscious-ness is developed and extended. This has been attained at the close of the penultimate phase, and becomes the *motif* of the whole cycle from the opening of its successor to its close. Universalised conscious-ness is itself subject to evolution and extension of range. It begins with the capacity for awareness at will throughout the whole physical body and is then extended successively throughout the superphysical bodies, from the lowest up to the highest. These are seven in number, and the attainment of universalised awareness in each of them occupies an evolutionary period or " day ".

The Adept has forcibly achieved this universalisation of con-sciousness far in advance of the Race. Instead of the normal, relatively slow and painful process through Race, Round, Chain and Planetary

[1] *Jn.* 12 : 24.

[2] *Rev.* 13 : 8.

[3] *Ex.* 13 : 7.

[4] In occult science the Solar System is said to consist of ten Planetary Schemes, each composed of seven successive Chains of Globes, superphysical and physical. Each Chain is composed of seven Rounds during each of which the life-stream, bearing with it the evolving beings, travels round the seven Globes. The period of occupation of one of the seven Globes is called a " World Period ". See Glossary—Chain.

Scheme, he attains to this state by a deliberate effort, maintained throughout several lives and consists largely of the practice of *Rāja Yoga*, which includes prolonged contemplation of the divine Self, the *Paramātma*, of the Universe and of the unity therewith of the human *Ātma*. Ultimately these are known to be not two but one, and thereafter the Adept *Yogi* affirms with full realisation: " The *Ātma* and the *Paramātma* are one ".

The process of enforced self-illumination is at least dual. On the one hand the Adept-to-be forces himself progressively to surrender the sense of I-ness, to deny to himself every sensation of individual identity and to relinquish every trace of personal possessiveness, and even the sense of personal identity as a separate being. The denial and relinquishment of self constitute part of the figurative " death " of all Initiatory rites. On the other hand, he extends the experience of harmonious attunement with the life of all beings around him until self-identification or at-one-ment (the true Atonement) with them is achieved, and by practice becomes normal. Thus successively attained in vehicle after vehicle, the Adept becomes at one with the life in all beings at all levels of existence. This culminates at the close of the seventh " day ", or major *Manvantara*, of his manifestation as a cosmic entity in at-one-ment with the totality of the appointed field of evolution. In the case of a Solar Logos conscious omnipresence throughout the whole Solar System is implied.

There is no finality to this process of extension of self-identity with other selves. Manifested Cosmoi are innumerable, since all are themselves evolving through the continuous process of emergence from the Absolute and withdrawal to it. The Absolute may therefore tentatively be defined as self-awareness in space and time, both potentially in *Pralaya* and actually in *Manvantara*, without cessation and without limits. Yet awareness itself is a denial of absoluteness. Absolute consciousness includes every possible phase, from transcendence in *Pralaya* to immanence in *Manvantara*. Absolute awareness must include unconsciousness as well as all possible consciousness, and therefore is inconceivable to the mind save by theory. The highest beings ascend to the very threshold of this state, which is the evolutionary summit. In one sense to eat unleavened bread is to transcend individuality, or to partake of the one life in its eternal self-existence in homogeneity.

FIRE has at least a dual significance in the Sacred Language. When destructive, it refers to the hypercritical attributes and activities of the human mind. When a source of illumination, as upon a mount or as a pillar of fire guiding through the darkness, it refers to the sublimated creative force in man, sometimes called the Serpent Fire,[1] by means of which the darkness of the unillumined, worldly state of mind is displaced by the light of wisdom. The wilderness, the arid state of consciousness, then gives place to the " Promised Land " of spiritual fruitfulness and realised union with God. This power is also universally symbolised by the serpent.[2]

THE FIRST-BORN is a symbol for the newly Initiated man or woman. After the first of the great Initiations, which itself marks a passage from one phase of human evolution to its successor, the superphysical vehicles used by the now Initiated Ego at the mental and emotional levels do not, as formerly, disintegrate after death. Throughout all successive rebirths the Ego retains the personal mento-emotional *psyche*. In this sense personal relative immortality (though not yet of the physical body) has been attained. Death passes over these forms (houses) in which Initiated Egos continue to abide. They are marked with " the blood of the Lamb " in the sense that the Christ-nature has been awakened into self-conscious activity, and the Christ influence and attitude to life are characteristic of the outer man. These vehicles are referred to as the houses of the Israelites which are passed over by death.

The Egyptians, on the other hand, represent normal humanity, which in the present epoch is still in the pre-Initiate stage of evolution. In consequence, the normal procedure of the disintegration of the three personal vehicles—the physical with the conjoined etheric, the emotional and the mental—occurs after physical death. The mento-emotional nature was the first-born of the preceding epoch and, until the man or woman is touched by the Thyrsus, is doomed to die with the physical. If this view be accepted, the affront to both the Deity and the human mind inseparable from the literal

[1] Serpent Fire—see Glossary under *Kundalini* and *Kundalini Shakti*.
[2] See heading " Serpents " later in this Chapter.

reading of the Scripture disappears. The Lord God is not, in truth, a bloodthirsty, tribal deity inciting His followers to slaughter lambs, eat the flesh and sprinkle their houses with the blood; neither is He a ruthless murderer. The Lord God can now be seen as a personification of law, and His deeds as allegories depicting cosmic, racial, individual, and both natural and Initiatory progression from one phase of evolution to the next.

THE FISH is a universally used symbol with many meanings. In one of these it refers to human passions refined to a harmless state, sublimated, transmuted to produce illumination and realisation of the oneness of all life, or to become " food ". Only sublimation is necessary, as the driving force behind passion is the same as that behind compassion. The Christ-consciousness, wisdom born of the union of will and universal love, which is personal love rendered all-inclusive, is represented by the fish.

This denizen of the waters (emotions) symbolises that condition of consciousness, and the mitre of a bishop is shaped like a fish's head with open mouth, possibly as a symbol that such a high dignitary has attained to this intellectual illumination (head) and his life is consecrated to its expression.

Apart from the astrological attribution of characteristics— Christlike compassion and intuitive wisdom—to the Zodiacal sign Pisces, a fish seems to have been used as a secret sign by which the early Christians could mutually identify each other during the time they were being persecuted. In addition, the letters of the Greek word for fish, *ichthys*, are the letters in Greek of the phrase " Jesus Christ, Son of God, Saviour."

GEOGRAPHICAL FEATURES, which are used constantly as topographical symbols, refer to waking states of consciousness whether normal (level ground), debased (valleys) or exalted (mountains). Palestine and Jordan, for example, as also Egypt and the Nile, are endowed with spiritual significance. Macrocosmically, the country is the Universe and the river is the stream of divine life perpetually flowing through it for its vivification. Pre-Initiate consciousness (" them that are without ") [1] is aware only of the material Universe and the material symbols.

[1] *Col.* 4: 5.

At the First Initiation self-conscious awareness of the existence of the one life, and dawning realisation of spiritual unity with it, are attained. In addition, symbols are then replaced by direct perception of that which they typify (knowing the mystery " face to face ", as in Christ's words to His disciples).[1] This self-unification with the eternal, omnipresent current of creative life is technically called " entering the Stream." Each Initiation deepens this reali- sation, until at the Fifth it is complete. The Adept knows himself as identical with the life-filling stream, the indwelling spiritual life, which like a river flows into and vivifies every form. He is then technically said to have " crossed the Stream ". Jordan, Nile and other sacred rivers are used as symbols of that timeless, spaceless, inexhaustible life of God. Consciously at one with it, the Adept achieves immortality.

Microcosmically, Palestine represents the physical body of man with Jordan as the spinal cord, the Dead Sea as the sacral region, the Sea of Galilee as the heart and the sometimes snow-capped moun- tains of Lebanon as the head, exposed to and receptive of the down- poured rain, symbol of the very waters of life. To separate by magical power the waters of Jordan (or the Red Sea) into two currents, one on the right and one on the left, to carry over the Ark of the Covenant (the Israelite nation), and to enable the people to cross dry-shod, is an allegorical method of describing certain bodily trans- formations, and the awakening and ascent along the spinal cord of the positive and negative currents of the Serpent Fire.

The two memorials built of twelve stones, one on the western bank of Jordan [2] and the other upon its bed,[3] represent the particular and the universal. They also represent, humanly speaking, the microcosm with its twelve zodiacal powers and the Macrocosm with its zodiacal belt, and reveal the exactitude of their mutual conformity. They are indeed, the same and are identical save for dimension. " The Universe is a man on a large scale." [4]

The holding back of the waters of Jordan also represents the uncovering of fundamental truth. The stones found in the bed

---

[1] *Matt.* 13: 11. cf. also I *Cor.* 13 : 12.
[2] *Joshua.* 4: 20.
[3] *Joshua.* 4: 9.
[4] *Lao Tze.*

below the waters represent both the supernal wisdom and the utter-most foundations upon which all creation is based. These roots of being, these truths and powers, these numbers and laws, upon and according to which the Universe and man are built, are normally concealed beneath the living substance of which they are composed. Matter-blinded man, the pre-Initiate mind, cannot see them under-neath the " flood ". Spiritually illumined man, the Initiate-mind, pierces the veil, symbolically holds back the waters of Jordan and perceives and forever after knows the twelve powers, principles and truths upon which, and of which, the Universe and man are built.

The Initiate consciously brings forth from within himself his human River Jordan, his spiritual life, and the same twelve powers, and develops them to perfection as an everlasting affirmation and memorial of their Macrocosmic existence. At this stage of their journey to the Promised Land, the Israelites under Joshua represent man at that illumined phase of his evolution at which he consciously takes his life and powers into his own hands and deliberately hastens their development to the perfected state. Truly it is also said that the memorials are there to this day, twelve-stoned and everlasting; for natural law is eternal, and when once a man is self-liberated and self-perfected he remains so for ever after. Thus, indeed, all is interior, all occurs within man. In their microcosmic, Initiatory interpretation, the great stories depict the training, the trials, the failures and the successes of those who find and tread the pathway to perfection, " the strait gate " and " the narrow way " which lead to life eternal.

GOLGOTHA may be interpreted as the place at which the physical, mental and spiritual " Crucifixion " occurs. The final, completed attainment of the Christ-consciousness, with all that it implies, must be achieved in full, waking, physical consciousness. The mind-brain itself must receive this illumination. The brain is situated within the skull and it is for this reason, it is thought, that the Crucifixion was made to occur on Golgotha, " a place of a skull." [1]

THE HAWK is the symbol of Ra, Horus and other Gods, and especially represents the " uplifting ", spiritualising, enlightening effect of divine power upon Nature, and also of the human Ego upon

[1] *Matt.* 27: 33.

mortal man. Macrocosmically the triple Deity " preys upon ",
" catches with its talons ", the material Universe and then absorbs
it, thus unifying the lower with the Higher and so spiritualising it.
Microcosmically, the Monad-Ego " preys upon ", " hunts ", catches,
elevates and absorbs the lower quaternary—hence divine hunters
(e. g. Eros), huntresses (e. g. Artemis), bows, arrows and other weapons,
many of them magical.

THE HEART. In the Sacred Language the heart, in the microcosmic sense, refers to the Causal Body, which is a centre in the higher
mental plane for the reception and the distribution (heart-like) of
the spiritual life-blood of the Ego to the lower man. This will-
charged life, which is the true *Christos* of the Soul, eventually floods
and completely dominates the outer man. Thus the Causal Body,
illumined and filled with *Ātma-Buddhi*, is a vehicle for the rhythmic
transmission of divine life throughout the whole nature of man. The
key-note of *Buddhi* is unity, love, kinship, compassion, and so the heart
is popularly used as a symbol for these qualities and experiences.
By the word " heart ", however, is meant not only the seat of affection,
the organ of tender emotion, but also the inmost Sanctuary, the
synthesis and source of all the energy, life, wisdom, love and will
of the Higher Self. The heart is thus an apt symbol of the central
life of the Soul, the Inner Ruler Immortal and its powers.

In ancient Egypt the heart bore a similar significance, and
invocations were addressed to it: " My heart, my Mother! My
heart wherby I came into being. May naught stand up to oppose
me at my judgment. Verily, how great shalt thou be when [at
Initiation] thou risest in triumph." [1] The still heart is a beautiful
and arresting Egyptian symbol for the illumined Higher Self in perfect
equipoise, utterly receptive to and hearing perfectly the divine
" Voice ". In those days prayers were offered to the still heart,
which was also interpreted as the divine love hitherto latent in the
Soul. Allegorically the heart, placed in a jar, was weighed against
a feather before Osiris (the Monad) in the Judgment Hall (of Initiation) in the Underworld after death. The heart in the jar represented
the Ego in the Causal Body and its influence as conscience, and the
feather referred to the personal life, the degree to which the latter

---

[1] q. v. *Book of the Dead*, Vol. 3, Ch. 30, E. A. W. Budge.

was illumined by the former being under test. Equilibrium of the two was demanded as a proof of worthiness. If attained, the Soul was pronounced " *Maa Kheru* ", meaning " true of voice " or " Gotrabhu ". [1]

The exposed heart of Christ (the Sacred Heart) symbolises the state of consciousness of the perfected man. His heart is ever exposed, meaning that the divine love of the Master is never withheld from any living being or thing. Perpetually through the centuries of His existence—through His heart, as it were—there radiates in all directions His divine, all-embracing love and compassion. That love flows out like a flood which engulfs the world. This is also symbolised by a rose blooming on the breast of a mystic.

A deeper meaning given to the emblem of the Sacred Heart is that in one of His activities the Adept voluntarily receives into His heart all evil, all the forces of hate, discord, disruption and ugliness, and by the magic of His love, which is selfless, He transmutes them into power and blessing and sends them out again through His heart as streams of benediction over the whole world. The spear with which the heart of Jesus was pierced may be regarded as representing the world's hate which He continually accepts, receives, changes into love within Himself by spiritual alchemy, and then sends out again for the blessing of the world and, no doubt, particularly for the blessing of those who are responsible for the hate. That is the difference between a Master and a man. The former never withdraws spiritually from humanity, and the fulfilment of the promise which Jesus made as He ascended into Heaven: ". . . lo, I am with you alway, even unto the end of the world ", [2] is beautifully expressed by the picture of the Christ with an open breast and the shining, pulsing heart within. Christ also exemplified this preserved unity with all mankind when He said of His tormentors: ". . . Father, forgive them; for they know not what they do." [3] The opened rose, with its beauty and its fragrance, especially when associated with the symbol of the heart, is regarded as an appropriate emblem of these powers, qualities and attainments of illumined man.

---

[1] *Gotrabhu*—a Buddhist term for one who has *Nirvana* as his aim.
[2] *Matt.* 28: 20.
[3] *Lu.* 23: 34.

THE HOLY GRAIL.   The Cup or Chalice may perhaps be regarded as a symbol of the superphysical bodies of both Universe and man. The foot of the Chalice would represent the etheric world and body of man. The stem would be the astral and mental planes and the human vehicles, the bowl the Causal Plane and man's Causal Body, and the wine the spiritual life of indwelling in the Universe and all beings.

At the First Initiation the *Buddhic* Principle and the power of intuition are further aroused. Gradually, sub-plane by sub-plane, the centre of self-awareness moves up into the *Buddhic* Plane. This brings the " wine " of the one life of God into the Causal Body or bowl of the Chalice. The inner Self of the Initiate then becomes spiritualised and the outer life deeply consecrated. As in the Adept, the centre of self-awareness ascends to the *Ātmic* level and the Fire of the One Will descends into the Causal Body, or symbolically the " bread " of Holy Communion is received.

The Quest of the Holy Grail is the search by the personality for the spiritual Self in the Causal Body. Thereafter the Quest leads to discovery of the inner Self (Logos) of the Universe, the Macrocosmic Chalice. This truth is only realised when the individual Holy Grail becomes known and its " wine "—*Buddhic* life and consciousness—is received. The Grail legend may thus be regarded as an allegory of the Paths of Discipleship and Initiation. All the events and adventures describe *interior* experiences of the neophytes, desciples and Initiates with King Arthur as Heirophant. The Knights are the attributes, qualities (for example, Galahad—purity) and weaknesses (Lancelot—sensuality) of each single Aspirant.

The Holy Grail, Chalice or Cup would thus seem to be a symbol of the Causal Body of man into which, at a certain level of evolution, the divine life of God is poured. The Quest is the search made by the human personality in a physical body for conscious experience of the universal wisdom-love within the inner Self. The Grail story tells of the drama of the Soul, in which the hero passes through the experiences and tests of the outer life, contends against ignorance and evil, and releases the highest qualities (captive maidens) from imprisonment in and by the lower nature.[1] When at last the personality

---

[1] q. v. *Idylls of the King*, and especially the stories of Sir Galahad and Sir Percivale —A. Tennyson.

becomes intimately linked with and knows itself as the inner, divine Self, " a higher power bringeth a Cup full of intuition and wisdom and also prudence and giveth it to the soul." [1] The symbolism of the Chalice and of the sacred Elements is thus dual, applying equally to the Universe and to man, the Host typifying the Deity, whole and indivisible—and particularly God the Father. The wine stands for God the Son, Whose life is poured down into the " Chalice " of material form.

THE HORSES of Pharoah represent the intelligent life-force which is the driving-power behind and within the activities of mind, emotion and body. When spiritually directed, this mental energy elevates the centre of consciousness towards the spiritual worlds just as Pegasus, the winged horse, carried his rider up into the air. When unrestrained, the mind-impelled life-force can lead to the indulgence of the lower nature, with its passions and desires. Thus, according to tradition an endeavour was made by sorcerers to have the child Zoroaster trampled to death by horses. The leading horse, however, stood over the child and preserved it from injury.

A white horse is a symbol of the Higher Mind illumined by intuition. The Lord Buddha, out of pity for the sufferings of the world, is said to have flown across the heavens on a white horse and entered into the regions of the demons in order to secure the happiness of mankind. The white horse is also symbolically associated with the sun, and so with the Dweller in the Innermost, the Monad of man. The World Saviour, or King Messiah, is described as riding on a white horse, holding a bow and wearing a crown.[2] The arrow is a symbol of the fiery darts or rays of the sun which physically give life, energy and fecundity to Nature. Spiritually interpreted it symbolises the thrust of Spirit, the fiery, electrical energy (Fohat) by which evolutionary progression is initiated and maintained. In man, the arrow is the will-force of the Monad which awakens the dormant intuitive faculty within the Higher Self and supplies the driving energy which causes a man to set forth upon the great quest, like a mountaineer who risks his life in order to conquer an hitherto

[1] q. v. *Pistis Sophia*, Trans. by G. R. S. Mead.

[2] The Coming *Avatar* to appear at the end of the present dark age, and referred to in Hinduism as the *Kalki Avatar*.

unknown and inviolate peak. The *Avatar*, or divine World Saviour, mounted upon a white horse, is thus the Christos; Vishnu among the Hindus; the Logos both of a Universe and of the human Soul.

In the choice of a horse rather than an ass, ox, elephant or other tamed quadruped, the attribute of speed is deliberately accentuated. Rapidity of movement suggests hyper-activity, and activity is one of the three basic attributes of all substance, the other two being rhythm and inertia. Activity or speed, when uncontrolled, leads to undesirable actions and excesses in self-expression. This is symbolised by wild, swiftly moving animals. Activity, controlled and inter-balanced with rhythm and inertia, leads to powerful and graceful motion, subject to mastery, and this condition is well portrayed by the horse.

The winged horse, Pegasus, in addition to the meanings already suggested, represents a still more advanced evolutionary condition; for a Pegasus can leave the earth and soar into the heavens. The four lower worlds in which, normally, form imprisons life, and the four lower vehicles of man, have become so completely subordinated to the indwelling consciousness and life and so permeated with awakened spritual power that they no longer confine to temporal and material limitations the being who is using them. The two wings of such a mount represent the co-ordinated, yet duly separated, abstract and concrete mentalities. Under these conditions Spirit is free of former material limitations, and man can soar in consciousness to realms beyond those where the human intellect is normally active and aware.

THE IBIS. This bird symbolises the Egyptian God of Wisdom, Tehuti, generally portrayed as being ibis-headed. The ibis feeds upon cobras, and so saves lives. The poisonous serpent means the creative force misused. This familiar phenomenon became translated into an allegory of the protection of man by the ibis-headed God from the misuse of the serpentine creative fire, particularly in the form of excessive sexual indulgence.[1]

Swamp and marsh mean both the lower astral and the primitive, primeval state from and within which life is created and formed. (cf. Moses in the bulrushes, and the Zulu tradition that " that ancestor, called Unkulunkulu, branched off from a reed, or came from a bed

---

[1] Serpent Fire: see Glossary—*Kundalini* and *Kundalini Shakti.*

of reeds "). In ancient Egypt Horus, the Younger, had been immaculately born to Isis and brought up in the marshes of the Nile Delta,
representing Macrocosmically the Universe " born " out of primeval
" slime " (pre-cosmic matter) as a result of active, creative power
—Osiris. As has been seen, when misused by man the Serpent Fire
become poisonous, evil, death-dealing. The ibis eats the snakes and
so reduces the danger. Tehuti, as Wisdom, illumines man and
" saves " him from this sin and its poisonous effects. This is probably
part of the reason for the ibis head of Tehuti.

> THE INTERLACED TRIANGLES. " The double triangles symbolise
> the Great Passive and the Great Active; the male and female;
> Purusha and Prakriti. Each triangle is a Trinity because pre-
> senting a triple aspect, [of the triune God, as also in man, knowl-
> edge, the knower and that which is known . . . Also the creative,
> preservative and destructive forces which are mutually cor-
> related"].
>
> (*The Mahatma Letters to A. P. Sinnett*, p. 346).

> " The way a triangle points determines its meaning. If
> upwards, it means the male element and divine fire; downwards,
> the female and the waters of matter."
>
> (*The Theosophical Glossary*, H. P. Blavatsky).

> A Master writes: " The true ' word ' may only be found by
> tracing the mystery inward and outward of the Eternal Life,
> through the states typified by these three geometric figures
> [the double triangle in the circle]."
>
> (*The Mahatma Letters to A. P. Sinnett*, p. 347).

THE HEXAGON. If the points of the figure of the interlaced
triangles, the Solomon's Seal, be joined up, a hexagon is produced.
This is a symbol of universal Creation, the Seven Sephiroth in creative
activity, their number being completed by their synthesis at the central
point from which all arises.

THE KISS involves the sense of touch. It symbolises the creative
contact of the positive agent upon the negative recipient, and portrays
a phase in the creative process. In human superphysical experience
the kiss is Astro-Buddhic. Physically it is given by the lips, which
are the entrance to the organ of taste. It is an expression of love and

desire, inspired by a realisation or instinctual recognition of unity, however fleeting and faint that realisation may be.

Since, however, unity behind apparent diversity is an unalterable fact, since the life in all is one and the same despite variety of form, the instinct for unity finds constant and continual expression in man. Therefore the kiss, or union of the higher creative " organs ", is the unchanging and ever continued expression of love. In a kiss on the lips, emotion predominates; the spiritual is implied by a kiss on the brow, over the pituitary gland and *Ajna Chakra*. The fact that paternal, maternal, filial, fraternal and sisterly kisses are hardly ever upon the lips is of interest, the element of desire being absent from all of these. In general, only between lovers is the kiss bestowed upon the lips.

The kiss which Jacob gave to Rachel, with its suggestions of attraction through sight, of contact by touch, of positive action by the male and acquiescence and response by the female, perfectly symbolises the Macrocosmic creative process which begins with the " kiss " of Spirit upon matter. The kiss of Judas is a betrayal leading to the imprisonment, the degradation, the suffering, the death and the entombment of the Christ in the sense that Spirit, which He personifies, is enfolded and so " betrayed " and imprisoned by matter, primordial freedom being temporarily restricted.

THE LOTUS. The open lotus bloom typifies the emanation of universal order from primordial chaos, the finite from the Infinite, Universes from the " waters " of unconditioned Space. The whole plant symbolises fertility, fecundation, growth, whilst the lotus seed which when cut across shows the perfect flower represents the Monad, the Immortal Germ—Macrocosmic and microcosmic. The lotus in full bloom portrays the perfectly expressed Monad, whether of Universe, angel or man—the God within fully made manifest.

If this symbolism is applied more particularly to man, then the lotus seed may be likened to the human Monad. This is appropriate because, when ripe, the seed is thrown off by the flower and sink into the muddy depths (incarnation in a physical body) and the roots draw sustenance therefrom. The stalk reaches up through the water (the emotional nature) and the leaves both rest on the surface of the water and are sustained above it, aptly representing the dual mind (concrete and abstrct). The beautiful bloom, with its pure white petals and golden heart opened towards the sun, is a fitting symbol of man's powers of aspiration and spiritual intuitiveness.

The formation of new seeds, which in their turn sink below the water into lake or river bed beneath, germinating and producing new plants, new flowers and still more seeds, portrays the unbroken succession of major and minor cycles (*Manvantaras* and reincarnations). The seasonal continuance of this natural process also indicates the deathless nature of the Spirit in man, with its assured resurrection from both bodily death and the limitations of existence in the human kingdom of Nature.

MARRIAGE and intercourse, whether legal or illicit, refer not to any carnal relationship but to a spiritual " marriage ", or blending of consciousness, at any level. The physical, waking consciousness can be elevated into union with that of the inner spiritual Self. A great teacher may blend his consciousness intimately with a disciple, while at the spiritual level the Supreme Teacher of All perpetually maintains an indissoluble union between Himself and all beings. The symbol of marriage is thus used in two senses. One refers to the conscious unification of the divine and the human in man. The other refers to the intimate, spiritual union established between a true Teacher and the spiritual Soul of a disciple or, in the case of Our Lord, with the whole of humanity. This latter is regarded by some Christian mystics as the true atonement, which might possibly be written as " at-one-ment ". Under such conditions a spiritual marriage might be said to have occurred, and thus Our Lord might permissibly be regarded as the Bridegroom.

Even illicit relationships may be used to indicate this same fusion of the lower and higher natures, and of the higher with the Divine. In many allegories the persons of harlots, and the practice of adultery, are introduced with the object of indicating enforced or premature attainment of union, or fully realised unity, with the innermost Self and the Most High God.

Since all characters in inspired allegories are personifications of principles and attributes of the single human being, frank Biblical references to legitimate or illicit procreative activity lose their repulsiveness; for such " marriage " is not physical but psycho-spiritual or heavenly, and such conceivings are of the Spirit, and so immaculate.

9

Marriage and the woman partner are used as symbols in two senses. In one the woman—or the womb, ark or cradle—is the abstract mind in its vehicle, the Causal Body. Marriage refers to the descent of the fructifying Monadic (the husband's) Ray, as a result of which the Higher Mind becomes pregnant with the faculty of intuition and the power to perceive the oneness of life amidst diversity of form. When these powers are developed to the degree at which they are consciously realised and employed, a son is said to be born. This is the Initiatory interpretation and is employed in all accounts of divine and semi-divine nativities.

In another meaning the woman is the outer personality, and more especially its formal mind. Marriage portrays the phase in its development at which the mentally fructifying influence of the inner Self (the husband), through the abstract intelligence, is finding a response in the hitherto wholly analytical, and therefore spiritually barren, formal mind. As a result of this type of union or marriage the faculty of abstract thought is added (conceived) to those of analysis and deduction, and when this is recognised and consciously used a son is said to have been born. Earlier people saw nothing obscene or impure in the procreative power, process and organs, and nothing indecent in their use as physical symbols of both divine creative power and cosmogenesis, and mystical unions and their fruits as attained by Initiated men. Phallicism is not necessarily an indication of evil-mindedness.

MOUNTAINS, upon which so much of importance occurs in the Bible and other Scriptures, refer in the main to a state of spiritual upliftment during consciousness in the physical body. Plains indicate the normal, necessary, work-a-day state of the mind, while valleys represent deliberately chosen, grossly material ideas, thoughts and activities. Volcanoes, and mountains whose summits are temporarily on fire or ablaze with light, symbolise both the head and the exalted state of consciousness of advanced Souls in whom the Serpent Fire has been aroused and has enfired the whole head, and opened (rolled away the stone of the sepulchre) the spiritual channel or whirling vortex at the crown of the head. When this has occurred the whole nature becomes illumined and transfigured, as did Moses on Sinai,[1]

_____
[1] *Ex.* 19: 3.

Elijah on Mount Horeb,[1] and Christ on the mount of Trans-figuration.[2]

The mechanism of human consciousness consists physically of the body itself and its cerebro-spinal system, with the seven nerve and glandular centres situated at the sacrum, the spleen, the solar plexus, the heart, the throat and the pituitary and pineal glands. At the etheric level, the etheric counterparts of these centres and glands and the etheric vortices called *chakras*[3] link the inner Self to the physical body. Seven *chakras* also exist at similar locations in both the emotional and mental bodies of man. Biblical references to these force-centres in the superphysical bodies of angels and of men are to be found in *Ezekiel*, Chapter one, verse fifteen, Chapter three, verse thirteen and Chapter ten, verse nine, and indirectly in *Revelation* Chapter six as seals which were opened.

Glyphs of floating in the air, or rising above the earth, are sym-bolical of ascension to superphysical and spiritual states of conscious-ness and being. Where fire is the elevating agency, as in the case of Elijah and, in a measure, Moses (the pillar of fire and the burning bush), the sublimated creative energy is indicated as the exalting agency. The Ascension of Jesus in clouds of glory is susceptible of a similar interpretation. In His case the ascent culminated in en-thronement at the right hand of the Father and this implies attainment of Christhood, Adeptship; for unbroken and fully conscious unity with the Supreme Deity—Nirvana—is entered into by the liberated Adept.

NATIVITIES refer to the process of the opening of new cycles, whether solar, planetary, racial, individual, psychical or spiritual. The children of such unions typify the new state of consciousness which follows, especially the faculty of spiritual intuitiveness. Those who thus attain are sometimes variously referred to as " little ones", children, youth, and the new-born. Even the process of abortion is given a spiritual significance, under which it indicates the forcing of spiritual evolution, the deliberate adoption of a mode of life which quickens spiritual " rebirth " and the realisation of unity.

[1] 1 *Kings* 19 : 11.
[2] *Matt.* 17 : 1-2.
[3] *Chakra*—See Glossary.

NIGHT, death, blindness and sleep refer cosmically to periods of non-manifestation, and humanly to mental states in which spiritual awareness is temporarily lost. Day, on the other hand, represents a period of manifestation and a state of spiritual illumination, constant for the inner Self but difficult of attainment by the outer man. Dawn, or daybreak, represents the process of return to manifestation and illumination. This change and its effects are well illustrated in the incident of the denial of his Master by Peter in the night, and his repentance and remorse as soon as day broke.[1] The story of this episode is one of those luminous cameos of condensed revelation of psycho-spiritual experiences on the path of discipleship.

OIL is one of many symbols used to denote: a special characteristic of spiritual wisdom; universal, sanctified and sacrificial love; the universal life principle; and the bliss, the harmony and the deep understanding which flow forth from these states of consciousness. An example of the use of oil as a symbol occurs in the following passage from the Bible:

> " Now there cried a certain woman of the wives of the sons of the prophets unto Elisha, saying, Thy servant my husband is dead; and thou knowest that thy servant did fear the LORD: and the creditor is come to take unto him my two sons to be bondmen.
>
> " And Elisha said unto her, What shall I do for thee? tell me, what hast thou in the house?   And she said, Thine handmaid hath not any thing in the house, save a pot of oil.
>
> " Then he said, Go, borrow thee vessels abroad of all thy neighbours, even empty vessels; borrow not a few.
>
> " And when thou art come in, thou shalt shut the door upon thee and upon thy sons, and shalt pour out into all those vessels, and thou shalt set aside that which is full.
>
> " So she went from him, and shut the door upon her and upon her sons, who brought the vessels to her; and she poured out.
>
> " And it came to pass, when the vessels were full, that she said unto her son, Bring me yet a vessel.   And he said unto her, There is not a vessel more.   And the oil stayed.
>
> " Then she came and told the man of God.   And he said, Go, sell the oil, and pay thy debt, and live thou and thy children of the rest." [2]

[1] *Lk.* 22 : 55-62.
[2] 11 Kings 4 : 1-7.

If, in consciousness, one has come to a realisation of spiritual wisdom, sanctified and sacrificial love and the universal life principle, and will share that realisation with others, the experience (or the supply of oil) is not only not diminished, but is increased.

This is also the esoteric meaning of all allegories which describe the multiplication of a small quantity into a large one. Here a fact in Nature, and not a miracle, is revealed. This fact is that when once an individual has become consciously at one with the universal life and a channel for its harmonising, healing and mentally nourishing influence, the experience of unity is deepened and the capacity to serve is increased. In addition, the recipients of this ministration receive a similar expansion and recognise and ratify the same law. In these ways not decrease, but increase, follows such expressions of divine love.

The widow, then, is the Higher Self of the spiritually awakened man or woman. Her widowhood and her poverty represent her detachment from external means of happiness and support, and her possession of one jar of oil indicates that the consciousness is becoming universalised. Her two sons are the mento-emotional and the physical constituents of the outer personality. Their danger of poverty and bondage indicates that the processes of self-universalisation and renunciation are as yet incomplete. They have not yet found expression through the mental, the emotional and the physical body and life.

At this profoundly important juncture in human evolution assistance, if wisely sought (v. 2), is always readily available. A Sage, a spiritual Teacher, unfailingly responds to a sincere appeal for aid, and propounds and exemplifies the law that spiritual increase (the addition to the widow's supply of oil) invariably follows the wise expression of universal love (the oil). If the pupil is able to respond, the household and the offspring (the mortal nature) become filled with an abundance of spiritual wisdom, life and love. When once universalisation of intellect has been attained and accepted by the mind-brain, the two sons (mind and body) are freed from the threat of slavery.

The theurgic act of increase or " multiplication ", as it is technically called, is well within the power of so high an Initiate as Elisha. Such multiplication is a not uncommon feat among qualified theurgists.

The narrative may therefore be accepted in both its literal and its symbolical reading.

THE PEACOCK represents that state of ignorance and foolish pride into which man can fall. The outer display of the peacock, especially of the form and colours of the male, does not appear to be matched by a corresponding intellectual power. Nevertheless the life-force finds expression even in so foolish a bird, which in reality is only following the ways of its own species. These ways prove to be adequate; for, like the rest of Nature, the peacock species is perpetuated and preserved on Earth.

Innate wisdom operates successfully despite intellectual limitations. Indeed, in some cases pure, natural wisdom finds a fuller and freer expression in a less active mind-brain. Man, himself, also passes through the " peacock " phase of his evolution. This was chiefly during the Fourth Root Race, in which the emotional nature and aura of man underwent their long development. Mind still slept save in the more advanced, and not until the later sub-Races, when the Fifth Root Race was already advanced, was mind added as a faculty and a power possessed and used by the Fifth human Race upon this Earth.

The peacock well symbolises the Fourth Root Race, in which the radiant colours of the astral aura and the faculties which they represent were the subject of Nature's handiwork. The aptness of the symbolism becomes plain when it is remembered that the male peacock displays his brilliant hues partly as a means of winning the favours of the female; for the brightly coloured astral aura of man is also the seat of procreative desire, and certain of its colours also shine more brilliantly than normal when feelings of love, whether platonic or sexual, are aroused and find expression.

Whilst the unicorn has a dual significance, representing an early and a later Root Race (the Third and the Sixth), the peacock symbolises the relatively mind-free Fourth Root Race and also both the later Sixth and Seventh Root Races when, without the intervention of the deductive intellect, the splendour of the intuitive faculty will be made manifest and man will live less in his mind than in his spiritual nature, and so possess both an intuitive wisdom and an implicit insight into every first truth.

This racial attainment also is foreshadowed in the Initiate, who attains to the powers of later Races and must possess and be able to display the appropriate faculties.   His aura shines, indeed, with the peacock's brilliant hues.   His intuitive wisdom is as a hundred eyes, which makes him relatively omniscient, and though regarded by his fellow men outside the Sanctuary as intellectually negligible, he is in reality the adornment of the Race.   The shining, silken feathers and the bejewelled neck and tail of the peacock aptly represent both the aura and the powers of future Races of men on Earth, as also of those individuals who outstrip their fellows and attain to a regal, spiritual splendour far in advance of their own Race and age.   The peacock is also regarded as a symbol of royalty.

THE PELICAN.   Rosicrucians used the female pelican to represent the maternal and the preserving aspects of Deity.   The mother bird is portrayed as feeding its seven young from its own opened breast whilst floating in a nest upon water.

Macrocosmically, the pelican is emblematic of the divine power of procreative Nature.   Water refers to Space, which explains why aquatic birds floating on water are chosen as symbols of Deity.   The nest is the differentiated substance of the Universe organised and insulated by the Ring-pass-not.[1]   The seven fledglings are the seven procreative Powers, Builders and Sephiroth, the Scheme, Chains, Rounds, Planes, Races and sub-Races; the Rays, the kingdoms of Nature and the human Principles—all of which are nourished and sustained by the divine life.   Blood stands for that universal life which, as portrayed in the glyph, the Logos pours forth sacrificially in the Eternal Oblation.

Microcosmically, the pelican represents the human Monad, the nest is the Auric Envelope[2] and water is the elemental essence of the planes of Nature and the bodies of man.   The seven young are the seven Principles or vehicles, all being perpetually nourished by the outpoured spiritual life of the Monad—the " blood " of the God within.   Blood is *Ātma-Buddhi*, the Christ Principle, the indwelling life, the elixir (Sk. *Amrita*).   By this outpoured life and light from the Monad the more material and sensual proclivities are gradually

[1] Ring-pass-not—see Glossary.

[2] Auric Envelope—see Glossary.

outgrown and the soul is purified. Symbolically, it is fed and its mental and emotional vehicles (robes) are made " white in the blood of the Lamb." [1]

THE PHOENIX. This was a fabulous Egyptian bird said to live for 500 or 1,000 years and then to kill itself by sitting on a burning pile of aromatic woods, its ashes giving birth to a young phoenix. Macrocosmically, it represents Logoi withdrawing from Universes at the end of their cycles of objective manifestation and reappearing at the opening of successors. Fire symbolises the creative, destructive and regenerating force of the Universe. It both creates and destroys. The Deity, in one sense, destroys Itself by releasing the creative fire; that is, It then ceases to exist as a purely spiritual, free and eternal Principle.

H. P. Blavatsky writes:

" The Phoenix, although generally connected with the Solar Cycle of 600 years—the Western cycle of the Greeks and other nations —is a generic symbol for several kinds of cycles, ciphers being taken out or more added according to which cycle is meant. . . The Phoenix—called by the Hebrews Onech, from Phenoch, Enoch, the symbol of a secret cycle and initiation, and by the Turks, Kerkes— lives a thousand years, after which, kindling a flame, it is self-consumed; and then, reborn from itself, it lives another thousand years, up to *seven times seven*, when comes the Day of Judgment. The ' seven times seven', or forty-nine, are a transparent allegory, and an allusion to the forty-nine Manus, the seven Rounds, and the seven times seven human Cycles in each Round on each Globe. The Kerkes and the Onech stand for a Race Cycle, and the mystical Tree Ababel, the ' Father Tree ' in the *Qu'rān*, shoots out new branches and vegeta-tion at every resurrection of the Kerkes or Phoenix; the ' Day of Judgment' meaning a minor Pralaya. The author of the *Book of God* and the *Apocalypse* believes that:

' The Phoenix is . . . very plainly the same as the Simorgh of Persian romance; and the account which is given us of this last bird yet more decisively establishes the opinion that the death and revival of the Phoenix exhibit the successive destruc-tion and reproduction of the world, which many believed to be

[1] *Rev.* 7 : 14.

effected by the agency of a fiery deluge [and also a watery one in its turn]. When the Simorgh was asked her age, she informed Caherman that this world is very ancient, for it has been already *seven times replenished*, with beings different from men, and *seven times depopulated* [the tense is past, because the book is allegorical, and has to veil the truth it contains]: that the age of the human race in which we now are, is to endure *seven thousand years*, and that she herself had seen *twelve* of these revolutions, and knew not how many more she had to see.'

" The above, however, is no new statement. From Bailly, in the last century, down to Dr. Kenealy, in the present, these facts have been noticed by a number of writers; but now a connection can be established between the Persian oracle and the Nazarene prophet. Says the author of the *Book of God:*

‘ The Simorgh is in reality the same as the winged Singh of the Hindus, and the Sphinx of the Egyptians. It is said that the former will appear at the end of the world . . . [as a] monstrous lion-bird . . . From these the Rabbins have borrowed their mythos of an enormous Bird, sometimes standing on the earth, sometimes walking in the ocean . . . while its head props the sky; and with the symbol, they have also adopted the doctrine to which it relates. They teach that there are to be seven successive renewals of the globe; that each reproduced system will last seven thousand years (?); and that the total duration of the Universe will be 49,000 years. This opinion, which involves the doctrine of the pre-existence of each renewed creature, they may either have learned during their Babylonian captivity, or it may have been part of the primeval religion which their priests had preserved from remote times.'

" It shows rather that the initiated Jews *borrowed*, and their non-initiated successors, the Talmudists, lost, the sense, and applied the seven Rounds, and the forty-nine Races, etc., wrongly.

" Not only *their* priests, but those of every other country. The Gnostics, whose various teachings are the many echoes of the one primitive and universal doctrine, put the same numbers, under another form, in the mouth of Jesus in the very occult *Pistis Sophia*. We say more: even the Christian editor or author of *Revelation* has preserved this tradition and speaks of the *Seven* RACES, four of which, with part of the fifth, are gone, and two have to come. It is stated as plainly as can be. Thus saith the angel:

‘ And here is the mind which hath wisdom. The seven heads are seven mountains, on which the woman sitteth. And there are *seven* kings; *five* are fallen, and one *is*, and the other is not yet come.'

" Who, in the least acquainted with the symbolical language of old, will fail to discern in the *five* Kings that have fallen, the four Root Races that were, and part of the Fifth, the one that *is;* and in the *other*, that ' is not yet come ', the Sixth and Seventh coming Root Races, as also the sub-races of this, our present Race?. . ."

(*The Secret Doctrine*, Vol. IV, pp. 188-189)

PILLARS generally represent a vehicle for the creative force, both in Nature and in man.   In the latter, the spinal cord along which the creative force flows is denoted.   In illumined man this force has been wholly sublimated and made to flow up into the brain and mind, where it manifests as a great illuminant and means of liberation, exaltation, inspiration and genius.   Thus Moses was guided over the wilderness to the Promised Land by a pillar of fire by night. All upright objects are susceptible of the same interpretation.

PLANT SEEDS are symbols of spiritual truth, or the " Word " of God.[1]

RIVERS.   Some rivers are used as topographical symbols with various meanings.   The evolution of the divine Self of man from a purely material mode of physical life, through successive stages leading to the adoption of a wholly spiritual life is referred to as " entering the Stream ".   The spinal cord along which, after its awakening, the Serpent Fire or *kundalini* flows from the base of the spine into the brain is also on occasion symbolised by a river.   cf. Jordan, Jabbok, the Nile, the Ganges, and the four Rivers that flowed out of Eden—Pison, Gihon, Hiddekel and Euphrates.

ROCKS represent the physical body and level of awareness.

THE ROSE.   The spiritual symbolism of the rose is traceable principally to the Persian mystical Sect of the Sufis, a Mohammeden Order which arose during the Seventh Century under the leadership of Abu Said.   They are supposed to have been called Sufis on account of their woollen robes, the word " Sufi " meaning " wool ", but H. P. Blavatsky traces the word to *Sophia* (Wisdom)[2].   They embraced

---

[1] *Matt.* 13: 20.

[2] q. v. *The Theosophical Glossary*, H. P. Blavatsky.

a monastic life, devoting themselves to contemplation, and developed a poetical, mystical form of language which concealed their spiritual teaching. The poet Hafiz who lived at Shiraz, Persia, during the Fourteenth Century, was called " Interpreter of the Mysteries ", and his works have been designated as the Scriptures of the Sufis. The city of Shiraz was famous for its exquisite rose gardens and for its marvellous weaving. In Persian carpets, woven in the design known as " Shiraz ", the predominating shade is a wonderful rose pink or rose red, and roses are frequently seen in the design. When the early Crusading Knights contacted Eastern thought in the Holy Land, they also contacted this Eastern mysticism and philosophy. Throughout succeeding centuries, when wave after wave of crusading knighthood and soldiery swept over Europe into Palestine, the chivalry of the West joined with the mystical philosophy of the East and a new civilisation of the West came into being, the emblematical flower of which was the rose, this symbolism finding expression in troubadour poetry.

During the same period Master Architects from the Comacine College in Northern Italy, created a new architectural style, a development of the Romanesque, which was given the name of " Gothic ", perhaps because it found its birthplace among the descendants of the Gothic peoples. In this new style the most exquisite rose windows in stained glass introduced the symbol of the rose into architecture, first into Northern France, then into England, Germany and Italy. In the year 1614 the story of a Brotherhood of the Rosy Cross and of its reputed Founder, Christian Rosenkreutz (the German word means " Cross of Roses "), was published.

The poems of Hafiz are typical of Sufi mystical imagery, introducing the emblem of the mystical rose (*Buddhi*), the rose garden (Causal consciousness), and the nightingale or " singer of the rose " (the Ego). The symbol of the rose typified the Second Aspect, God as the true Beloved, and the garden a state of union with God, or God's presence. This mystical literature was adopted by the Sufis centuries before the days of Hafiz as a guard to their secret teachings, and was expressed as follows:

" Hafiz meditates in his rose garden:
Every rose in the garden reveals Thy Face . . .

> Every rose which adorns the garden bears traces of His
> [sic] colouring and perfume . . .
> The rose garden of my thoughts is full of pictures and
> images of Thee;
> No one hath beheld Thy Face; and yet there are thousands
> watching for Thee. . .
> Thou art still folded up in the rosebud hidden from our
> sight and hundreds of nightingales are waiting to see
> Thee, their Rose, unfold and display Thy Face."

It was said of Hafiz that " all the couplets of his odes are Divine
Knowledge."

About 1,200 A. D. a Knight named Guillaume de Lorris wrote
Roman de la Rose, in which the rose symbolises love. The story is,
very briefly, that of a lover who dreams of a beautiful garden (Causal
consciousness) which he enters, and where he discovers a magical
fountain (Buddhi). He knows it to be the fountain into which the
Greek youth, Narcissus (the personal Ego), fell and was drowned (to
the temporal worlds) because of his absorption in his own beauty
reflected in its shining waters (the Ego in its own world).

In *Roman de la Rose* the lover fears to look into the fountain and,
raising his eyes, beholds a rose bush of great beauty (*Buddhic* consciousness) growing beside it, on the top of which there is one exquisite
bloom (the experience of union with God). The sight of this flower
fills the youth with rapture. While he ardently contemplates it
(practises Yoga), the God of Love (*Ātma*) with winged arrows shoots
at him six of his darts (the idealism of the Path). These darts are
(exoterically) Beauty, Simplicity, Courtesy, Honesty, Comradeship
and " *Beau Semblant* ", which is difficult to translate but which might
mean Perfect Manners—Well Seeming.

The lover thereupon becomes the liegeman of the God of love
and offers to Him his heart, which the God locks (renders it incapable
of—locked away from—purely sensual love) with a golden key
(Initiation and its fruits). A voice tells him that if he wills to possess
the rose he must obey the commandments of the God of Love, and
that he can only succeed with the aid of Hope, Gentle Thoughts,
Gentle Words and Gentle Looks. As the lover remains alone gazing
upon the beauty of the rose, a noble youth (a senior Initiate) called
Bel Accueil (Loving Welcome) approaches and helps him to climb

the bush (tread the Path), so that he can pick one of the petals to lay against his heart. The guardian of the rose (the difficulties of the Path) awakens, however, and chases both the lover and *Bel Accueil*, putting them to flight. The further story of *Roman de la Rose* tells of how the lover, after many hardships and adventures, acquires the rose.

The symbol of the rose is eternal because it represents a life to be lived and a spiritual experience to be attained by every pilgrim on the Pathway to Perfection. When thus interpreted, this story applies to every aspirant who seeks to attain to perfection, as symbolised by the rose. Allegorically, all are journeying to the Heavenly Rose Garden, wherein they will one day find the Perfect Rose.

THE ROSE AND CROSS OF THE ROSICRUCIANS. The rose is the symbol of " Nature, of the ever prolific and virgin earth, or Isis, the Mother and nourisher of man, considered as feminine and re-presented as a virgin woman by Egyptian Initiates."

(*The Secret Doctrine*, Vol. V, p. 293.)

In ancient days the rose was dedicated to Venus, who is the personification of the generative energy of Nature. In this sense the rose and the cross together symbolise universal generation and all that it produces. In man the rose may be regarded as the spiritual Soul in its vesture of light, the Causal Body, after its impregnation by Spirit (Sk. *Ātma*), to produce, be illumined by, and shed abroad the " fragrance " of pure Wisdom. This is said to be the condition of the Initiate of the Greater Mysteries, the interior generative process being described in allegorical narratives as Annunciations, Imma-culate Conceptions and Nativities of World Saviours.

The rose is guarded by thorns. The Mysteries are approached through and guarded by dangers, just as spiritual sovereignty is only attained after suffering. The crown of thorns portrays the true royalty of Spirit ever unperceived by the unrecognisable to unillumined man, and in consequence is thought to be a crown of thorns, since only the suffering is seen and not the triumph. The thorns also symbolise the painful development of the lower, concrete mind through which, in the process of evolution, consciousness must pass in order to reach the higher mental and intuitional states. Activities, when Egoistic and separative, inevitably cause pain and sorrow—the pricks of the thorns—and since the head is the centre of mental life the thorns are appropriately placed as a crown thereon, as at the Crucifixion of Jesus. Furthermore, before perfection the abstract or idealistic and the formal or acquisitive minds in man strive continually for mastery, and the pains and wounds of that mystical conflict are also symbolised by the thorns.

Microcosmically, the opened rose in one aspect represents the Higher Self in the Causal Body of Initiated man, in which and from which are born universal love, wisdom and bliss, more particularly represented by the fragrance of the flower. The cross is generally interpreted as the symbol of self-sacrifice, immortality and holiness. Esoterically, however, the cross describes the whole mystery of creation. Spirit as the positive, masculine potency, the Great Breath or " Word " (Sk. *Purusha*[1]), descends vertically into and penetrates matter as Space, the feminine creative potency, the Great Deep (Sk. *Prakriti*[1]). The point of intersection is the critical centre at which generation occurs and from which the product—the Universe—arises. In this sense the rose upon the cross symbolises that new Cosmos, at whatever level and of whatever degree.

The descent of Spirit into matter, the vertical into the horizontal —the cross—and as a result the rising of self-conscious and perfected life—the rose—suggests the two great processes of involution and evolution, forthgoing and return. The whole procedure occurs within the circumscribed region of differentiated matter in which the new Universe is to appear and its perfecting to be achieved. This area is surrounded by a mystical " Ring-pass-not " or " Rope of Angels ", and is symbolised by a cross within a circle. The walls of Temples and Churches, the Auric Envelope of man, and the membranes and matrics enclosing bodies and cells, all correspond to

---

[1] *Purusha - Prakriti :* These two Sanskrit terms are used throughout this work partly because of their rich metaphysical significance and partly for brevity, since both possess so many connotations, all of which have their place in the procedures of Cosmogenesis. The meanings are given in the Glossary. Since both the positive (*Purusha*) and the negative (*Prakriti*) creative potencies are inherent in *Prakriti*, both male and female characters are used in allegories of creation, sometimes confusingly, to personify each of them. Thus in the present case Esau, who is " red and hairy ", is made to represent the positive and his twin, Jacob, the negative elements in the production of Universes. In other Biblical allegories the female represents the negative, as in the case of Sarah, Rebecca, Rachel, and Mary the Mother of Jesus. See also Pt. Three of this Vol.—Cosmogenesis.

this Macrocosmic and microcosmic protective veil and are represented by both the rose upon and the circle round the cross. In man *Ātma*, the vertical arm, descends into and penetrates Higher *Manas*, the horizontal arm, to produce individualised, then awakened, and later perfected or arisen, *Buddhic* consciousness, the *Christos* of the Soul, the opened rose.

This Rosicrucian symbol is susceptible of a still more occult interpretation, for the stem of the rose tree is generally wound round the vertical arm of the cross. Whenever a perpendicular is entwined by a spirally winding stem of a plant, by a current of force or by a serpent, then the spinal cord with the ascending Serpent Fire is implied. A result of this ascent of the creative fire in man is to open successively the seven " flowers ", " lotus blossoms " or " roses "—the *chakras*[1]— in man. One of these seven is situated at the heart, which is midway between the two arms. This great force centre, the seat and expression of awakened spiritual wisdom and love in Initiated man, is symbolised by the opened rose. It is sometimes referred to as the mystic rose blooming on the breast of the spiritually new-born.

Man himself is perfectly symbolised by the cross, the vertical arm representing the Spirit in him and the horizontal arm the material nature. Even man's physical body is cruciform in certain ways. For instance, the spinal column is a vertical support from which, at right angles, the ribs extend horizontally. Furthermore, the spinal cord is as an electro-magnetic cable, from which at right angles and horizontally large numbers of afferent and efferent nerves carry nervous energy throughout the body. With arms outstretched in love and sacrifice, man's body makes a perfect cross. In a symbolical sense he only assumes this posture when—rose-like—his heart is open in love and compassion for the whole world. The rose upon the cross is therefore a beautiful and a dynamic symbol, and also represents an ideal to which to aspire.

THE SACRIFICIAL LAMB or kid is ever the symbol of the Logos in Its aspect of Preserver, while the blood represents the one life in its vitalizing, sustaining activity. This life is the foundation of the Universe. It is the electrical potency of the Logos which is the active basis of all atomic substance. The sacrificial lamb refers to the

[1] *Chakras*—see Glossary.

primeval and great sacrifice of Spirit at the foundation of the manifested worlds, when the spiritual is gradually "smothered" and
"killed" within the material Universe. This is a law of life under
which the seed ". . . is not quickened, except it die ".[1]   In the Hindu
Scripture, the *Rig Veda*, the "thousand headed Purusha" was
slaughtered at the foundation of the world, so that from its remains
the Universe might arise. The relationship between the Hindu and
the Christian use of the symbol of the lamb is further indicated by
the fact that in Sanskrit the word *Aja*, for *Purusha* or eternal Spirit,
also means "lamb". In the cosmic sense, then, the symbol of the
sacrificial lamb may be regarded as a reference to the metaphorical
disappearance of Spirit as it becomes involved in matter, or is sacrificed.

THE SCARAB beetle was intimately associated with the creative
Deity, Amen Ra, one of whose titles was Khepera, meaning "he who
rolls". Why this association of a lowly insect with the creative
Lord of All? The life habits of the scarab suggest an answer, for
it encloses its egg, its seed of life, in a ball of mud, rolls the ball to
a sunny spot and leaves it to the warming influence of the sun. Ultimately the egg hatches and brings forth a larva, which finds itself
surrounded by its necessary food. Consuming this, it passes through
its transformations and ultimately emerges as the winged scarab,
to become in its turn the parent of further eggs, the cycle thus being
continually repeated.

The creative Logos similarly produces from within Himself the
seed-thought of the Universe-to-be, sometimes described as the Golden
Egg or the Egg of *Brahma*. This dynamic, archetypal idea (egg)
is brought into association with (laid upon) pre-cosmic matter (sand),
or the virgin sea of Space, just as the scarab's egg is deposited in the
mud and rolled into a depression in the sand. The next step in the
creative process is the operation of the major cycle of forthgoing
and return, with its innumerable sub-cycles, not inaptly represented
by the scarab's action of forming a ball of mud round its egg and rolling
it to a sunny spot. Just as the larva of the beetle finds itself surrounded
with the essential sources of nutrition, so also are all living beings
from the beginning of their objective manifestation provided at all
levels of existence with both interior sustaining life and the external

[1] 1 *Cor.* 15: 36.

food which Nature supplies.   Furthermore, the larva passes through its metamorphosis to become winged and free of the limitations of its ball of mud, and in like manner the body of man dies, thereby freeing the Soul.   The symbolism is susceptible of further application, since in due course man as mystic progresses from the matter-blinded to the spiritually illumined state, thus achieving the so-called flight of the Soul.   The physical body and *ahamkaric* limitations no longer entomb illumined devotees.

As the newly formed scarab becomes in its turn a parent, setting in motion the same cyclic procedure, so do the Souls of men reincarnate, at death shake off the bodily " chrysalis ", and thereafter withdraw to their Source.   Thus in two senses at least the life habits of the scarab portray the resurrection of the Soul of man—naturally after death, and also during life by successful contemplation of the Divine. Hence the scarab is indeed an apt symbol, both for the Logos as Initiator of the law of cycles, and for the immortality and the resurrection of the Spirit of man.

SEA MONSTERS represent the coarser emotions, while smaller fish typify the Piscean or Christ-consciousness of unity, kinship, from which spring Christlike love, tenderness, compassion, healing grace and ministration.   The mitre of the bishop is shaped like a fish's head with open mouth, possibly as a symbol that such a high dignitary has attained to this state of consciousness and his mind and life are consecrated to its expression.

SERPENTS.   The first reference to the serpent is made in Chapter Three of the *Book of Genesis*, where it is intimately associated with the fruit of the tree of knowledge of good and evil and the symbolical eating of that fruit by Adam and Eve.   In one of the many possible interpretations, and particularly in this allegory, the serpent is the *fohatic* energy itself, and the tree is the consciousness and its vehicles in which that force is active.   Together they constitute creative power, Macrocosmic and microcosmic.   The serpent by itself is the undulatory, triply-polarised force in the Cosmos, in a Universe, in all Nature, on any plane and in every vehicle of man.   The tree of life is impregnated substance, fructified matter forming the vehicles of any being at any level, from a Logos to an amoeba, charged as that matter is with the vivifying life-force.

10

When not active the neutral current by itself, the trunk of the tree, represents the latent divine presence. When active the positive and negative serpentine, inter-active currents of the Serpent Fire are present and in operation. As previously stated, the symbols for this energised condition are the serpent and the tree. Sometimes a single serpent is coiled round the trunk of the tree and sometimes two are indicated, one on either side.

The symbol of the serpent is susceptible of many interpretations, exoteric, esoteric and most deeply occult. In general, it is the symbol both of wisdom and of the wise, who in the Sacred Language are frequently referred to as serpents. The *Nagas* of Hindu literature are none other than *Rishis*, liberated *Yogis*, Adepts. The serpent is chosen as a symbol of wisdom for various reasons. It glides secretly, and for the most part unseen, on the surface of the globe just as wisdom, whether revealed from on high or inborn, is a concealed power potent either to illumine if rightly employed, or to destroy if misused. The smooth sinuosity of the smake and its movements not inaptly portrays the harmonious and rhythmic self-expression of wisdom in both the Universe and the man in whom it is awake and moving. He is enlightened from within, or secretly.

The serpent regularly sloughs its skin. Despite this seasonal change, the reptile itself is unchanged and appears in a new and glistening covering. So wisdom, while remaining the same in essence, is self-manifest in ever new forms, none being able to hold it permanently. The serpent's tongue is forked or bi-polar. So, also, is wisdom, being susceptible of degradation into low cunning employed for meanest motives, or of elevation into lofty intuition in accordance with unselfish ideals. Snake venom can destroy or heal, depending upon its use and dosage. This is also true of wisdom. Degraded, it poisons the soul; rightly used, it is an antidote for many ills.

The eyes of the serpent are compelling, even hypnotic. Wisdom, once awake in an individual, brooks no resistance, breaks all bonds, and ultimately rules with impelling power. The wise, also, are irresistible in their might, even though appearing to be lowly and making no claim to high regard. Nevertheless they live near to the Source of life, just as the serpent lives near to the roots and seeds of living things.

The serpent is represented in man in both its constructive and its destructive aspects. The Higher Self, the will-wisdom of the spiritual Soul, corresponds to the serpent of light, while the desire nature contains destructive potentialities. The mind is the balancing force, or rod, between these two oppositely polarised energies, or serpent, in man. The serpent on the cross lifted up by Moses in the wilderness to heal the Israelites of their sickness[1] is a symbol of wisdom united with the mind to purify and elevate the lower self, and heal it of its material tendencies and the effects of their expression.

The serpent is used also to portray the harmonising influence of the Christ-nature in man, which has power to heal and raise the dead to life. This implies the power to transmute the lower aspects of human nature into the higher. Aesculapius, the God of Healing, frequently appeared in the form of a serpent and the caduceus, the staff of Hermes, has been regarded as a symbol for a curative force.

Serpents were described as three-headed, as winged, as having human legs, being loud-breathing, hissing, poisonous, and having yellow poison flowing over them. In the higher aspects this symbolises the action of the threefold Higher Self, especially the principle of pure wisdom within it. The lower, destructive activities of the serpent of ancient symbology refer to the predatory and destructive desires and passions of man. The hero who destroys the latter personifies the Initiate who has transmuted the lower into the higher, and has himself attained to perfect equilibrium between them.

When the serpent's tail is in its mouth an endless circle is made, implying the eternity of wisdom, and even eternity itself. Esoterically, however, processes of cosmogenesis are indicated by the union of a symbolised positive and negative, or the entry of the tail into the mouth. All generative processes are, indeed, indicated in that form of the symbol. This leads to the deeply occult significance of the serpent, namely the universal, divine, creative and ever-active life-force. This is *Fohat* in its dual polarity, and is sometimes symbolised not as one serpent with tail in mouth, but as two mutually intertwined. Here the laws of electricity, under which all generative processes occur, are indicated.

[1] *Num.* 21 : 9.

The driving force from within which leads to creative activity in organic forms, and chemical affinity in inorganic, is indeed bi-polar. The aptness of the choice of the serpent as a symbol for this power would seem to be supported by the fact that its tongue is forked. It is the positive and negative currents of the Great Breath, continually breathed forth as *Fohat* into and through every atom of every world, to become omnipresent and perpetually active through-out the whole Universe. This fact was both concealed and revealed in ancient allegories in which Jupiter, and other male creative deities, changed themselves into snakes for the purpose of seducing goddesses. In cosmogenesis such goddesses personify matter, the waters of Space, the feminine receptive and reproductive principle. Microcosmically the human Monad corresponds to God the Father, and the spiritual Self in its vesture of light corresponds to the goddess. When evolu-tion has brought the spiritual Self of man to readiness for the " birth " into dominant power of the Christ-nature in man, a descent occurs (the mystical Annunciation) of the *fohatic* or fructifying power from the Monad into the hitherto " virginal ", awaiting spiritual Self. This is the Heavenly Marriage, the Immaculate Conception, from which Christlike consciousness and power are " born ". A serpent with tail in mouth, two serpents intertwined, or one encircling a rod, staff or pillar, all symbolise the electric, creative energy of *Fohat* in action in the material Universe, and therefore in man, the micro-cosmic temple of the Universe.

In man the rod refers both to the spinal cord and to a canal, or etheric and superphysical channel, in its centre passing from the root of the cord in the sacrum, along its whole length, into the *medulla oblongata* and brain. This canal is the vehicle for the creative life-force, a measure of which plays down from above in the generative act. This current is uni-polar, or even of neutral polarity, since it plays and produces its effects in both the male and the female organism. The historic occult name for this canal is *Sushumna*,[1] usually only applying, however, when by occult means the same neutral force is made to play not downwards, but upwards along the spinal cord. Before this reversal of the flow of creative energy can be achieved, positive and negative currents must be aroused and themselves, like

[1] *Sushumna (Sk.)*, tube.

twin serpents, flow upwards, inter-twining as they flow to induce
an ascent of the accompanying neutral energy. Entering the brain,
this triple power so illumines the mind of man that he becomes, as
it were, a god (possessed of theurgic powers). This fact is revealed
in *Genesis* [1] where Adam and Eve represent the oppositely polarised
currents, the tree of knowledge of good and evil (particularly the
trunk) corresponds to the rod, and the tempting serpent to the creative
force ascending along the *Sushumna* canal. Thus Adam and Eve
are forbidden to eat of the fruit of this tree, since by so doing they
would become as gods.

The intensely heightened vibrations of the brain, the glands,
the cells and the aerial substance in the ventricles, cause the brain
and cranium to be responsive to Egoic and Monadic life and consciousness. Spirit then predominates in the individual. Matter loses its
power. Symbolically, through the agency of an interchangeable
serpent and rod, the Israelites are freed from bondage in Egypt.
The shaft of *Ātmic* fire which forms the core of the force which plays
along the *Sushumna* canal is brought down to the densest physical
level, or symbolically " cast upon the ground ". When that occurs
the relatively dormant, positive-negative, creative life-force resident
in the sacrum is awakened into activity. Each polarity then pursues
a mutually intertwining, serpentine path around the *Sushumna* canal.
Symbolically stated, the rod becomes the serpent.[2] This process is
not unproductive of a certain shock and some pain. The Initiate
momentarily shrinks from it, but still persists. Moses is therefore
made to flee before the serpent. When, however, he unites his own
will with that of the Hierophant Himself and sublimates the creative
force, compelling it to flow upwards from the pelvis, it becomes in
his hand the magician's wand of power. Symbolically, Moses takes
the Serpent Fire by the tail and it becomes a rod in his hand.

As portrayed in the Egyptian symbolical figures in which serpents
are intertwined around rods or pillars, the tail is at the foot of the
pillar, meaning the sacrum. The head of the serpent is at the upper
end, whence frequently a lotus flower is blooming. This, too, is
a universally used symbol. Rods which blossom, as did Aaron's,

[1] *Gen.* 3: 5.
[2] Ex. 4: 2-4.

have a similar significance.[1] The opening of the force-centres in the superphysical bodies, consequent upon the arousing and the upward flow of the serpent power, is depicted by such symbols. The historic occult names for the positive and the negative currents of force are *Pingala* and *Ida*, and the triple upward flow is most perfectly revealed by the Greek symbol of the caduceus. Hermes is the Moses of the Greeks, in that he is a messenger from God to man by virtue of holding in his hand the caduceus, just as Moses held in his hand the rod. Hermes also delivered Persephone from the under-world, Hades, even as Moses delivered Israel from bondage in Egypt.

The dark and light coloured serpents of the caduceus symbolise the dual power of the secret wisdom—black and white magic. Tehuti, Mercury, Hermes, possessing (having mastered) the triple serpent fire, personify pure wisdom guiding the Soul after death, both natural and figurative (at Initiation), and calling to life that which has been dead. This power is possessed by all Adepts or " serpents ". The ancient Chinese symbol of the Emperor's throne—the " Dragon's Seat "—and the dragon embroideries on his dresses of State, also refer to this sublimation and its results. Jesus advised His disciples, saying ". . . be ye therefore wise as serpents, and harmless as doves."[2] This may be taken as a veiled reference either to the Serpent Fire or to the wisdom and the prudence of the Adept or " serpent ".

The two serpents symbolise all apparently opposing and hostile pairs in the world's allegories. They embody the idea of dualism and the supposed struggle between good and evil, Spirit and matter, light and darkness, gods and demons, Saviours and serpents and dragons, Cain and Abel, Esau and Jacob, and Osiris, Apollo and Python. The heroic Saviour represents the pure wisdom by which alone the conflict, as it occurs in man, may end in victory for Spirit, light, good. The divine messengers sent to save mankind, the Christos as Son of God and the Celestial Virgin, sent down from Heaven to Earth to save a perishing humanity, are all personifications of the pure wisdom by means of which the conflict of the opposites may end not in the defeat of one by the other, but in their perfect harmonisation or equipolarisation. The result is the retention of

---

[1] *Num.* 17: 8, *Neb.* 9: 4.
[2] *Matt.* 10: 16.

the full powers of both of the opponents, the light and the dark serpents, and the attainment of the capacity to use either or both of them while the user remains in a condition of dynamic equilibrium. This attainment is symbolised by the crushing of the head of the serpent by Sri Krishna, and the victories over reptiles by the Saviours and heroes of other ancient peoples.

Contemplation of the symbol of the caduceus will reveal how perfectly it portrays that process and that attainment. This saving power, the Christos, entered into the man Jesus, the human vehicle, at the moment of his baptism in Jordan, and from then on Jesus began to work miracles by divine authority. The holding of the caduceus (or rod or serpent) in the hand is itself a symbol implying mastery of a power, and the possession of knowledge and skill in its employment.

The transmutation of rod into serpent, be it noted, could only occur at the command of the Deity and by His magical power. Actually, the descent of the Monadic *Ātma* through all the vehicles and down the spinal cord into the sacrum is essential to the premature full-awakening of the triple creative fire and its successful sublimation and use as a magical tool. To bring this power of *Ātma* down is one part of the office the Hierophant of the Greater Mysteries. Since thereafter a new life is begun, the act has ever been correctly termed Initiation. The Initiate is one in whom has been aroused the power to liberate himself from the limitations of matter, desire and self-separateness into the freedom of universal consciousness, life and power.

The Serpent Fire, or *kundalini*, is in essence creative and, though as yet but slightly aroused, with all other forces and powers of Nature is represented in the physical body of man. There, at this period of human evolution, it manifests itself as the source of both the sex impulse and the nerve fluid. It resides, coiled serpent-like, in the sacral *chakra* or " wheel " at the base of the spine, which in its turn is a relay station for the similarly coiled up energy in the centre of the Earth, itself a storehouse of solar *kundalini*. When fully aroused, either by yoga or as a natural result of evolutionary progress, *kundalini* flows up an etheric canal in the spinal cord called the *Sushumna nadi*, passing through each of the other *chakras* on its journey. As it passes through the spinal centres in which the *chakras* arise, some of its force flows down the axis of the funnel of each, vivifying it occultly and thereby awakening the individual to self-conscious awareness in the superphysical worlds.

When *kundalini* touches the spleen centre, it gives to man the power of travelling at will on the astral plane while away from the physical body.   When it touches and opens the heart centre, the forces of the *Buddhic* or Christ-consciousness in man resident in the vehicle of intuition, if sufficiently unfolded, begin to flow through the neophyte at the physical level and the " mystic rose "—the heart *chakra*—" blooms " upon his breast.   The powers of the Christ-consciousness—knowledge of the oneness of life, direct intuitive spiritual perception, wisdom and a profound compassion—then begin to manifest themselves through thought and word and deed.   The throat centre, when vivified, bestows the power of clairaudience, or of responding to superphysical sound vibrations as well as to those physical sounds which are beyond the normal auditory range.   The brow centre, when occultly vitalised, bestows the faculty of clair-voyance, and when the coronal *chakra* is opened the neophyte acquires the faculties of using supersensory awareness while still awake in the physical body, and of leaving and returning to the body at will without any brake in consciousness.   The pituitary and pineal glands then function somewhat as do the valves or the amplifiers of a radio receiving set, thereby enabling consciousness within the brain to pick up and become aware of superphysical forces and phenomena. Indeed, the cerebro-spinal system of man, when occultly vivified, resembles in many respects a television receiving set.   One difference, however, is that subtle broadcasts are projected upon the screen of the mind-brain and clairvoyantly perceived.   The full manifestation of these occult faculties during waking consciousness demands a long and arduous training, and depends upon the complete vivification of the pituitary and pineal glands by means of *kundalini* and its comple-mentary forces.

SHIPS, ARKS, CRADLES, refer to any containing and conveying vehicle of consciousness, whether physical, intellectual or spiritual— or human, superhuman, divine or cosmic.   Their passengers—animal, human and superhuman—symbolise the varied powers and qualities of human nature.

THE SKULL. A profound interpretation may be given to the symbol of the skull for it is the receptacle of the brain, in its turn the vehicle of the mind—abstract and concrete. It is the mind which becomes illumined by intuition during the Rite of Initiation, and it is the immortal Self in its higher mental vehicle which becomes the Adept. Within the skull, therefore, the whole mighty drama of the perfecting of man is performed. This is clearly implied by the four Evangelists, who make the Crucifixion of Jesus (the death of the illusion of separateness and the consequent illumination of the mind) occur on a hill of doubtful existence and location called Golgotha, " a place of a skull ".[1]

THE SPHINX. The great Sphinx of Giza, " guarding " the entrance to the Nile Valley, is in the form of a gigantic carved lion with the head of a man. Whilst it is the most famous single monument of the ancient Egyptians, strangely enough its origin is unknown. The Greek Sphinx, however, unlike the Egyptian, had wings and a human female torso. Sphinxes exist all over the Near East—in Egypt, Cyprus, Asia Minor, Persia (on gems) and Assyria. There appears to be a direct relationship between the ancient winged griffons and the winged Sphinxes—and through them with the Egyptian Sphinxes. There is an ancient legend that the Spirit of a beautiful woman lives in the Sphinxes at Gizeh. She was a famous courtesan, Nitocris or Rhodophis, and while she was bathing one day an eagle snatched one of her sandals from the hands of a woman attendant and carried it to Memphis, where the King was administering justice in an outside Court. The eagle released the sandal and it fell into the lap of the Pharaoh. He was so struck by the coincidence, and by the shape of the sandal, that he ordered a search for its owner, and found and later married her. After her death Nitocris, or Rhodophis, was buried in the third Pyramid, and her Spirit is supposed still to haunt the nearby Sphinx and occasionally to appear outside it in the form of a naked beauty who seduces travellers and causes them to lose their senses and wander about demented. Nitocris may be thought of as the human soul, the sandal as evidence of her personal identity, the eagle as her aspiring thought, and her marriage to the Pharaoh as the fulfilment of her aspirations.

[1] *Matt.* 27: 33; Mk. 15: 22.

Another famous Sphinx existed at Thebes. It had the face of a woman, the feet and tail of a lion and the wings of a bird, and lived on a rocky mountain called Phicium. The Muses taught it a riddle, and whenever anyone failed to answer correctly the Sphinx would carry them off and eat them. Wisdom misunderstood can destroy. The Mysteries are not without their danger to the unprepared. The riddle was: " What is that which is four-footed, three-footed and two-footed? " Oedipus guessed the riddle by reasoning that the answer was man; for the child crawls on hands and feet, the adult walks upright and the old man aids his steps with a walking stick. When Oedipus guessed the riddle the disappointed Sphinx threw itself down from the mountain and was crushed on the rocks below.

If the riddle be interpreted as referring to the sevenfold man, the four feet would represent the mortal quaternary and the three feet the triple Ego. The two feet portray the Ego and the Monad. When these two are united, as in the Adept, the mystery or riddle of life is solved. Symbolically, the Sphinx as a mysterious being passes out of existence. The Sphinx may also refer to that great event in Nature known in occult philosophy as individualisation. The animal body represents the former purely animal condition wherein group consciousness exists. The head of man upon the animal body indicates the attainment of an individualised, self-conscious intelligence typical of mankind. When the Sphinx is winged, future flights into mystical and spiritual states of awareness are foreshadowed.

SPRINGS and fountains refer to the inexhaustible and upwelling spiritual life within the Higher Self. Rivers and streams represent the flow of that life throughout the various regions of Soul and body.

STARS refer to cosmic Intelligences, Ministers of the Most High God, Builders of the Universe. The twelve zodical Signs refer, microcosmically, to the totality of man's nature and powers, the twelve principles, faculties and forces inherent in man. The twelve tribes personify, Macrocosmically, the Regents of the twelve Signs, as also do the twelve disciples, with the Lord Christ as the sun in the midst.

THE SUN and its fructifying rays symbolise both the very loftiest spiritual state and the spiritual Soul of man, the Monad, the Dweller

in the Innermost. The sun is, however, so important and so oft-
used a symbol and has so many significations, that Chapter V of
Part One of Volume I of this work is devoted to the subject. As
both a physical and a spiritual source of power, the sun provides an
example of the law that the effective outpouring of essential light
and life is followed not by exhaustion, but by perpetual and abundant
renewal. Although from all the seven principles of the sun, one on
each of the seven planes of Nature, spiritually and physically nourishing and sustaining life-force is continually outpoured to fill all the
forms of the Planetary Schemes, their component Globes and their
inhabitants, the power, the light and the glory of the sun are in no
wise diminished. Renewal from an inexhaustible, universal, interior
source continually occurs.

The seven-principled sun and the Seven Mighty Spirits before
the Throne are also symbolised as ". . . a Lamb as it had been slain,
having seven horns and seven eyes, which are the seven Spirits of
God sent forth into all the earth ",[1] and as the Christos from whose
crucified body, blood and water flow down to the earth perpetually
to save and purify, or spiritualise, the souls of men. The miracles of
Christ, who twice fed a great multitude with a little bread and a few
fishes and had more left afterwards than before,[2] also exemplify the
same law of inexhaustible supply.

In terms of ordinary human life no sincere, genuine, sensibly
devised and sensibly delivered gift is ever lost or wasted, whatever
the apparent result. To give wisely and selflessly is to achieve a
greater fullness of self-expression, an enhanced capacity for effective
service and a continual increase of the wherewithal—spiritual, intellectual and physical—to go on giving and serving. Wise sharing,
especially of life, love and happiness—the great Soul nutrients—
increases the giver's supply of those blessings. All sacrificial actions,
all surrenders and all martyrdoms of divine personages, Saviours
and Saints recorded in the Mythologies and the Scriptures of the
world exemplify this law in both its solar and human manifestations.

THE SWAN (Sk. *Hamsa* and *Para-hamsa*): In its nature and habit
the swan symbolically portrays a complete system of Cosmogony.

---

[1] *Rev.* 5: 6.
[2] *Matt.* 14: 19-21, 15: 34-38.

The Logos in maternal, productive aspect lays the golden egg (Sk. *Hiranyagarbha*) on the " water " of Space. By the rhythmic beating of its wings it hatches the egg, whereupon the Universe appears. The egg thus represents the Universe-to-be, the golden embryo, the germ of the Solar Logos and all that will be produced. The shell is the Ring-pass-not [1] and the contents are the germinal life within, the abstract ideation of the Universe in the Universal Mind (Sk. *Mahat*). All this begins in an inceptive state. Evolution thereafter brings fructification of the germ and its development into a reproduction of the parent bird. Human unfoldment similarly consists of successive hatching out of primitive consciousness into wider awareness, as from physical to astral, mental, Causal, *Buddhic* and *Ātmic* levels successively. In Mysticism such ascent is called the flight of the Soul, and all of this is implied in the symbols of the egg and the bird.

THE SWORD is a symbol of spiritual Will in man (Sk. *Ātma*). St. Paul refers to " the sword of the Spirit, which is the word of God ". [2] The conflict between light and darkness, virtue and vice, order and chaos, is also implied in the arming of Saviours, heroes and Hierophants with swords. By the aid of the sword or spear of Will, when directed by intellect, controlled by brain and mind and propelled by arm and hand, truth fights against falsehood.

In no part of the Universe can the Spirit be passive. Everywhere it is the foe of evil and the friend of good. Everywhere, therefore, throughout the perplexed, tumultuous world is seen " the flashing of the spiritual sword " in the hands of true crusaders and servants of the light. The religious motif is also introduced by the symbol of the sword held by the blade with the hilt uppermost, thus presenting the sign of the cross.

THE TEMPLE, Macrocosmically, is a symbol of the Universe as a whole, including its outer physical form or walls and its indwelling Deity, or Cloud upon the Sanctuary. Microcosmically, human nature from physical body to Monad is portrayed. The symbol of the temple will be interpreted in its due place whenever it occurs in the Old and the New Testaments, and this will apply especially to

[1] Ring-pass-not—see Glossary.
[2] *Eph.* 6: 17.

the building, the measurements and the embellishments of King Solomon's Temple,[1] which will be considered in some detail.

Christ appeared in the temple at the age of twelve.[2] He later performed miracles in the temple: " And the blind and the lame came to him in the temple; and he healed them."[3] Christ cleansed the temple: " And said unto them, It is written, My house shall be called the house of prayer; but ye have made it a den of thieves."[4] Christ prophesied the destruction of the temple: " And Jesus said unto them, See ye not all these things? verily I say unto you, There shall not be left here one stone upon another, that shall not be thrown down."[5]

Whilst the historicity of these verses is not here discounted, their mystical interpretation draws attention to important ideas. In general, a temple is a symbol of the whole human being, physical, intellectual and spiritual. The outer walls, for example, represent both the physical body and human consciousness when limited to physical awareness. The courtyard with its various subsidiary buildings represents the *psyche* or personal soul. The people passing into and from the temple personify the day by day emotions and thoughts by which the inner man is partly expressed through the lower quaternary (the four sides of the complete edifice). The building of the temple itself, as distinct from its outer walls, and including particularly its foundations, walls, roof, embellishments, domes, minarets and spires, represents the inner individuality, the Inner Ruler Immortal, the spiritual Soul with its developed qualities within its vesture of light, the Causal Body, itself symbolised by the material structure.

The interior of the temple represents the intellect of man, and more particularly that aspect of the mind which responds to abstract and spiritual ideals and ideas. The people who are present personify mental activities, the traffic of the mind, and more especially the aspirations, the illuminations and the intuitions received when the mind is in an elevated mood, or in the temple state of consciousness.

The Sanctuary, or the Holy of Holies, is a symbol of the vehicle of spiritual intuition, the " Shrine " of the God within, the Dweller

---

[1] 1 *Kings* 5: 5 *et seq.*
[2] *Lk.* 2: 46.
[3] *Matt.* 21: 14.
[4] *Matt.* 21: 12-13.
[5] *Matt.* 24: 2.

in the Innermost. The tabernacle and the sacred objects within all represent the seventh principle of man, the ray and the radiance of the Monad with its spiritually creative powers, the true divine Presence above and within the Sanctuary of the Soul.

The veil of the temple represents the protective region, at whatever level, between the innermost and the outermost. The true glory must itself ever be veiled, both as protection against profanation from below and as a safeguard against premature discovery and misuse of the truth of truths and the power of powers.

The truth of truths is that God and man are one. The power of powers is that of spiritual creativeness. Both are dangerous to man until he is wholly sanctified, and therefore incapable of misusing them. The chariot of fire in which Elijah disappeared from the sight of Elisha,[1] the appearance of the Lord in a cloud to Moses,[2] the bright cloud which overshadowed Jesus upon the mount,[3] and the cloud into which Jesus was received at His Ascension,[4] in one interpretation symbolise this protective veiling of the highest spiritual truths and the virtual omnipotence bestowed upon those who possess them.

Ordination, consecration, sanctification, which permit a priest to enter the Sanctuary, ideally imply both complete transcendence of the sense of separateness from God and all His other manifestations and also the final renunciation, because outgrown, of personal possessiveness and pride. When this has been achieved, the veil of the temple is rent.

The account of the twelve-year-old Jesus in the temple[5] (like every other allegory, an interior experience of one individual) portrays the threefold (by addition 12 equals 3) spiritual Soul thus illumined, and therefore able to display superior wisdom and bestow illumination upon the mind, represented by the doctors with their memorised knowledge, traditional beliefs and formal methods of thought.

Mary and Joseph were away from the temple. In consequence, they missed and feared they had lost their son.[6] They represent

---

[1] 2 *Kings* 2: 11.

[2] *Ex.* 24: 16, 34: 5; 40: 34, 35.

[3] *Matt.* 17: 5.

[4] *Acts.* 1: 9.

[5] *Lk.* 2: 46.

[6] *Lk.* 2: 45 *et seq.*

the higher aspects of the personal consciousness, the mind-brain which had for a time been allowed to become too greatly absorbed with material considerations. Their return to the temple in search of the temporarily lost light indicates successful meditation by which the personal consciousness had been elevated into self-realisation, self-discovery of the immortal, spiritual Being within the *Augoeides* or " temple " of light. The discovery of their son[1] portrays the success of the quest and the resultant illumination which is received by the mind-brain from the higher, abstract mind, the intuition and the spiritual will. Mary's reproof of Jesus for his absence[2] indicates the not unnatural reaction and lack of comprehension exhibited by those who, when they are brought into the presence of spiritual truth, are often necessarily concerned with mundane and possessive considerations. Most people tend to apply worldly standards of judgment to spiritual laws, truths and activities.

The explanation of Jesus: ". . . wist ye not that I must be about my Father's business? ",[3] corrects this error and directs the mind upward to the innermost Self, the Father, and to the impersonal principles and purposes by which the Higher Self is animated. A mystical experience is also described and guidance in its attainment is given. The mind-brain, it is shown, discovers that illumination demands a universalisation of consciousness and outlook. In other words, the temple state of consciousness must be entered. Spiritual rather than worldly values must be accepted. The mind must become flexible in order to receive wisdom, as did the doctors in the temple, however much it may at first appear to contravene traditional ideas and modes of thought. Then the realisation will be attained of the ever youthful, ever new, divine Presence within the temple— the power, the wisdom and the knowledge of the Christ-nature— symbolised by the twelve-year-old Jesus.

In the Initiatory interpretation the truth is revealed that the new-born, the Initiate, can no longer be bound by personal ties of family, nation or race. He is a citizen of the world and a servant of the whole of humanity. The mothers of Moses and of Jesus

[1] *Lk.* 2: 46.
[2] *Lk.* 2: 48
[3] *Lk.* 2: 49.

learnt and acquiesced in this law, though doubtless not without some
pangs experienced by the maternal heart. In their microcosmic
interpretation, all the recorded visits of Christ to the temple together
constitute an allegorical description of the way of illumination.

The outer temple and courtyards must be cleansed. The money-
changers must be cast out,[1] meaning that the daily life must be free
from acquisitiveness and especially from the profanation of spiritual
things. Ultimately all sense of separated individuality will have been
outgrown—the temple will have been demolished—and the spiritual
Self within liberated or " saved ", as is indicated by Christ's affirmation of His ability at will to destroy and rebuild the temple,[2] and by
His prophecy of its destruction.[3] As this state is approached, the
outer man becomes almost miraculously perfect. Symbolically,
the lame and the sick are healed in the temple.[4]

The parental search and the discovery of the youthful Jesus
in the temple giving illumination to the doctors is thus seen as a
beautiful allegory of the Soul's (Mary and Joseph) successful quest
for spiritual light. Success is assured for all who similarly search;
for the young Christ ever sits in the temple which is the spiritual
Soul of man. Wisdom is always available to those who will enter the
temple self-cleansed, self-healed, and seeking light as ardently as
loving parents seek their only son who is temporarily lost.

TREES. Throughout the Bible this symbol is employed to represent the omnipresent, ever-active, prolific, creative life-force
inherent in all substance, whether superphysical or physical—meaning
Nature herself. It is well chosen, for the tree draws its sustenance
from the earth (Prakriti), the roots being the means by which it is
drawn up, collected and individualised into a single localised area
of activity. The extracted nutriment and natural energy become
concentrated therein, later to flow along the vertical trunk. Withdrawn from the earth, the element of air is entered and at a certain
height from the ground the general shape of the root system is partially
reproduced in the pattern of the branches.

---

[1] Matt. 21: 12.
[2] Matt. 26: 61; Jn. 2: 19.
[3] Matt. 24: 2.
[4] Matt. 21: 14.

Trees, whether deciduous or evergreen, are obedient to the law of cycles, as is evinced by their successive, regularly spaced, seasonal periods of creative activity and quiescence. The principle of growth from a potential or seed-like condition, characteristic of spiritual as well as of physical evolution, is also displayed. Each phase culminates in the production of new seeds, and in this may be discerned that universal principle under which minor cycles contribute to the fulfilment of a major cycle. Leaves, by their inbreathing and outbreathing, also represent the phases of alternation through which all objective manifestations pass.

Microcosmically, trees refer to the creative life individualised in man as the procreative force. To climb a tree to see the Christ, as did Zacchaeus,[1] and to be hung upon a tree,, indicate the full sublimation of that force and the attainment of God-consciousness which this makes possible.[2] Fruits symbolise the products of the action of the life-force in Nature and in man. The apple more especially would seem to typify self-conscious, individualised experience of the creative process, as in the case of the fruit of the tree of knowledge of good and evil partaken of by Adam and Eve, the eating of which brought about the so-called (and miscalled) " Fall ". When the apples are golden the attainment of Christ-consciousness is definitely symbolised, for such attainment is the " fruit " in man of the activity of the intuition.

THE TRUMPET and the trumpet sound are also used as symbols in the Bible, and their significance is sufficiently great to justify an interpretation at length. The voice of the trumpet in the Universe is the power of the " Word ", the fully emitted, focused and directed creative force. The trumpet sound, however, indicates the same power made manifest, or sounding forth, through all the vehicles of man, from the Monadic to the physical. The trumpet is a tube down which the breath, another symbol for the self-same power, is forced and by which it is limited to the space within. As a result of this empowered, concentrated and contained expiration, the whole trumpet vibrates and therefore emits the note or sound of the

---

[1] *Lk.* 19: 4.

[2] *Acts* 5: 30; 10: 38, 39—". . . Jesus of Nazareth. . . whom they slew and hanged on a tree."

11

compressed air or breath, which is a symbol of creative energy or the cosmogenetic " Word ".

Macrocosmically, then, the trumpet itself is the substance of the Universe before and after being moulded into form, and also of any highly responsive component. Microcosmically it symbolises man, and especially his vehicles of consciousness, spiritual, intellectual and physical, in a similar responsive condition.

Whenever it may, truthfully but symbolically, be said that on the mount the sound of the trumpet waxes louder and louder,[1] and that before Jericho the people hear the sound of the trumpet,[2] then man has brought all his seven principles and his whole nature into attunement with the Monad, and through that with the Logos, with which the Monad is for ever at one. At that consummation the divine " Voice " is heard and resounded in seven forms or modes of sound, one for each vehicle of consciousness, throughout the higher and the lower selves of man. Then ahamkara[3] (the walls of Jericho) is shattered. The personal chord, hitherto often discordant, is submerged and extinguished as a separate tone within the great trumpet sound produced by the divine Breath.

When this condition is attained, communion between the Higher Self and the Monad occurs. Moses speaks to God and God answers by a " Voice ". Yet voice it is not, nor any sound. It is pure will expressive of the purpose or intent of the divine Father-Mother in bringing forth the Universe. It is the irresistible, all-pervasive, inherent impulse to self-expression, expansion (hence the name of *Brahma*, from the word *brih*, to expand or grow) and fullness which reigns at the heart of all Nature and all creation, from the highest to the lowest. It is the *Brahmic* will to fullness which as *Vach*[4] sounds forth at that cosmic moment when divine Ideation first emanates as will-light-sound from the Absolute. Throughout the cosmic days and years which follow, that will-light calls into existence suns, planets, beings, in obedience to law. Level after level, plane after plane,

---

[1] *Ex.* 19:19.

[2] *Joshua* 6:20.

[3] *Ahamkara* or *Ahankara* (Sk.). The conception of " I ", self-consciousness or self identity; the " I ", the egotistical and *mayavic* principle in man, due to our ignorance which separates our " I " from the universal ONE-SELF; personality, egoism. *The Theosophical Glossary*, H. P. Blavatsky.

[4] *Vach* (Sk.). Voice, speech. A reference to the Logos doctrine.—See Glossary.

of increasing density come into manifestation and gradually embody and show forth the will-light. Monads flash forth their Rays. Beings emanate and inhabit the planes. Deeper and deeper penetrates the cosmic will-thought-Word, awakening the sleeping substance, forcing its atoms to answer, to echo or re-sound the cosmic " Word ". The light shines forth from the creative centre to illumine the darkness and render visible the hitherto invisible robes in which the cosmic Mother is enwrapped.

The will becomes more potent, the sound louder and the light brighter as the aeons pass. The Monads become more radiant and their Monadic Rays flash forth as wider and more brilliant beams. The denser regions assume the intended forms, the outer darknesses give way to light, and where once there was chaos divine order rules.

In each and every being thus called into existence as dweller and toiler in the created worlds, the cosmic processes are microcosmically reproduced and fulfilled in parallel. As the whole responds, so does every part. In man, as one such dweller and toiler in the worlds, the inertia and silence inherent in matter give place to rhythmic motion (the walls of Jericho fall down) and the heard and answered cosmic " Voice ". In man, as in the Universe, darkness is displaced by light. It is this stage in the creative and evolutionary process which is allegorically described by the sound of the trumpet waxing loud and strong, and by the verbal intercourse between Moses and God upon Mount Sinai.

The summit is not yet attained. Unity is not yet achieved; for when there is unity there is no need for, or even possibility of, external interchange. The realisation of unity is described generally by the death or magical ascension (Enoch,[1] Elijah,[2] Christ,[3]) of the body, as the Soul is caught up and absorbed into its God. The Israelites in the allegory are the varied attributes, powers and capacities developed by, and now inherent in, the Higher Self as a result of the long series of successive lives.

Thus developed, thus evolved and enriched, the Higher Self becomes attuned to its Lord or Monad, ascends the " mount " or higher

[1] *Gen.* 5: 24.
[2] 2 *Kings* 2: 11-13.
[3] *Mk.* 16: 19.

levels of evolution and consciousness, and there hears and repeats throughout its whole nature the Monadic " Word ", or the trumpet sound now grown loud and strong. An Initiation into the Greater Mysteries is then conferred to constitute a recognition in the outer, objective worlds of the evolutionary attainment of the Higher Self in the inner and subjective realms. " The way of holiness " is being trodden. " The strait gate " has been found and " the narrow way " ascended. The Noble Eightfold and Razor-Edged Path is successfully being climbed and the mountain-top is in full view.

UNICORN. The assumption that much of the Mythology of ancient peoples, with its many glyphs and symbols, is Adept and Initiate inspired for the purpose of preserving to the Race and revealing, while yet concealing, power-bestowing knowledge, is supported by the remarkable aptness of the symbology. The unicorn or horned horse, for example, in one of its many possible meanings, is a symbol for the sublimated creative force in man. The horn, emerging from the brain, indicates that the expression of the creative power and desire occurs through the will-inspired intellect and its cranial organ, which is chiefly the pituitary gland. The horn is occultly phallic and the horse is an oft-used symbol for the lower quaternary. It is also the Pegasus which the hero Bellerophon, the Initiate Ego, catches and masters with a golden bridle. This bridle is a symbol for the developed will-thought by means of which the personal nature of man (Pegasus) is controlled and guided. The winged horse was caught near a fountain, typifying the source of life. Mounting it, Bellerophon rose into the air and slew the Chimaera, a fire-breathing monster (the passions). Thereafter the Initiate Ego is no longer limited to the surface of the earth and the physical body; he soars, as if winged, into the empyrean, the higher states of consciousness.

In one Old Testament story[1] Job is being tested throughout a long interrogation between the Deity and himself. The unicorn in him must no longer be wild, even though its universal nature, symbolised by wildness and freedom, remains and is recognised.

In *The Book of Job* the change from the wild ass to the unicorn is also significant, for the ass is a symbol of stubbornness and in its wild state all its qualities are unharnessed. The Candidate for

[1] *Job*. 39: 9-12.

Initiation must tame the hitherto wild ass so that thereafter, as a docile quaternary, it may bear the threefold Ego onward to its goal, even as the ass bore the Holy Family to Egypt and the Christ in triumph to Jerusalem.

Egypt is a topographical symbol for the Sanctuary of the Greater Mysteries and the Hall of Initiation wherein Jesus, like every Initiate, was sanctified and consecrated to His mighty task. Jerusalem is the immortal Self of man, the spiritual Triad, in which the Initiate is fully conscious. This " Jerusalem " state of consciousness is achieved while wide awake in the often resistant quaternary. Symbolically, the Christ triumphant rides into Jerusalem upon an ass.

The unicorn is a fabulous animal whose spinal cord is presumed to extend beyond the *medulla oblongata*, through the pituitary gland and out between the eyes, after which it becomes hardened into a horn. Occultly interpreted, this refers less to the physical spinal cord than to the interior etheric canal which runs along its length and, as previously stated, is called *Sushumna*. The equi-polarised creative fire, Serpent Fire, or *kundalini*, flows along this canal from sacrum to brain and in its flow, in man, it is accompanied by the separate positive and negative currents which follow each their own pathways known as *Pingala* and *Ida* respectively, intertwining the *Sushumna* as they flow.

This sublimation of the creative force, this ascent of the whirling, serpentine, creative fire, occurs as a result of the sublimation of the sex-force by the continued practice of *yoga*, aided by passage through valid Rites of Initiation. Such knowledge was for a long period of time part of the closely guarded secrets of the Mysteries, and even now the technique whereby it is thus aroused is kept secret from the world.

This secrecy is designed not to withhold valuable information, but to protect the profane and the unready from the danger and the strain inseparable from the premature awakening of *kundalini*. Many symbols are therefore employed to refer to this redeeming, liberating power in man. In most of them serpents, often intertwined, figure largely. The stories of the transformation of the rods of Moses and Aaron[1] into serpents to win freedom for the Israelites, and the

[1] Ex. 4: 2-5 & *Num.* 17:1-11.

glyphs of Laocoon and his two sons; of the brazen serpent on the cross held up by Moses; of the caduceus in the hands of Hermes who frees the soul (Persephone) from Hades (imprisonment in the physical body and world)—all these portray this sublimation of the creative force and the resultant liberation of consciousness from the restrictions of bodily life.

The authors of *The Book of Job* [1] used the conjoined symbol of the wild ass and the unicorn to indicate that Job had progressed through the wild, stubborn and sexual phases of human development and, Moses-like, was horned,[2] if with but one horn. The horn of the unicorn is sometimes pictured as helical, which is a veiled reference to the spirally intertwining forces of *kundalini*, " the power that moves in a serpentine path ".

In this sense the unicorn (conjoined mind, emotion, vitality and physical body of the man in whom the Serpent Fire is fully aroused) is willing to serve him (" abide by thy crib "), can be bound and made to " harrow the valleys ". The horned animal (controlled personality) is to be trusted. It is also mighty in " strength ". Labour can be left to it. The owner can believe in it, knowing that it will " bring home (sublimate) thy seed (the procreative power) and gather it into thy barn " (the brain and the Causal Body).

The unicorn is also a symbol of that early Race of men in whom the pineal eye was at the surface of the head. These were the so-called Lemurians, the Third Root Race in the succession of Races upon Earth, but the first to wear physical bodies and to renew human physical life on this planet. They were gigantic men, heavily built and clumsy, unskilled in the management of a physical form, but possessing still that psychic vision which was instinctually and naturally employed by the first two Races on Earth, which were astro-etheric. Their physical vision was limited, for the two eyes were still rudimentary, yet their psychic vision was at first remarkably clear.

As the Third and Fourth Root Races developed the bodies became smaller, more compact and more readily controlled. The present two eyes developed, to bestow clearly focused and sterioscopic vision, and the so-called third, pineal eye retreated to become the

[1] *Job* 39: 9-12.
[2] According to Michelangelo.

present pineal gland. The unicorn is said metaphorically to have roamed the earth until the time when this process was complete. Thereafter it disappeared (symbolically), remaining only as an emblem of humanity's past, as a mysterious racial memory of man, who had attained to a physical body and in his mortal nature was then a quaternary, a quadruped, a horned horse, a unicorn. The unicorn, however, did not die. Like the pineal eye, which has retreated into the brain, it retreated to become for long ages quiescent, yet remaining as a glyph within the memory of the Race.[1] The less symbolic and more actual Lemurian Race is referred to as the Cyclopes, the one-eyed giants of Greek Mythology. The fact of the early existence of a one-eyed Race slept as both a memory and a power within the subconscious mind of successive Races.

The wheel turns. All that ever was, after sleeping for a time, reappears. The unicorn and cyclopean man are awakening from their long slumber. The human quaternary finds its vestigial horn reappearing at the surface of the forehead, not as hardened tissue but as whirling, creative fire. Modern man, becoming giant once more, if only as yet in mind, finds his closed third eye of psychic vision and intellectual intuitiveness opening once more. Man's inherent psychic faculties, his innate seership, is no longer a dimly remembered, racial power waking fitfully in children and simple folk. It has forced itself upon the human mind, has been scientifically investigated, and now is recognised as an almost universal and an active power which has been christened " extra sensory perception", or ESP.

Thus, as a symbol, the unicorn, white and gleaming with fire which coruscates, whirls and shoots forth from between the eyes, again roams the mountain sides, the rocky crags and the dim forests. Polyphemus frees himself from his mountain cave (the psychically unresponsive physical bodies of the later Fourth and early Fifth Root Races) and, with the fires of Etna burning more fiercely than ever,

---

[1] The existence in the remote past of single-eyed men is suggested by classical allusions to the Cyclopes, such as Polyphemus, and the occasional appearance of abnormalities in the form of babies born with a single eye. This is regarded as an example of atavism. Reptiles still exist, particularly tuataras found in a few small islands off the North Island of New Zealand, which possess a third eye, generally referred to as a pineal body, in a cavity between the eyes covered by a thin skin. Occult science states that the first physical men on earth were one-eyed giants.

stands upright once more. The Cyclopes are here on Earth again, but no longer one-eyed. Rather are they endowed with three organs of vision, two physical and one superphysical. They are partly represented by the men and women of today who are already possessed of these intuitional and psychic faculties, which will be natural to later Races.

Ulysses personifies the evolutionary procedure, and the stake which he thrust into the eye of the giant in the cave (the head of man) is the downward thrust of Spirit-life bringing the Monad-Egos of men through the temporary blindness of the physical, emotional and early lower mental phases of human development.

The Adepts and Initiates of old thus enshrined in allegory and symbol their ethnological, historical and occult knowledge, leaving it apparent for all that had eyes to see and yet veiled, because temporarily not needed and not without danger, until the time of unveiling should arrive. The present is the time, and in this age the modern Adepts are re-awakening the slumbering memories and long sleeping powers of their younger brothers, the humanity whom the Adept Brotherhood has never ceased to care for and to guide.

THE VEIL is used in both the Old and the New Testaments. In terms of consciousness, the veil symbolises the mental barrier which restricts awareness and thought during physical incarnation to the limitations of the formal, concrete brain-mind. On account of this " veil ", transference of intellectual light, creative genius, inspiration from the Higher Self to the lower, is normally both diffi-cult and rare. When it is achieved, distortion and severe " privation " of the transmuted abstract ideas are likely to occur. Barrenness symbolises this restricted condition of mind. The heavenly marriage and conception, as the ultimate full union of the Higher and lower selves is symbolically called, has not yet been achieved. Here an example is quoted of the use of the symbols of the barrenness and later conception of a woman in advanced age, which may usefully serve to illustrate the principle of the veil: " Then the woman came and told her husband, saying, A man of God came unto me, and his countenance was like the countenance of an angel of God, very terrible: but I asked him not whence he was, neither told he me his name." [1] Herein is allegorically described both a prerequisite for successful passage through the first of the great Initiations (seeing a man of God, the *Augoeides*), and the psycho-spiritual condition (conception) to which the fully prepared Candidate has attained. This consists of the establishment of an intimate relationship (fruitful marriage) between the inner Self, whose " name " is then known, in its vesture of light—vehicle of the abstract intelligence—and its self-manifestation below that level in the vehicle of concrete, analytical thought (the wife of Manoah and all other barren women who become fruitful). The former is represented by the man of God and the latter by the wife and mother-to-be.

Up to the time of preparedness for the first Initiation in the individual, and of the general unfoldment of the intuitive faculty in the Race, a barrier or veil exists between these two aspects of human nature, the Egoic and the personal. This barrier and cause of intellectual and spiritual barrenness is like the veil before the Sanctuary in that temple which is man himself, in whom abides the Spirit of the Highest, the innermost divine Power and Presence, called the Monad.

In the Fifth Root Race of the Fourth Round on this planet, this veil of the human temple is penetrated only by men who are in advance of the Race, or subjected to special Egoic and mental stimulation by either seniors in evolution or members of the Angelic Hosts, or as a result of unusual astrological aspects to which they are able to respond. As the sixth sub-Race of the Fifth Root Race appears and develops, the veil between Higher and lower minds becomes thinner, and in consequence the intuitive faculty shows itself. In the Adept of this period, and in humanity as a whole at the end of the Fourth Chain, the veil is " rent " or dissolved, as is made plain in accounts of the Crucifixion of Christ.[2] The rending in twain of the veil of the temple is an allegory descriptive of a state of consciousness rather than of a supernormal phenomenon in a physical temple.

The statement that the woman of Zorah came and told her husband, Manoah, of the experience of annunciation, reveals the intimate intercommunication already established between the two

[1] *Judges* 13: 6.
[2] *Matt.* 27: 51.

aspects of mind in the individual who is fully prepared to be received into the Greater Mysteries, to be initiated, and to experience the " birth " of the intuitive faculty or *Buddhic* consciousness.

The story of Pilate is of interest from this point of view. His wife had a dream[1] in the daytime, during waking consciousness— meaning Egoic illumination. She did not herself go to Pilate, as did the woman of Zorah to her husband. She sent a messenger, implying the absence of personal communication between them, the existence of a barrier of space or distance (a veil). Pilate did not heed the warning, however. He was not yet open to the light of intuition. As the lower mind not yet fully illumined, but approaching that state, he committed Jesus (intuition itself and the Christ-nature within man) to be crucified by the rabble. The bloodthirsty crowd represents the numerous anti-spiritual attributes of the outer man, including fanaticism, mob psychology, orthodoxy and blood lust, whether for physical flesh and blood or the contemptuous murder of new ideas and principles. A man in the condition typified by Pilate, capable of such surrender and heedless of the voices of conscience and intuition, even though he hears them, is as yet unresponsive to his spiritual Self. A veil exists between them, shutting out the inner God in the Sanctuary of his being from the sight of the man still outside the Holy of Holies.

The veil may also be interpreted as the silence imposed on every member of the Greater Mysteries concerning the secrets therein revealed. In one interpretation, the Initiatory, the finger on the lip of Horus Harpocrates refers to this vow of silence. Nevertheless Initiates have spoken, but it is no secular tongue they use, comprehensible to the profane; for to do so would be to break their solemn vow and to cast pearls before swine.[2] When the illumined ones did speak they used a language especially invented for the purpose. This was the Sacred Language of allegory and symbol, which is itself a veil concealing from view that *gnosis* which is power.

VINEYARDS, gardens and fields indicate, cosmically, the material evolutionary field; and humanly, fruitful conditions of consciousness, especially as at the opening of new cycles of experience and

---

[1] *Matt.* 27: 19.
[2] *Matt.* 7: 6.

development. Thus the Biblical story of the creation of the Earth and of man begins in the Garden of Eden, and it was in a garden that Mary Magdalene met and eventually recognised the risen Lord. Wildernesses and deserts, on the other hand, refer to those states of spiritual aridity to which all mystics bear testimony.

THE VULTURE. The symbolism in this case is much the same as for all birds of prey, with the additional meaning of the revelation of truth by taking off excrescences, or eating flesh from bones, as portrayed by the scavenging function of the bird and by its use by the Parsis, at their Towers of Silence, for the devouring of corpses. Vultures in their purificatory and scavenging functions also symbolise the transmuting power of the Spirit in man whereby lower personal grossnesses and delusions (flesh) are consumed, or transmuted into intuition (the upper air). The head-dresses of Egyptian Goddesses and Queens originally indicated that this process had been achieved in consciousness. A golden amulet in the form of a vulture, when placed on the neck of a mummy, represents the Ego as purifying the emotions and thereby freeing the soul from their restrictions.

WATER refers, in general, to universal, pre-cosmic, root substance (the waters of the Deep). Applied to man, water typifies the emotional world, the emotional or desire body, and the varied manifestations —calm, troubled or stormy—of the feeling aspect of human nature. Wine, blood, saliva and tears generally refer to the sublimated and spiritual expression of the forces of desire. This takes the forms of enhanced will-force, of spiritual intuitiveness and wisdom, and of universal love and compassion.

WINE refers to the intuition, and especially to the transmuted and purified emotional instincts when self-consciously used as means of intuitive, direct perception. When the lower is united with the Higher Self and the divine Principle is realised and present, water (the emotions) is automatically transmuted into wine (the intuition). This is clearly portrayed by means of these particular symbols in the account of the marriage feast at Cana.[1] The magical action whereby bitter waters were made sweet is susceptible of a similar interpretation.

[1] *Jn.* 2: 1-11.

CHAPTER II

SYMBOLS WHEN STATIONARY AND SYMBOLS WHEN MOVING

THE addition of movement to a symbol both bestows upon it an increased significance and indicates its intended application to a particular level and state of consciousness, whether in Cosmos or in man. This Chapter contains preferred interpretations of symbols, both with and without movement.

When a movement occurs, either of a symbol itself or of beings who are associated with it, then an additional dimension of meaning is being revealed. The First Logos, however, would be typified as stationary upon the most lofty peak, because He had attained to the highest possible degree of evolutionary development. This attainment would for Him include all the resultant expansions of awareness, planetary and extra-planetary, and the corresponding powers of both self-expression and command over Nature's processes and forces, and the Intelligences associated with them. This is also true of those Archangelic Beings who are known as " The Mighty Spirits before the Throne ". These receive and transmit throughout their varied Hierarchies both the formative impulse and, at the loftiest level of Principle alone, the idea (Archetype) of ultimate development in every kingdom of Nature. Such Beings, when represented symboli-cally, are depicted as stationary but all below them, whatever the kingdom to which they belong, ascend and descend [1] the " ladder " of divine consciousness.

When the central figures in Scriptural narratives ascend moun-tains, both general evolutionary progress and the attainment of supernormal powers of consciousness are implied. Descent to the foothills and the plane below refers to a return to normal states of

[1] *Gen.* 28: 12.

awareness. To the reader possessing the keys, voluntary descent into a valley reveals that a human being has fallen below the attained standard in both motive and conduct.

In Greek Mythology the God Zeus on Olympus represents the Cosmic Logos Itself, whilst Zeus manifested on Earth—engaged in *amours* of different kinds, for example, each with its occult signification—is an allegory of the manifestation of the divine life in Nature and in man. The kingdom of Nature—mineral as in the shower of gold which fell upon Danaë, plant as in the transformation of Daphne into a laurel tree, bird as when Zeus in the form of a swan visited Lida, and animal as when Zeus took on the semblance of a bull and carried away Europa—all in their turn refer to the self-manifestation of the Logos. The nature of the action—protective, destructive, taking captive or physical intimacy—describes the form of the divine manifestation. Applied to human beings, the attainment of mystical union with the Logos—God-consciousness—is being symbolically described.

Ideally an alphabet of symbols should include an interpretation of the symbol itself, and a statement of its meaning when movement is associated with it. Thus aided, the Scriptures and Mythologies of ancient peoples come to life for the student who possesses the necessary keys.[1]

World Scriptures and Mythologies all contain—may be said almost to consist of—epic accounts of journeys by land or sea. Not infrequently these journeys take the travellers for long distances and amidst great perils interspersed with triumphs. When included in inspired allegories and metaphorical histories, such voyages by land and sea all symbolically describe processes of the emanation of Cosmoi with their hidden life, presiding and directing Intelligences and myriads of Monads, each an "Immortal Germ". Accounts of experiences passed through conceal the occult laws under which Solar Systems and all that they contain are produced, whilst those describing return journeys—very often triumphant and wealth-conveying—tell of the fulfilment of the evolutionary process.

---

[1] Four of these keys are set forth in Pt. II, Ch. II of this Vol.

AGRICULTURE

Those Deities, demi-gods and men who in Scriptures and allegories are portrayed as engaging in agriculture, represent Logoi of Universes and the assisting Sephiroth Who, like Heavenly husbandmen or gardeners,[1] " plant " Monads in both the substance of the Universe and in the vehicles or bodies in which they will evolve.

In the Eleusinian Mysteries Demeter or Ceres presumably personifies the Supreme Deity, whilst her daughter Persephone, and also Triptolemus, personify the Sephiras. The ears of wheat supposedly bestowed upon the latter refer to the seed-like potencies in the Monads which can only germinate after planting. Therefore Triptolemus is sent throughout the world to teach mankind the science of agriculture, or in other words the " planting " of the Monads in matter.[2] The mission of Triptolemus to travel throughout the world in his (significantly) winged and serpent-powered chariot and teach humanity the science of agriculture may also be interpreted as an instruction to found Temples of the Mysteries wherein the psychological and spiritual significance of " wheat " was to be taught. If this may be carried further then, as already stated, in one aspect the Deity is as a divine " Farmer " and the Sephiroth and other assistants are as His husbandmen.

This use of metaphor can lead into a much wider development of both the idea and the interpretation of symbols. For example, every spiritually awakening and awakened human being who serves unselfishly in some field of activity thereby becomes as a husbandman or labourer in the fields of the one great " Father "—God. At first this service is but intuitively conceived. In the Adept, however, it is carried out in full and unbroken experience of unity with the universal life and its divine Source. The activity of husbandry offers a good example of the value and meaning of motion when added to a more or less static symbol.

---

[1] For example, ". . . the LORD God planted a garden eastward in Eden. . ." (*Gen.* 2: 8).

[2] Admittedly a microcosmic interpretation is also possible. The fact is fully recognised, however, that little or nothing is positively known about the Ceremonies of the Eleusinia. A study of all available literature in English, and of the archaeological discoveries at the site—especially the famous plaque and the Triptolemus vase—have led me to suggest the above interpretations.

BEASTS OF PREY

These sometimes represent undesirable human characteristics, such as cruelty and over-accentuated sensuality, which attributes must be transcended and the force which animates them sublimated. In symbology such animals are sometimes destroyed without the use of weapons, as were the Nemean lion by Hercules and the roaring lion by Samson,[1] presumably implying that vices must be transmuted into virtues without any external aid. If the hide or head of the animal is thereafter worn by the victor, as in the case of Hercules, successful sublimation is being described, since that which once existed as a danger is thereafter turned to helpful, as well as symbolical, use.

BURIAL

Macrocosmically burial, whether temporary during human life or permanent after death, refers to the descent of Spirit into the deepest depths of matter—the mineral kingdom. Microcosmically, both the involution of the Monadic Ray into forms and of the human Ego into bodies at each reincarnation are indicated. Thus the Hebrew Patriarchs, Abraham, Isaac and Jacob, were buried in the cave of Macphelah, Joseph was lowered into a pit and Jesus was buried in a rock tomb, all of these being underground.

CALVES

Because of its almost infinite potentiality as either bull or cow in-the-becoming, the calf became a symbol of the prodigal abundance in which Nature provides for man.

The cow, in its turn, came to be regarded almost reverentially because of its unfailing and providential supplies of milk, flesh and hide. It has become especially associated with the Principle of divine Motherhood (Hathor), perhaps on account of its continuing maintenance of successors by the production of calves.

CHALICE

A consecrated cup or Holy Grail refers to the vesture of light (the *Augoeides*[2]) in which the threefold spiritual Self of man is

---

[1] *Judges.* 14: 5, 6.

[2] *Augoeides*—see Glossary.

manifested, and through which it is expressed in the spiritual worlds. The receipt of the gift of a cup, and the vision of a chalice or Grail, imply that one has reached the stage of Monadic and Egoic unfoldment at which wisdom (wine) has been attained and compassionate goodwill, which leads to continuous selfless service to others, becomes a perfectly natural way of life; for this latter is born of ever-deepening realisation of the unity of the life in all forms and of the identity of an individual's own life-essence (wine) with that by which all other beings are nourished, sustained and preserved. The Cup or Grail and the actions of seeing, following and drinking from it, and of administering the Sacramental Wine to others, offer illustrations of the effectiveness of including movement in the symbolical presentation of ideas.

CORN

Corn and seed symbolise the universal potentiality for generation, growth, and the infinite production of new seeds. For man, as Monad, seed also implies innate capacity for the fulfilment of evolutionary destiny—the attainment of Adeptship.

(a) PLANTING: In the Macrocosm planting refers to the opening of *Manvantaras* and the emanation from within the Logos of the projected Rays of the Monads into the " field " of evolution at whatever level, from the most spiritual to the mineral kingdom of a physical planet.

For man, as Monad, the sowing of seeds has a similar significance. In addition a state of human consciousness is being described, namely that at which the spiritual Self is beginning to reach and influence the motives and the conduct of the mortal personality. One example of this is readiness to allow the husks—the external appearance of things—" to die ", meaning to cease to influence attitudes and actions. This applies to both personal position and prestige and to worldly possessions, all seen as " husks " which must no longer either deceive the mind or prevent the recognition and unfoldment of the true ideal. The person thus illumined has discovered the truth that life is fulfilled by renunciation, and not by perpetually grasping for possessions.[1]

---

[1] *Jn.* 12: 24—admittedly a rendering not readily discernible in the text.

(*b*) RIPENED CORN: Naturally this matured state indicates the fulfilment of evolutionary destiny up to the degree ordained for any particular period. For man this implies the completion of human evolution, culminating in Superhumanity. Since every matured and healthy seed contains the potentiality of the repetition of the cycle of further planting, ripening and harvesting, so Adeptship when achieved leads to still greater developments up to the stature of a Solar Logos, a Cosmic Logos, and beyond in infinite degree. All this possibility of ever increasing attainment is implicit in the symbol of corn and of its passage through various stages of its existence.

(*c*) STORAGE: Storage of corn, as in a granary, refers to periods between *Manvantaras—Pralayas*, in fact—when seeds remain intact but ungerminated.

THE CROSS AND CRUCIFIXION

When conjoined, the Cross and the process of Crucifixion portray both matter itself, with its four directions of space (the Cross), and the voluntary self-limitation accepted by a Logos (the Christos) and all that follows from the beginning of the divine manifestation up to its close at the end of *Manvantara*. The man who on the threshold of Adeptship voluntarily accepts " crucifixion ", portrays a state of consciousness in which every faintest trace of personal possessiveness and of the delusion of self-separated individuality is transcended. This is not, however, an actual sacrifice, since the realisation of unity has already been attained to a very considerable degree, as exemplified by the acceptance of the " cup " by Jesus in Gethsemane. Whilst each symbol is susceptible of interpretation by itself, when motion is added an interior experience, either degrading or uplifting according to the circumstances, is being described.

GARDENS

Applied to mystic states of mind a garden implies fruitfulness,. whilst working in gardens, vineyards and fields allegorically describes the successful pursuit of the contemplative life, and this is especially true when corn is being grown or harvested. The stories of Ruth and Boaz in the wheat field, of Mary Magdalene in the garden, and

12

of Triptolemus being sent out into the world, as related in the Eleusinian Mysteries, all imply phases of self-illumination.

GRAIN

The great nutritional value of all cereals to the body of animal and man may be interpreted as the provision by Nature of a complete supply of spiritual power, life and wisdom, and of the faculty of comprehension. Prodigality of supply, spiritual beneficence and material well-being are all indicated by harvested corn. A grain of corn, as distinguished from its enclosing husk, is used by Jesus as a symbol for the essential spiritual life of man and for the importance of permitting the " husks " of possessiveness and egoism to " die " in order that the essential life principle may " live "; for He said: ". . . Except a corn of wheat fall into the ground and die, it abideth alone; but if it die, it bringeth forth much fruit." [1] The choice of the essential rather than the unessential, the Real rather than the unreal, and the application of the results of such choice to motive and conduct are here indicated, whilst the readiness to sacrifice temporal possessions and gain in order to be enriched by the eternal " treasures in Heaven " is accentuated. St. Catherine of Sienna expressed this in the words: " We must become the wheat of Christ."

GRAVES

Graves are naturally the antithesis of heights, and Macrocosmically designate the opposite position in space, namely the depth, or phase of involution, at which the manifesting power, life and consciousness of the Logos have become " robed with a garment " of densest matter. In the Earth Planetary Scheme, Chain[2] and Round this consists of the mineral kingdom of Nature with its indwelling inhabitants, who are the Sephiras[3] and the nature spirits of that kingdom,[4] by whatever name they may be known in different ages and amongst different peoples. With regard to man himself, the physical body, and partic- ularly the organ of awareness known as the cerebrospinal system—

---

[1] *Jn.* 12 : 24.

[2] See Glossary—Chain.

[3] See Appendix—The Sephirothal Tree.

[4] q. v. *The Kingdom of the Gods*, Pt. II, Ch. IV. esp. pp. 107-109, Geoffrey Hodson.

especially the portion within the skull—is as a grave to the reincarnating Ego. Since the Crucifixion and Resurrection of Christ are susceptible of interpretation as being descriptive of self-liberation from the limitations imposed by the substance of the brain, may it not be significant that the former of these, which allegorically describes the final stages of human evolution, should have taken place on Golgotha, " the place of a skull "?

HORSES

The horse is a quadruped and, like all other four-legged animals, when referred to in an epic story has two possible meanings, whether applied to the Macrocosm or the microcosm.   On the one hand these are the four worlds of thought, desire, vital energy and physical action, and on the other the driving force by which they are moved to produce objective results.   These results can be either immediately or eventually beneficent, pleasure-giving, and in accordance with the Will of Cosmos as a whole, tamed and domesticated animals then being used as symbols.   If, on the other hand, the effects of the interior energy and its objective results are inimical, destructive and painful, then the symbolism is that of wild horses and—as earlier indicated—of beasts of prey.

The winged horse Bucephalus—and indeed all animals which co-operate with man, whether serving him or providing him with nutriment and clothing—is an example of the former symbology, whilst monsters—such as Ammit of the Egyptians and the Chimaera and the Theban Sphinx of the ancient Greeks—and predatory lions, tigers and wolves, are examples of the latter.   Horses, however, are most frequently used to represent beneficent forces.   When winged they portray the Macrocosm in later phases of development; for at that stage matter has become spiritualised and bodies built of it are symbolically " winged ", as are the horses which were said to draw the chariot of Helios, the Sun-God.   In the microcosm they represent the four vehicles of Initiated man, which no longer imprison but aid consciousness in gaining free access to all areas and all levels of the Universe within the attained range of omnipresence.

JEALOUSY AND HATRED

These human traits generally arise from envy and, for example, are usually felt by the less favoured towards the more favoured members of a family. Their conduct towards others is used in allegories of creation and procreation to delineate the resistance of matter to Spirit, of substance to the moulding influence of the Archetype, and of the body of man to the direction of the indwelling human Spirit.

LIONS

The king of beasts is a notable example of a symbol used to denote that interior alchemy whereby undesirable human characteristics must be transcended and the force which drives them sublimated. Also indicated is the need for self-preservation and success throughout the whole procedure. An additional element exists, in that the lion has long been regarded as an earthly representative of the King of the Universe, the Solar Logos. When the skin of the animal is worn with the head resting on the head (seat of mental awareness) of the hero, then both *conscious* union with the Solar Deity and the ability to draw upon the spiritual energies of the sun are being referred to.

MACROCOSM

All components of Universes, including groups of both super-physical and physical planets and their central sun, and the evolutionary phases during which Monads unfold their potentialities in the course of cyclic passage through all the kingdoms of Nature— are referred to allegorically in the Sacred Language. Each life-bearing planet in its turn also passes through manifold experiences, which include involution towards increasing materialisation, the development and growth of species, their highest possible evolution and their ultimate dissolution, all being similarly described by means of allegory and symbol. Thus is depicted the whole field of Macrocosmic forthgoing and return, culminating in the inevitable triumph of Spirit over matter, of life over form, and of Archetype over all material resistances.

MALE ANIMALS

The ram and the bull were thought by primitive peoples to be appropriate manifestations of the potent creative and procreative power of the Deity; hence the worship of these two animals.

MAN THE MICROCOSM

At the dawn of every era of cyclic self-manifestation the human Monad (often personified by a Saviour or a hero) sets forth on the great journey to far-off lands. It awakens from the " sleep " which precedes fructification, passes through pre-gestatory and later post-fructification developments within the vast " womb " of Mother Nature, is born into self-conscious existence within the ever-changing, illusory worlds of forms and phenomena in which shapes appear and disappear, and finally reaches maturity and old age. The imprisoning vehicles ultimately pass away, thereby granting release into freedom and a return to the unchanging, eternal worlds from which the great pilgrimage first began.

METALS

According to their classifications these have their several signi-fications. Silver, for example, refers to spiritual will, gold to spiritual wisdom and copper to spiritual intelligence, in which last is included capacity for the comprehension of underlying principles and dis-crimination between that which is Real (timeless) and that which is unreal (purely temporary).

MONAD-ADEPT

Some journeys are made to end miraculously, either by apparent bodily death followed by resurrection, or by seemingly miraculous translation from Earth to Heaven, from bondage to freedom or, as in the *Book of Exodus*, from Egypt to the Promised Land. Such journeys by intrepid travellers are sometimes undertaken in pursuit of goals which in ordinary terms seem unworthy of the immense efforts involved, the dangers encountered and passed through, and the results and attainments. These goals include the discovery and possession of a Golden Fleece, Golden Apples, crossing a stream and reaching the further shore, and the overcoming and slaying of incredibly fantastic enemies. As heretofore suggested, the very incongruity and incredibility of these stories may permissibly be regarded as hints from author to reader to look beneath the surface and there find the hidden truths which have been so cleverly and effectively concealed.

As a result of the forthgoing and return of the indwelling life, of the informing Spirit-Essence, and of the directive Intelligence, both Macrocosmic and microcosmic, the attainment of self-liberation from all encasements and conscious manifestation of all inherent powers to the highest possible degree is assured.

When miraculous events are associated with final departure from the visible worlds and the sight of men, whether in a chariot of fire or in clouds of glory, then the implication is that a home-coming in advance of the Race, by means of deliberately hastened progress towards the attainment of the standard of perfection set for an epoch or a cycle, has been achieved. As part of the symbolic account of this procedure miracles are generally performed, non-existent, fabulous creatures are encountered, whether as friends or foes, and the central character is victorious. In all such cases the attainment of Initiate-ship and Adeptship by the human Monad-Ego is being allegorically described.

MOUNTAIN TOPS

Ascent to the summit of a mountain signifies the attainment of the highest level of human consciousness. In the Macrocosm this refers to the first plane of manifestation after emanation from the Absolute has occurred. The most highly developed and therefore most powerful Being in the Cosmos, the Director of the emanation, the First Logos, symbolically is met—as by Moses on Mount Sinai —on the top of a mountain.

NATIVITY

Birth implies the degree of development at which not only the higher intellect or abstract intelligence, but also the faculty of spiritual intuitiveness, are exerting an increasing influence upon the outlook and conduct of the illumined person. Thus the mystical Nativity is an interior illumination,[1] a Christmas of the Soul, in which an ever deepening compassion for and realisation of union with the newly born life in all kingdoms of Nature is experienced. The allegorical descriptions of Nativities, with their concomitant supernatural hap-penings, portray the early stages of the manifestation of the Christ-consciousness in a spiritually evolved person.

[1] *Gal.* 4: 19.

PRECIOUS STONES

All of these have their specific spiritual and occult implications. The diamond, for instance, symbolises the Spirit-Essence of Universe and man, as well as its expression as dauntless courage and undefeatable will. The sapphire refers to wisdom; the emerald to intelligence; the jaspar to balance, rhythm and unrestricted interplay between the inner and the outer selves; the topaz to the rationalising intellect, and especially to the will to discover truth and fact; the ruby to the flame of dedication to the Highest and to selfless devotion to humanitarian Causes; whilst the amethyst symbolises the power to express the triple Self in man. In allegories the giving and the receipt of any of these jewels imply that the corresponding quality has been developed.

RESURRECTION AND ASCENSION

In contradistinction to burial, which is an allegory of the involution of Spirit into matter, these two procedures refer to phases of the evolutionary pathway when the de-spiritualising influence of matter is progressively reduced until it is entirely transcended (Ascension). In an Initiatory interpretation, rising from the grave implies the attainment—as a result of occult progress and the Rites of Initiation —of the ability both to leave the body at will and to outgrow the necessity for further enforced reincarnations. The resurrected and ascended Initate is free of the wheel of birth and death, and also of the limitations imposed upon consciousness by the delusions of self-separateness and egoism and by incarnation in a physical body.

SACKS OR OTHER CONTAINERS OF FOOD

These symbols are susceptible of a number of interpretations, such as: the outer edge or so-called Ring-pass-not[1] of Universes; the auric envelope or limit of the range of radiation of semi-sentient or sentient products of Nature, including man; the skin of the physical form; the womb; the seed capsule; the enclosing membranes of cells. The nest of the self-sacrificial pelican (a Rosicrucian symbol) has the same significance.

SPHINXES

This non-existent creature—generally portrayed in sculpture —has many profound significations. As in the case of the Centaur,

[1] Ring-pass-not—see Glossary.

a human head or body on an animal form indicates that the evolution
of the Monad through the animal into the human kingdom of Nature
is being portrayed.   A winged animal with a human head thus aptly
depicts one of the great " miracles " of Nature which, I repeat, is
the evolution of the Monad out of the group and instinctual consciousness of the animal into the capacity for individualised, reasoning
intelligence as possessed by man.   The Sphinx, with its animal body
and human head, is an appropriate symbol of this progression.
Furthermore, the animal attributes and attainments are not immediately lost, and so in the symbol an animal body is retained.   If
winged, then a reference is being made to man's ability to reason,
and later both to conceive of abstractions and to gain knowledge
by means of spiritual intuitiveness.

The quality of mysteriousness and impenetrability associated
with the Sphinx hint at the fact that to the strictly formal mind the
gaining of knowledge by the exercise of the abstract intelligence and
the intuition is incomprehensible.   Thus the Sphinx at Thebes
propounded a normally unanswerable riddle to those who passed by.
" What creature goes on four feet in the morning, on two at noonday,
on three in the evening? "   " Man ", answered Oedipus.   " In
childhood he creeps on hands and feet; in manhood he walks erect;
in old age he helps himself with a staff."   It was the right answer.

VEHICLES

Chariots—whether winged or dragon-borne, aerial or physical
—great ships and little boats, arks and fishing vessels, are often made
to convey hero, heroine and crews to far-off destinations in this world
or the next, and sometimes from Heaven to Earth and back to Heaven
again.   All these are symbols of vehicles, forms or bodies—whether
a Ring-pass-not of a Logos[1] and His Universe, the aura of an Adept
or a human being, or the form of some natural *genus* in the organic
kingdom.   This last includes the physical body of man, its skin,
and also the bodily cells together with their enclosing membranes.
Spirit needs a body, life needs form, intelligence needs mind and brain
in order to become self-expressed in ever-increasing fullness, beauty
and nearness to the Archetype.   In the Sacred Language all vehicles

[1] Logos—see Glossary.

refer to these enclosing, preserving and conveying *media*. Indeed the world itself, the physical Globe, may be regarded as the chariot of the mysterious, indwelling Spirit of the Planet, or the " shell " of a so-called " Heavenly Snail ".[1]

WAR

Engagements between armies and duels between men all indicate the battle which Spirit must allegorically fight in order to become fully self-manifest in matter, whether this be in its lowest and densest state or in its most tenuous and highly spiritualised condition.

WILDERNESSES

A desert or a wilderness may refer to pre-cosmic matter, meaning space or substance not yet impregnated with Spirit and, in consequence, non-productive. When, however, characters in metaphorical stories enter wildernesses, then in a microcosmic interpretation emanative and formative processes have begun. The Great Breath is being breathed upon the Great Deep, after which pre-cosmic substance— no longer a wilderness—becomes pregnant with and productive of material Universes and all that they bring forth. Christ in the wilderness, for example, is a Macrocosmic allegory of the entry of the Logos-to-be upon hitherto virginal space. In this context Satan personifies the inertia of matter, and his allegorical temptings and defeats indicate amongst other things the assurance of the " victory " of the Logos, as conjoined Spirit-Mind-Word, over matter with its resistant tendencies. Thus the whole drama of creation is magnificently portrayed in the passages in the Gospels which tell of Christ being tempted by the Devil in arid, non-productive conditions— the wilderness.

In a microcosmic interpretation, however, when a man or a nation enters or leaves a wilderness, states of mind are being described. Used as a symbol for a state of consciousness, a man said to be in a wilderness is as one barren of spiritual realisation and idealism; for as a result of this his mind, and so his life, become desert-like so far as inspiration and unselfish love and service are concerned. Spiritual deadness and loss of enthusiasm and of aspiration for achievement

---

[1] A term used in occult philosophy for the Regent of a Planet.

in any field of human endeavour—especially that of search for and discovery of the Divine within—all these are portrayed by the movement of intelligent beings into a wilderness or desert. Departure from a wilderness or desert, in its turn, implies eventual recovery from these limitations.

*   *   *   *

The foregoing, in outline, are some of the interpretations which can be applied, not only to the symbols themselves but also when action is involved, such action frequently designating the particular revelation which the author wished to convey.

CHAPTER III

THE SYMBOLISM OF NUMBERS

" The World is built upon the power of numbers ".
—Pythagoras.

INDICATIONS are found in ancient literature of a development which gave to numbers their real significance, and employed them in a system of symbolism which referred to something more than enumeration alone.

Numbers can be used as symbols, because the Universe is established upon a co-ordinated plan in which quantitative relations are repeated through different states and planes. Number is common to all planes of Nature, and thus unites them. By the study of numbers, therefore, one may learn the fundamental laws of the creation, constitution and progressive events in the lives of both Universes and men; for man is a modification of cosmic elements, a concentration of cosmic forces.

Every number has a certain power which is not expressed by the figure or symbol employed to denote quantity only. This power rests in an occult connection existing between the relations of things and the principles in Nature of which they are the expressions.

All numbers are represented by ten symbols, beginning with 0 and ending with 9. In this series:

0 stands for infinity; the Infinite, Boundless Being, the *fons et origo* of all things, the egg of the Universe, and the Solar System in its entirety. Universality, cosmopolitanism, circumambulation, voyaging, the cycles, negation, circumference, limitation and privation are implied. Zero also denotes the infinitely great and the infinitely small, the circle of infinity and the point at the centre, the atom, the absence of quality, absolute freedom, and the infinite and eternal Absolute which can only be described as No-Thing, because it is nothing that man can name. Zero also indicates boundless, infinitely potential, living light, the Rootless Root, the Sourceless Source.

The principle of forthgoing and return, which is expounded in Chapters II and III of Part Four, is also portrayed by the circle or ellipse of Arabic notation. The descending arc represents involution, the lowest point of the mineral kingdom, and the returning arc portrays evolution through mineral, plant, animal and man to Superman and Deity.

1 symbolises manifestation, assertion, the positive and active principle. It is zero made manifest, and so is the symbol of the sun. It stands for the Logos, the manifestation of the Infinite and Unmanifest. It represents the Ego, self-assertion, positivism, egotism, separateness, selfhood, isolation, distinction, self-reliance, dignity and rulership. In a religious sense it symbolises the Lord. In a philosophical and scientific sense it is the synthesis and fundamental unity of all things, and in a material sense it is the unit of life, the individual.

Both the figure and the meaning indicate the vertical which connects extreme height with extreme depth; that universal Intelligence which is the primary form of all consciousness and is hidden behind all numbers and all symbols. 1 is the essence, substance, energy and consciousness of the Universe expressed in varying degrees in all its forms. In man it is the Monad and the Spirit-Self manifesting as individuality; the unfolding unit or immortal, reincarnating Ego.

2 expresses antithesis; all opposing polarities including active and passive, male and female, positive and negative, profit and loss. In the Universe it stands for the dualism of manifested life—God and Nature, Spirit and matter, and their relationships. Duplication, reflection, alternation, sympathy and antagonism; pure wisdom, as the mirror in which the Divine in both Universe and man sees Itself; these are also implied in the number 2.

In man it is the spiritual intuitiveness which illuminates the mind and manifests in the personality as grasp of inner principles, abstract ideas and basic formulae, as also of the fact of the inevitable duality of being on all planes of manifestation. Uniting in itself opposite terms or principles, it denotes creation, production, fruition, combination, the manifest and the unmanifest, the explicit and the implicit.

3 signifies the trilogy; the trinity of life, substance and intelligence, of force, matter and consciousness. Creation, preservation, transformation, multiplication, development, growth, and therefore expression, are all implied.

3 denotes the outworking of the principles reflected from 1 by 2. This suggests sanctifying intelligence, understanding in contrast to wisdom, which reflects knowledge of the inmost Self. The family —father, mother and child; the three dimensions—length, breadth and height; the three postulates—the thinker, the thought and the thing; are also represented by the number 3.

4 is the number of reality and concretion, order, measurement, classification, recording, tabulation and memory, the measuring intelligence. 4 typifies the material Universe, physical laws, appearance, physiognomy; also logic, reason, discernment, discrimination, discretion and relativity; cognition by perception, experience, knowledge and science. The cross, segmentation, partition, order, classification, the swastika, the wheel of the law, sequence, enumeration, are denoted by 4. Applied to man it symbolises the personal nature —the lower quaternary.

5 being the middle number between 1 (beginning) and 9 (completion), implies mediation; as also adaptation, processes and methods. Law is seen by the wise as the manifestation of perfect justice, and they adapt natural conditions to the end of progressive liberation from all bondage. Expansion, inclusiveness, comprehension, understanding, judgment, increase, fecundity, propagation, justice, reaping, harvesting, reproduction of oneself in the material world, fatherhood, rewards and punishments under the law, are all represented by this number. The unchanging aspects, the strength and apparent severity of the operations of law, inspire fear in the uninstructed. Actually this law is the impersonal root of all operations of the life-force.

6 is the symbol of balance, equilibrium, symmetry, harmony of opposites, reciprocity, complementary activities and intelligent mediation. 6 represents co-operation, marriage, connubiality, the relations of the sexes, a link, reciprocal action, counterpoise, the interaction of the spiritual and the material, the mental and the physical, in man. The *psyche*, psychology, divination, psychism, telepathy and psychometry are symbolised by the number 6.

7 represents temporary cessation, but not final perfection, which is reserved for the number 9. Number 7 stands for the logical consequence of the ideas symbolised by the preceding numbers. This includes rest, safety, security, victory, but not final cessation or completion. It also implies time and space, duration, distance, old age, decadence, death, endurance, stability, immortality. The seven ages, days of the week, seals, principles in man (the triad and the quaternary), notes and colours, are also referred to by the number 7.

8 is the digit with the meanings of ebb and flow, alternate cycles, involution and evolution, the emergence of opposite forms of expression from a single cause, rhythm, and dissolution at the end of cycles. 8 also denotes reaction, revolution, fracture, rupture, disintegration, segregation, decomposition, anarchism, lesion, separation, divorce, expiration following inspiration, afflatus, genius, invention, deflection, eccentricity, waywardness, aberration and madness. The process of balancing accounts with Nature, receiving payment and paying debts, karmic adjustment in which, for example, both benefices and adversities may be received in preparation for advancement into a new cycle—all this is indicated by the number 8. It is the number of magic and occult science.

9 is the number of completion, but not absolute cessation, attainment, fulfilment, the end of one cycle merging into the beginning of its successor which will lead to greater attainment, since every end is the seed of a new beginning. 9 is thus the number of regeneration, spirituality, sense-extension, premonition, going forth, voyaging, reformation, nebulosity, pulsation, rhythm, reaching out, extension, publication, archery, prediction, revelation and mystery.

10 is a combination of the vertical line of self-consciousness and the ellipse or circle of superconsciousness. It is the number of perfection and dominion, and suggests the outpouring of the limitless life-force through a directive Logos. 10 indicates the resplendent intelligence, full of life and power, and consciousness of mastery founded upon the perfecting and organising power of understanding.

These are some of the links in the almost endless chain of associated ideas centering about the nine digits and the cypher. In some systems of interpretation the cypher is put last, so that the first and last are brought together to form 10, the perfect number in the decimal system; but in the Hebrew scheme the number 12 has that distinction, for it is the product of 3 multiplied by 4. The number 7, produced by their addition, is another sacred number. The foregoing interpretation of the numbers is applied to the unit value of any number— as $7+3+1=11=2$, in which 2 is the unit value. Thus all numbers have final reference to one of the nine digits.

The following minor key to the interpretation of numbers may prove useful, being in many respects more concise and easier of application than the foregoing. In this system the indications of the numbers are as follows:

0. All power—past, present and future—regarded as omnipresent and timeless.

1. Individuality and possible egotism, self-reliance, affirmation, distinction, the primal Emanator which directs the reappearance of and sustains and transforms the Universe; the Logos.

2. Unfailing wisdom expressed in thought and word. Relationship, psychic attraction, emotion, sympathy or antipathy, doubt and vaccilation, are also indicated.

3. Guidance on the pathway to liberation provided by understanding of law. Expansion, increase, intellectual capacity, riches and success.

4. The inexhaustible contents of boundless space, from which all spiritual and material needs can be met. Realisation, property, possession, credit, position.

5. Impersonal, undeviating justice in all human circumstances, recognised and acknowledged. Cause and effect, reason, logic, ethics, travelling, commerce, utility.

6. The conceived and manifested Universe expressed as beauty. Co-operation, marriage, reciprocity, sympathy, play, art, music, dancing.

7. Victory attained by spiritual will supported by perfect wisdom and understanding. Equilibrium, contracts, agreements, treaties.

8. Confidence born of realisation of perfect law, and eternal
light. Reconstruction, death, negation, decay, loss, extinc-
tion, going out.

9. Life in thought and word and deed unshakably established
in the Eternal Principle, the Spirit-Essence of the Universe.

10. The world of Spirit perfectly embodied in the world of matter.
In man, the Macrocosm perfectly expressed in the microcosm,
and the Spirit in the flesh.

PART FOUR

THE CYCLIC PATHWAY OF FORTHGOING AND RETURN

THE PARABLE OF THE PRODIGAL SON AS AN EXPOSITION OF THE LAW OF CYCLES

THE DIVINE LIFE AS THE PRODIGAL SON

THE MACROCOSMIC CYCLE

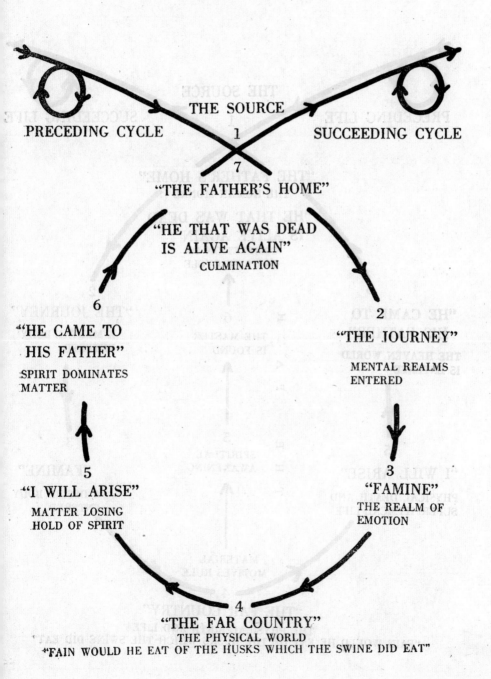

PRECEDING CYCLE

SUCCEEDING CYCLE

THE SOURCE
1

7

"THE FATHER'S HOME"

"HE THAT WAS DEAD
IS ALIVE AGAIN"
CULMINATION

6

"HE CAME TO
HIS FATHER"
SPIRIT DOMINATES
MATTER

2

"THE JOURNEY"
MENTAL REALMS
ENTERED

5

"I WILL ARISE"
MATTER LOSING
HOLD OF SPIRIT

3

"FAMINE"
THE REALM OF
EMOTION

4

"THE FAR COUNTRY"
THE PHYSICAL WORLD
"FAIN WOULD HE EAT OF THE HUSKS WHICH THE SWINE DID EAT"

THE MICROCOSMIC CYCLE

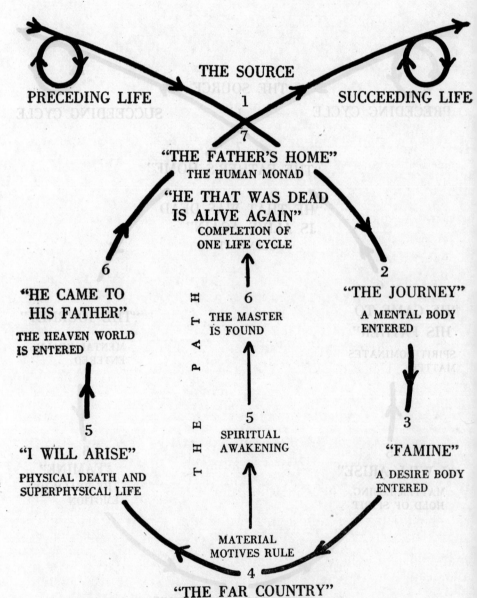

THE SOURCE

PRECEDING LIFE　　　　　　　　SUCCEEDING LIFE

1

7

"THE FATHER'S HOME"
THE HUMAN MONAD

"HE THAT WAS DEAD
IS ALIVE AGAIN"
**COMPLETION OF
ONE LIFE CYCLE**

6

**"HE CAME TO
HIS FATHER"**

THE HEAVEN WORLD
IS ENTERED

T
H
E

P
A
T
H

6
THE MASTER
IS FOUND

2

"THE JOURNEY"

A MENTAL BODY
ENTERED

5

"I WILL ARISE"

PHYSICAL DEATH AND
SUPERPHYSICAL LIFE

5
SPIRITUAL
AWAKENING

3

"FAMINE"

A DESIRE BODY
ENTERED

MATERIAL
MOTIVES RULE

4

"THE FAR COUNTRY"

THE PHYSICAL BIRTH AND LIFE
"FAIN WOULD HE EAT OF THE HUSKS WHICH THE SWINE DID EAT"

CHAPTER I

GENERAL INTRODUCTION

THE interpretation of the Parable of the Prodigal Son [1] which follows is intended to serve five purposes. The first is to illustrate the allegorical method of writing. The second is to suggest possible methods of interpretation and the significance of such Biblical symbols as the members of a family, the child, the kiss, baptism, crucifixion, the cross, burial, the tomb, prodigality and wasting of substance, garments and their parting, shoes, the ring, blindness and the recovery of sight, death and dismemberment, the " fall " of man, Egypt, Babylon, the pit, the prison, hunger, thirst, famine and swine. The third purpose is to offer information concerning the teachings contained in the parable. The fourth is to state some of the fundamental principles of the system of philosophic thought followed throughout this book, and the fifth is to share the fruits of long continued study of this wonderful story.

The Parable of the Prodigal Son is regarded as applicable equally to the Macrocosm, or the Cosmos as a whole; to the microcosm, or man as Spiritual Soul; and to his human personality; it being susceptible of interpretation in these three ways. To them are added qualifications to be developed and experiences to be passed through by those who choose the way of hastened unfoldment, seeking to enter in at " the strait gate " and tread " the narrow way ".[2] This last is sometimes referred to as the Initiatory interpretation. The subject of Initiation is considered in Chapter I of Part Six.

If it be questioned whether so complex an interpretation of the parable as is here offered is justified, and whether it was Our Lord's intention to refer to Macrocosmic and microcosmic procedures in

[1] *Lk.* 15: 11-32.
[2] *Matt.* 7: 13-14.

Nature, it could be answered that the processes of involution and evolution are cyclic, and that this fact is implicit in all references to forthgoing and return, whether direct or in parable.   In anything like a full exposition of the subject, extensions of the story to apply universally are, therefore, not only permissible but called for.   Moreover, only a very restricted range of possible applications of the principle of cyclic progression is included, the subject actually embracing the whole of objective existence.   It is on these bases that the following interpretations are offered.

A comparison may usefully be made between the Gospel version of the great parable and the Gnostic *Hymn of the Robe of Glory*,[1] which is an exposition of the same theme.   In this story Our Lord gives one of the master keys to the understanding of both Universe and man.   All allegories written in the Sacred Language are susceptible of application in a number of ways.   They may apply to the Cosmos as a whole, to each Solar System, to the human Race, to the Monad of man and its seven principles or bodies, to the Ego of man and his repeated incarnations in the flesh, and to every human being who embarks upon the mode of life which will hasten his evolution, called by Isaiah " The way of holiness ".[2]   This last includes admission to one or other of the Schools of Prophets [3], and passage through their Grades of Initiation to emerge as a Prophet, or one who both speaks from divine inspiration (*Heb. Nalie*) and is a seer (*Heb. rō'eh*).   Interpretations of allegories and symbols from this last point of view are termed " Initiatory " throughout this book.

The term " Cosmos " refers to the totality of the Sidereal Scheme, including all galaxies, all nebulae, all stars, all planets, all beings, and the divine Intelligences associated with them.   This totality is called throughout this work the " Macrocosm " or " Great World ".   Since man is an epitome of the whole and all creation is represented within him as seed powers and vibratory potentialities (" the portion of goods that falleth to me " [4]), he is sometimes referred to as the " microcosm " or " little world ".   These two, the Great and the

---

[1] *The Hymn of The Robe of Glory,* by G. R. S. Mead.
[2] *Is.* 35: 8.
[3] 2 *Kings* 2: 5, 4: 38, 6: 1 and *Dan.* 1: 4.
[4] *Lk.* 15: 12.

little worlds, are one in essence. All that is true of the larger, the Universal Existence, is equally true of the lesser, human existence as individual man. Lao Tze truly said, "The universe is a man on a large scale."

Perhaps the most profound of all the profound truths contained within the Wisdom Religion are those of the unity of the Macrocosm with the microcosm, and of the close similarity between the processes by which both become manifest and evolve. Man, in very truth, was created in the image of God. "The mystery of the earthly and mortal man is after the mystery of the supernal and immortal One." [1]

Man is described as that being in whom highest Spirit and lowest matter are united by intellect. Although this makes of him a triplicity, his constitution is said to be at least sevenfold. At the present stage of human evolution the seven bodies or principles of man, beginning with the most dense, are stated to be: the physical body, vehicle of thought, feeling and action in the physical world; the etheric double, the connecting link between the inner and the outer man, and the container of the vital energy or *prana* received physically from the sun and superphysically from the Spiritual Sun; the emotional or astral body, the vehicle of desire; the mental body, vehicle of the formal mind and instrument of concrete thought; the higher mental or Causal Body, vehicle of the threefold Spiritual Self at the level of abstract mind, called by the Greeks the *Augoeides* and frequently referred to as the Ego; the Buddhic body, vehicle of spiritual intuitiveness; the Ātmic body, vehicle of the spiritual will. Overshadowing and empowering the whole sevenfold man is the Dweller in the Innermost, the Monad, the Immortal Germ, a scintilla of the Spiritual Sun.

The contribution of occult philosophy—an aspect of the Wisdom Religion—to the problem of the emanation and constitution of the Universe is twofold. It consists first of an affirmation of the existence in Nature of a triune directive Intelligence, sustaining Life and creative Will, and secondly of information concerning the existence, the nature and the function of those individual embodiments of the powers in Nature called in Egypt and Greece "gods", in the East *devas*, in Palestine *elohim*, and in the West "Angelic Hosts".

---

[1] *Clef des Grands Mystères*, Eliphas Levi.

Occult philosophy shares with modern science the view that the Universe consists not of matter, as man's five senses would seem to indicate, but of energy, and adds that the Universe of force is the kingdom of the gods; for fundamentally these beings are directors of universal forces, power agents of the Logos, His engineers in the great creative process, which is regarded as continuous. Creative energy is perpetually outpoured; on its way from its source to material manifestation as apparent (to man) physical substance and form, it passes through the bodies and auras of the gods. In the process, the creative energy is " transformed ", " stepped down " from its primordial potency. In this sense certain Orders of the gods are thus " transformers " of power.[1]

All powers exist potentially within every man, and throughout his existence he gradually unfolds the whole pattern and image of Deity which is ultimately made manifest in him. Then he fulfils the Divine command: " Be ye therefore perfect, even as your Father which is in heaven is perfect "[2] and completes, as far as he himself is concerned, the Great Work.

[1] q.v. The Kingdom of the Gods, Geoffrey Hodson, T.P.H., Adyar.
[2] Matt. 5: 48.

CHAPTER II

THE PATHWAY OF FORTHGOING

THE PARABLE ITSELF

" *And he said, A certain man had two sons :*

And the younger of them said to his father, Father, give me the portion of goods that falleth to me.   And he divided unto them his living.

And not many days after the younger son gathered all together, and took his journey into a far country, and there wasted his substance with riotous living.

And when he had spent all, there arose a mighty famine in that land ; and he began to be in want.

And he went and joined himself to a citizen of that country ; and he sent him into his fields to feed swine.

And he would fain have filled his belly with the husks that the swine did eat : and no man gave unto him.

And when he came to himself, he said, How many hired servants of my father's have bread enough and to spare, and I perish with hunger !

I will arise and go to my father, and will say unto him, Father, I have sinned against heaven, and before thee,

And am no more worthy to be called thy son : make me as one of thy hired servants.

And he arose, and came to his father. But when he was yet a great way off, his father saw him, and had compassion, and ran, and fell on his neck, and kissed him.

And the son said unto him, Father, I have sinned against heaven, and in thy sight, and am no more worthy to be called thy son.

But the father said to his servants, Bring forth the best robe, and put it on him ; and put a ring on his hand, and shoes on his feet :

And bring hither the fatted calf, and kill it ; and let us eat, and be merry :

For this my son was dead, and is alive again ; he was lost, and is found. And they began to be merry.

Now his elder son was in the field : and as he came and drew nigh to the house, he heard music and dancing.

And he called one of the servants, and asked what these things meant.

And he said unto him, Thy brother is come; and thy father hath killed the fatted calf, because he hath received him safe and sound.

And he was angry and would not go in: therefore came his father out, and entreated him.

And he answering said to his father, Lo, these many years do I serve thee, neither transgressed I at any time thy commandment: and yet thou never gavest me a kid, that I might make merry with my friends:

But as soon as this thy son was come, which hath devoured thy living with harlots, thou hast killed for him the fatted calf.

And he said unto him, Son, thou art ever with me, and all that I have is thine.

It was meet that we should make merry, and be glad: for this thy brother was dead, and is alive again; and was lost, and is found." [1]

The Parable of the Prodigal Son describes the process of the forthgoing of the outpoured, conscious life of the Logos, which bears with it into the field of evolution the Rays or radiations of the Monads of all beings (the " journey into a far country ").

At the beginning of each new manifestation these Monads are at varying stages of development and awareness, according to the degree of unfoldment reached in preceding cycles. At the farthest point of the path of forthgoing, represented in the Earth Scheme of our Solar System by the mineral kingdom of the physical plane, the power, the life and the consciousness of the Monad are most deeply encased in matter. In the parable this phase is portrayed by the deepest degradation of the prodigal son, who fain would have eaten " the husks that the swine did eat ".

The parable also describes in allegory the pathway of return, or evolution, at the close of which all the seed powers of the Monads have become developed to the highest degree possible in any particular cycle. The bliss and the enrichment of the Spiritual Soul are symbolised by the welcome, the gifts and the feasting provided for the prodigal son on his return. This major cycle of involution and evolution is repeated in innumerable component sub-cycles of gradually diminishing degree and dimension. Man as Ego repeats it, for example, in each cycle of birth and death. Throughout this book the period of activity is called *Manvantara*, and the quiescence which always follows is termed *Pralaya*.

[1] *Lk.* 15: 11-32.

THE CHARACTERS

The Parable of the Prodigal Son is now considered in detail and interpretations offered from the points of view of both the Macrocosm, or totality of the Universe, and the microcosm, or man—as Monad, as Ego and as Initiate.

The chief *dramatis personae* consist of the father and his two sons. In their supernal significance, the father personifies the Absolute; the elder son, the First Emanation therefrom; the prodigal son, the outpoured, seed-bearing life, the Cosmic Christos.

THE FATHER

The father thus represents that eternal and infinite Parent from which the temporary and the finite are born. It is boundless Existence, ever unknowable and unknown, the changeless, infinite, Eternal All, the self-existent Causeless Cause, the Germ in the Root. This one Absolute Reality antecedes all manifested existence; it is the Rootless Root of all that was, that is and that ever will be.

When an epoch of manifestation (*Manvantara*) is to begin, the non-manifested condition in which " darkness was upon the face of the deep " gives place to manifestation. Quiescence, darkness, boundless " night ", then give place to activity, light, " day ". The elder son may be regarded as representing that cosmic Ideation which is the basis of the intelligent operations in Nature. This is the infinite Creative Spirit which through will, thought, and sound, and by the action of the hosts of Creative Intelligences, the *elohim*, produced all things, gave the first impulse to cosmic law and perpetually keeps everything in the Universe in existence and order.

When the evolutionary field has been prepared by this activity, it is entered by a third " person ", the younger son, the Logos, the " Word ",[1] the Cosmic Christ, Who in this interpretation is portrayed by the prodigal son. It is this Christos Who is " born ", " baptised " in the waters of the Great Deep, " betrayed " by intimate contact with the grosser worlds,[2] " crucified " on the cross of physical

[1] *John* 1: 1-5.
[2] Symbolised by the kiss of Judas.

substance,[1] " buried " in the rock tomb,[2] Who " rises " and Who ultimately ascends in clouds of glory to THAT whence He came. Yet these are not three separate eternal Beings; for That which ever was, That which ever is and That which is ever becoming is at the same time a unity. In the interpretations which follow no further reference will be made to these three subjective existences in one— the Absolute (the father), cosmic Ideation (the elder son) and cosmic Life (the prodigal son).

In the manifested Macrocosm, the father personates both the Cosmic Logos and the Presiding Deities of all stars, Solar Systems, and their major planetary components. He may also refer to the transcendent Aspect of Deity from Which all goes forth, to Which all returns, and Which exists as an overshadowing, rather than an indwelling, Presence. In the Hindu Scripture, the *Bhagavad Gita*, the Lord Shri Krishna as the transcendent Logos says: " Having pervaded this universe with one fragment of Myself, I remain." [3]

In the microcosm, the father refers firstly to the Monad in relation to the seven planes of Nature and the seven principles of man, composed of the matter of each of them, and secondly to the Ego in relation to the four vehicles of the personality.

THE ELDER SON

Macrocosmically, the elder son personates the *elohim*, or Creative Intelligences, Archangels and angels, who never lose consciousness of oneness with their divine Source. In this sense they remain at home. They are older than those Monads who embark upon the evolutionary journey which takes them through the physical plane, because they emanated first in the sequence of creative activities. These are the Seven Mighty Spirits before the Throne, the perfected Monads who reached their highest degree of development in the preceding cycle or incarnation of the Logos in Cosmos or Solar System. As previously stated, these great Beings and their Hierarchies of angels remain at home in the sense that they are perpetually self-identified with the Source of their being and life. A Biblical

---

[1] Composed of the four elements and extended in the four directions of space.
[2] Descent into the mineral kingdom.
[3] Op. cit. 10th *Discourse*, 42.

reference to them reads: " When the morning stars sang together, and all the sons of God shouted for joy." [1]

It may here be stated in advance that the suggestion of jealousy in the parable concerning the younger son is not to be taken seriously. It is possibly a cover or blind for the profound ideas revealed in the allegory, or even a deliberate direction of the mind away from such Beings and the power bestowed upon those who are able to be in contact with and to invoke them for thaumaturgic purposes. A measure of reserve concerning too direct a reference to these Beings is necessary, because they are agents for great cosmic forces. Human beings who communicate with the Angelic Hosts can learn to tap these forces and collaborate with their Angel Directors.

Like Ezekiel, the young Zechariah, son of Berechiah, " the prophet of the long vision ", evidently saw four at least of these Archangelic Creative Intelligences, sometimes associated with the four quarters of the compass. He refers to them as four chariots drawn by red, black, white, grizzled and bay horses, but his angel teacher told him: ". . . These are the four spirits of the heavens, which go forth from standing before the Lord of all the earth." [2] He went on to refer to the directions or points of the compass to which these chariots were drawn. These great Beings and their Hierarchies of angels remain at home in the sense that they are perpetually self-identified with the Source of their being and life.

Microcosmically, the elder son represents the human Monad, which also remains at one with the divine Source. The Monads of men are probably the so-called angels who " always behold the face of my (their) Father which is in heaven."[3]

THE PRODIGAL SON

Macrocosmically, the prodigal son represents the immanent Aspect of the Logos, the indwelling divine life which embarks on the great pilgrimage through matter, bearing the radiations or life-threads of the Monads out into the evolutionary fields which had already been prepared by the Hierarchies of Creative Intelligences,

[1] *Job.* 38: 7.
[2] *Zech.* 6: 5.
[3] *Matt.* 18: 10.

the Archangels and angels, who were thus older or precedent in time. This process of bearing the radiations of the Monads, with all their inherent powers, out into the field is described by the action of the younger son who " gathered all together, and took his journey into a far country."

Microcosmically, the prodigal son represents the projected Ray of the Monad, which eventually becomes manifest at the level of the abstract intelligence as the Monad-Ego in its immortal vesture of light, the Causal Body. This is the pilgrim God in man, his Higher Self, which goes forth during pre-natal life and from birth to death is embodied in the fourfold personality as its ensouling and spiritually vitalising principle.

Such are the three major *dramatis personae* in the great story, and such are some suggested interpretations of them. They might also be regarded as representing the fire (the father), the flame (the elder brother) and the sparks (the prodigal son), the triplicity which is at the heart of all objective manifestation. They are also representatives of the three mystical Aspects of both the primordial and the manifested Trinity. In addition they represent, as do all intimately related triple symbols, the three *gunas* or attributes of matter: activity (the father), rhythm (the prodigal son) and inertia (the elder brother who stays at home). The actions of the father and the two sons portray in allegory the interactions, and their varied results, of these three Aspects and attributes of Spirit and matter.

WASTING THE SUBSTANCE

The term " prodigal " is applied to the younger son because he is said to have wasted his substance in riotous living after he had arrived in the far country. This also is a veiled reference to the Eternal Oblation, as a result of which the Logos sacrificially pours out His life that His Universe may live. This voluntary self-crucifixion of the Cosmic Christos, the Macrocosmic prodigal son, upon the cross of matter shaped into Universes with their four directions of space, is referred to in Chapter I of Part Five of this work. Under certain conditions of heightened awareness, the universal, indwelling, divine life in Nature becomes visible as an all-pervading, glowing, golden life-force, omnipresent as an ensouling principle in every atom of every world. Physical forms then disappear. One is within and part of an all-pervading ocean of golden, glowing life, which appears to consist of myriads of points of light, inter-connected by lines of force, the whole being part of an apparently infinite, living web [1] of exceedingly fine mesh which pervades all beings, all things, all worlds. Each of the points is found to be a source of life, almost a sun, within which life-force wells up as from an inexhaustible fount. From these centres the golden power flows along the great web, vitalising all substance. There is no dead matter. All beings and all things are seen to be filled with the indwelling life or fire of God. An inspired poet truly described this state of consciousness:—

" Lo! Heaven and earth are burning, shining, filled
With that surpassing glory which Thou art.
Lost in its light each mortal weakness, stilled
Each rapt adoring heart." [2]

The process of limiting the universal life of a presiding Deity to a single Universe, and to the lines of force of which its web of life consists and their intersecting points, is referred to allegorically both as a wasting of substance and a forcible dividing into many parts of that which is essentially one. Thus, at the Crucifixion it is said of the crucified Christ: " And they crucified him and parted his garments, casting lots."[3] This causing of the one to become many in order that the manifestation of the hitherto unmanifest may occur, is described in other world Scriptures as the death and dismemberment of Saviours and Deities, such as Osiris and Bacchus. On the pathway of return (the prodigal son returning home) these temporarily separated parts are restored to unity, or fully recognised by perfected men as illusory; for form alone is discrete and diverse, while the life within forever remains an integral whole. This is partly indicated by the placing of a new robe—a whole or " seamless " garment—upon the prodigal son, and the reuniting of the several parts of the dismembered bodies of Saviours and Deities.

[1] q.v. *The Web of the Universe*, E. L. Gardner, T.P.H., London.
[2] *St. Alban Hymnal*, Rev. Scott Moncrieff.
[3] *Matt.* 27: 35.

THE FATHER'S HOME

The consciousness of a Logos of a Universe (its Father), is established in the highest spiritual world, called in Sanskrit *Adi* meaning " the first ". At this level one might possibly assume that the presiding Deity is transcendent above and beyond the Universe. Allegorically, the father remains at home with the cosmic Creative Intelligences who, in their synthesis, are the " first-born ", " the first fruits ", the elder son. This highest of all worlds, the plane of the most tenuous of all degrees of density of substance, is the celestial abode of the " Father which is in heaven ". This is the " holy habitation ",[1] " heaven thy dwelling place ".[2]

Here in *Adi* abides in indivisible unity the primeval creative Force, eternal and uncreated, but manifesting periodically. This is the abstract Aspect of the Supreme—infinite, absolute, attributeless. It is an impersonal, nameless, universal Principle, the God Transcendent which periodically becomes the God Immanent (the prodigal son).

The Monads as microcosms have their abiding-place in the Monadic world, called in Sanskrit *Anupadaka*, meaning " the parentless ". This level of manifestation is but one degree denser in the consistency of its substance than the first, or *Adi*.

In the case of the immortal Ego of man, as also of its vehicle —the *Augoeides*, the Gnostic " Robe of Glory ", the Causal Body— the father's home is the realm of the Higher Mind, the abstract, intellect of man.

THE PRODIGAL SON TAKES HIS PORTION AND JOURNEYS INTO A FAR COUNTRY

Macrocosmically, the " portion " represents both the volume (if such a term may be used) of cosmic life, apportioned to a single unit of manifestation, such as a Solar System, and the inherent potentialities of the Monads which are to issue forth from the parental Source, the Logos (the father). Before manifestation the potentialities of the Monads were not apparent, though present as their spiritual Essence. This is the condition obtaining in the father's

[1] *Deut.* 26: 15.
[2] I *Kings* 8: 30.

home before the prodigal son " journeys into a far country ". When manifestation begins, the Monads project their Rays into the evolutionary field.   In due course these projected Rays become individualised into immortal human souls, using vehicles more especially expressive of the faculty of abstract thought.   Plato in the *Timeus* says: " Now when the Creator had framed the soul according to his will [the Monads as miniature replicas of himself] he formed within her the corporeal universe. . ."   These are the divine seeds of the parent Tree of Life, within which infinite cosmic potencies reside.

Neither the miscalled " fall " of man nor the forthgoing of the prodigal son are in the least degree errors or sins, such attribution being entirely fallacious.   The process of " planting " alone is indicated; for just as the gardener must place his seeds in the darkness below the surface of the soil, where they are out of his sight and left to the mysterious operations of the creative life-force within them, so the Divine Gardener (the father in the parable) must " plant " or send out into the universal field or garden His Monads, seeds of His very existence.   Only by being planted can seeds bring forth from within themselves reproductions of the parent plant.   Only by journeying "into a far country" or, allegorically, "falling", can the infinitude of inherent, deific powers latent in the Monad become manifest as perfected and consciously employed theurgic faculties.

The seed-like attributes are the " portion ", and the going out afar refers to embarkation upon the path of forthgoing.   In man as Ego, the " portion " refers to those particular embryonic, divine characteristics which are germinal in the Monad at the time of emanation from the divine Consciousness.   In the personal sense the " portion " refers to the powers stored in the Ego in the Causal Body, to those faculties and capacities which after rebirth, or the Egoic going out afar, will be brought down into the new personal nature and expressed in numerous ways, some of them temporarily unfruitful, unsatisfactory, excessive or " prodigal ", and therefore " wasted ". At this point in the narrative movement, and so time and space, are introduced.   Macrocosmic and microcosmic processes of emanation have begun.

14

" A FAR COUNTRY "

From the point of view of the first Emanation from the Absolute, the Alone-Begotten Son, the " far country " is the Great Deep as opposed to the Great Breath; it is virgin space, the substance of which the new Solar System is to be built. Spirit and matter are the two primeval Aspects of the One, the Unknown Deity. This abstract, deific, feminine Principle, this pre-cosmic, undifferentiated substance, is the root out of which manifested Nature will later emanate, grow, evolve. The evolutionary field, which the Creative Intelligences (the elder son) specialise from the pre-cosmic to the cosmic, from the non-atomic to the atomic condition, and later arrange into seven successive gradations of density, is also represented in the parable by the " far country ". This term is, perhaps, more especially applicable to the seventh and densest of these gradations or planes, namely the physical world.

In our Planetary Scheme,[1] in which the Earth is the densest Globe, the deepest point of descent reached by Spirit and life on the path of forthgoing is, in fact, the mineral kingdom of physical Nature. There the life-wave, personified by the prodigal son, is farthest away from its Source or " father "; there the deepest degradation occurs. If the adjective " far " be stressed, then the physical world represents the " far country ", which also proved to be the land from which the pathway of return was entered upon.

Microcosmically, the " far country " has at least three significations. In one of them, in which the Monad is the prodigal son, the whole Solar System is away from " home " and the physical level is farthest away, or " a far country ". The Monadic radiation, in its turn, reaches the deepest point of descent as a result of incarnation in a mortal personality, and especially in its dense physical body.

If the Spiritual Soul or Ego of man be regarded as the prodigal son, then the mental, the emotional, the etheric and the physical planes and levels of consciousness are the evolutionary field. Again, the physical body, being the densest, is " a far country ". There the immortal Ego is most deeply imprisoned. There it is least conscious of its heavenly nature or is, symbolically, farthest away from the father's home.

[1] q.v. *The Earth and Its Cycles*, E. W. Preston, T.P.H., Adyar.

As has already been mentioned, and as will be more fully explained as the Books of the Bible are successively interpreted in later volumes, the Monadic seeds of life, the journey of life, and the greatest distance which is reached on that journey, are all portrayed in the Bible by means of various allegories and symbols.   Egypt and Babylon, where the Israelites (the nation typifying the prodigal son) were made captive, the pit into which Joseph was lowered, Samson's prison, and the rock tomb of Christ, are all emblematical of the densest phases entered upon, as also of the turning points at which the direction of the pilgrimage is reversed and the " prodigal son " arises and makes his way home.

In a third possible microcosmic interpretation, the " far country " is represented as the physical body of a baby at birth and through early infancy.   Whilst birth in a physical body does mark the limit of the distance to which the Egoic Ray of life and consciousness descends, and is also a turning point, during the early months little or no self-manifestation of the Ego in its new vehicle is possible.   In this sense, for the reincarnating immortal Self the baby form represents " a far country ".

" A MIGHTY FAMINE "

Macrocosmically, famine represents the inertia temporarily resulting from the equilibrium of Spirit and matter.   When the deepest density is reached, neither of them is able greatly to influence the other.   " God sleeps in the mineral ", it is said, meaning that the extreme density of the encasing mineral form prevents external awareness and activity by the entombed, " sleeping ", ensouling Spirit-Life.

Microcosmically, the famine refers to the absence of spiritual understanding from the brain-mind.   During the physical, the emotional and the early mental racial epochs, the bodily man is not consciously sustained by any spiritual impulses or soul nourishment, as it were.   In later evolutionary phases this condition can also be temporarily experienced as, for example, during times of self-indulgence and deliberately chosen selfish and sensual ways of life.   Both of these conditions are portrayed in the Sacred Language by famines.

Hunger and thirst are also sometimes used as symbols of the absence of, and the longing for, truth. After the unsatisfactory character of mere externals as food for mind and heart has been realised, manna as the " bread of heaven ", or truth directly perceived, becomes an urgent necessity; it is hungered and thirsted for, and is urgently sought. In this sense famine represents deprivation, and even ignorance of that true wisdom for which the awakened soul is longing, or for which it is ahunger and athirst.

As is so often the practice in the Sacred Language, when a physical symbol is translated into its mystical import the meaning becomes reversed. Famine, for example, is a physical disaster, but the hungry and thirsty condition of the soul can prove to be a prelude to the search for truth. Thus the Lord Christ said: " Blessed are they which do hunger and thirst after righteousness: for they shall be filled." [1] Similarly, the statement " he began to be in want ",[2] though descriptive of a painful experience, is in reality a most favourable sign; for such " want " is the precursor of the search for food, meaning nutriment for the mind and Spirit.

HE HIRES HIMSELF AS A SWINEHERD

Swine are used as symbols of the lowest and most sensual instincts and desires of man. Association with them, feeding them, and particularly eating them, represent a most unclean and depraved or swinish state, in which the passions are " fed " by continual indulgence.

A FARMER HIRES HIM AND SENDS HIM INTO THE FIELDS

The Macrocosmic journey of forthgoing is described by the words: " he sent him into his fields to feed swine ".[3] The farmer, or " citizen of that country ", represents the Creative Logos Who prepares or " tills " the fields of space in readiness for the sowing of the seeds, or the descent of the Monad-bearing life-wave—the prodigal son. The reference to feeding the swine here indicates the near approach of this life-wave to the lowest point of descent, swine being regarded, if perhaps unfairly, as somewhat unclean and lowly beasts.

---

[1] *Matt.* 5: 6.
[2] *Lk.* 15: 14.
[3] *Lk.* 15: 15.

To tend them, therefore, would be one of the most menial forms of service.

Microcosmically, the Monadic Ray penetrates deeper and deeper into the evolutionary field and the Ego draws near to the time of birth. The Egoic Ray, in its pre-natal descent, has penetrated the etheric world and become attached to the embryo.[1]

HE FEEDS THE SWINE IN THE FIELDS

Macrocosmically, the one life (the prodigal son) vitalises gross material forms (the swine). Without this inner sustenance they would die of inanition (famine). Similarly, the Monad as microcosm empowers and spiritually " feeds " the Ego, which in its turn inspires and vitalises the personality. Both of these manifestations of the Monad would be lifeless or " famished " without their indwelling, divine life. Also, for the first seven years of each new incarnation the Ego cannot use the new body very much; it thus experiences a metaphorical famine, which it does its best to mitigate by putting forth as much of its power, life and consciousness as the growing vehicles can receive, assimilate and express. In the Sacred Language the same symbols are susceptible of opposite meanings. Thus, in the personal application of the symbol, feeding the swine means giving life-energy to animal-like propensities, indicating the grossness due to arrival at the extreme of density on the evolutionary journey.

HE HUNGERS

Macrocosmically, the upward turn is now fore-shadowed. The attraction of Spirit is beginning gradually to overcome the grip of matter and draw the outpoured, manifested life back towards its Source. This is sometimes symbolised as hunger and thirst, which are made to represent the longing for the bread of esoteric truth and the waters of sacred knowledge, the inexpressible longing of the inner man for the Infinite. Thus the Psalmist sang: " My soul thirsteth for God, for the living God ".[2]

Thirst is also oppositely used as a symbol for a longing for the illusion of self-separated existence and for the gratification of the

[1] q.v. *The Miracle of Birth* and *The Kingdom of the Gods*, Geoffrey Hodson.
[2] *Ps.* 42: 2.

lusts of pride and sense—the cause of human suffering, as the Lord Buddha taught. These chain the Immortal Ego to the wheel of birth and death; for it is this thirst for life, this clinging to life on this Earth, which causes rebirth or reincarnation. When, at last, it is replaced by the thirst for freedom from the round of birth and death, for liberation or salvation in order to be more effective in the service of God and man, then such thirst becomes the very force which strikes away the fetters from the soul.

The microcosmic meaning of the condition of hunger thus emerges. It implies that the Ego, as prodigal son, has become sufficiently evolved to aspire to the Monad, and the personal man in his turn to reach up to the Ego. The great Quest—as for the mystical Holy Grail—is about to be embarked upon. The impulse is beginning to stir within the man thus moved, as a result of which, as mystic, he will make the irrevocable resolve expressed in the words of the prodigal son: " I will arise ".[1]

HE FAIN WOULD EAT OF THE HUSKS THAT THE SWINE DID EAT

Macrocosmically, the husks are outer physical coverings, or temporary forms, which have been cast off by the involving and evolving life. When travelling along that arc of the great cycle which is farthest from the starting place, life and consciousness are so materialised and spiritually insensible as to be ready complacently to remain within the forms of the past. The involutionary and evolutionary thrusts are so nearly balanced, that throughout the epoch of equilibrium no particular impulse backwards or forwards is strongly felt (one form of the " famine "). In consequence habit rules instinctual impulse, if not deliberate action.

In another sense, the yearning indicates that the one life has reached the outermost husk or crust of the Universe, the mineral kingdom of a physical planet. Husk-eating, then, implies existence and the receipt of experience within that densest, outermost form.

In the microcosmic, Monadic sense, the corn of wheat represents the Immortal Germ—the Monad—which, borne out into the field of evolution by the outpoured Spirit-Life, must descend into the

[1] *Lk.* 15: 18.

deepest depths of matter and there lie latent (die) before that Germ can produce a reproduction of its parents.

In terms of the human intellect, this phase of the journey of the prodigal son corresponds to the evolutionary stage at which the human mind is unable to comprehend (famine) abstract and spiritual ideas, truths and laws. In consequence, concrete, rigid forms (husks), both in thought and in action, are sought and chosen *faute de mieux*. In religion, for example, formalism and the dead-letter, literal reading (husks) of the Scriptures would be hungered for and insisted upon. Allegory, symbol and the purely historical view (husks) would be preferred to mystical interpretations and the eternal truths (the grain within) which those interpretations reveal.

In another sense the symbols of famine, hunger and thirst apply to the later stage when these outer forms cease to satisfy, and the mind yearns for the living waters of truth. In this more mystical significance the famine is an essential precursor of the culminating spiritual feast, or *agape*. Until this awakening occurs, forms and formalism in every aspect of life are sought.

Symbolically, the prodigal son, as the Ego in the mind-brain, fain would eat of these husks, knowing nothing else. Eventually, however, realisation of the husk-like or totally unsatisfying nature of outer forms produces a yearning for the permanent realities within. This is the true " hunger " for God, the longing of the soul for union with its true Source. The husks, from which emotional, mental and spiritual satisfaction have for so long been vainly sought, are then seen for what they are and renounced in favour of the true " bread of life " by which alone the soul's famine may be relieved, its hunger satisfied and its thirst quenched. This metaphysical use of the term " hunger " and " thirst " frequently occurs in the Bible, as in the texts: " For he (the Lord) satisfieth the longing soul, and filleth the hungry soul with goodness ",[1] and " Blessed are they which do hunger and thirst after righteousness: for they shall be filled." [2]

To sum up, famine, hunger, thirst and yearning for the husks have two main significations. One is descriptive of the mental and spiritual phases of human evolution at which the mere gross

[1] *Ps.* 107: 9.
[2] *Matt.* 5: 6.

covering or " husk " of life, thought and religion—the Lesser Mysteries
—is chosen and its value insisted upon.   The other refers to a later
phase when these things are at last perceived for what they really
are, mere husks, and the golden grain—the Greater Mysteries—
alone is hungered for and sought.

In one other sense, *tanha* (Pali), thirst for life in form, is indicated
by yearning for the husks.   The eternal, formless, universal life is
as yet unknown, and even inconceivable.   The temporarily concrete,
the particular with its outer form, is clung to as the means of satisfying desire and the only rock of salvation.   Form inevitably fails
the seeker for reality, who must outgrow the desire for it, recognise
its temporary nature, and be ready to renounce it in order that the
eternal, universal life within may be known.   Our Lord, as so often,
chose an analogy from Nature to express this truth, saying: ". . .
except a corn of wheat fall into the ground and die, it abideth alone:
but if it die, it bringeth forth much fruit.   He that loveth his life
shall lose it; and he that hateth his life in this world shall keep it unto
life eternal." [1]

"NO MAN GAVE UNTO HIM "

Macrocosmically, this may indicate that although the forthgoing,
Monad-bearing life-wave (the cosmic " prodigal son ") had reached
the deepest depths and had begun to conceive the return journey
towards its Source (hungered), the human kingdom of Nature had
not yet been formed (no *man* gave unto him).   The Monadic radiations still shone forth universally as the not yet individualised, ensouling life-principle of the sub-human kingdoms of Nature.   The famine
condition still obtains, in the sense that the return can only be consummated after the phase of Monadic individualisation as human
Egos has been entered upon and passed through.   The animal kingdom is, as it were, the portal to this stage and, whether intended or
not, the prodigal son's association with animals (swine) does seem to
indicate that this phase immediately preceding individualisation
had been entered upon.

In the microcosm, man's discovery of reality is accompanied
by recognition of the facts that the soul's hunger can never be satisfied

[1] *Jn.* 12: 24-25.

by " food " from without, and that the journey home cannot be completed as long as there is dependence upon any external support. Only by virtue of the indwelling life within, and by reliance upon that alone, can human limitations be left behind and Superhumanity (the new robe), or fully conscious union with God (the return of the prodigal son), be attained.

The loneliness of the mystic is also indicated. When spiritual awakening occurs and the pursuit of the eternal is decided upon, family, friends and erstwhile intimate associates sometimes fail, not unnaturally, to understand the change of motive for living, and the mode of life which must be followed, when at last a man says: " I will arise ". This experience, rightly received, can be salutary, painful though it may at first prove to be; for it leads to the realisation that only by complete self-dependence and obedience to unchanging, spiritual laws can the " return home ", for which the aspirant is now athirst, be achieved. In these various ways both the Macrocosmic and microcosmic prodigal sons find that " no man gave unto him." [1]

HIS FATHER'S SERVANTS EAT WHILST HE HUNGERED

The outpoured life has now turned towards its Source. The prodigal son thinks of home. Manifestation as man has been achieved. Both the Race and the individual are now able to realise the existence of the spiritual Source (the father's home) and to yearn for it. The mystic, ahunger for divine food, contemplates the Father's home, the spiritual worlds, and the Creative Intelligences who are established there as servants or ministers of the Most High.

Man, now awakening spiritually, begins to realise that only by service may the homeward road be found and trodden to its end; only through the apparent lowliness of menial service can a man become a Lord of All. When, however, this spiritual awakening occurs, no useful service is ever regarded as either lowly or menial. Indeed, ministration then becomes the unfailing rule or life. By this means the Inner Self, so long obscured by personal craving or hunger for temporal dominion, is revealed and is the only true greatness attainable by man. This does not consist of power or position,

[1] *Lk.* 15: 16.

but of becoming a selfless servant of that Supreme Splendour which is also named " The Eternal Sacrifice ".

The necessity for the subservience of the lower nature and self of man to the Higher, the Spiritual Self, is also implied. Bodily actions, emotions and thoughts must become the servants of the Monadic will. This subservience brings not loss but gain, not deprivation of faculty but increased efficiency. This addition is the result of the elimination of that resistance to the inner will which was inevitable as long as thoughts, feelings and conduct were directed towards the gratification of self-desire (feeding the swine and yearning for the husks).

" I WILL ARISE "

From the point of view of the Macrocosm, the deepest point of the descent or involution of the one life (hiring himself as a swineherd) has now been reached and passed. Ascent begins. In racial evolution humanity, in both its major and its minor component cycles, grows out of the primitive, the pioneering and the acquisitive phases. Cultural and spiritual activities begin to be foreshadowed, and individuals commence to seek and find " The way of Holiness ". They consciously and deliberately decide to embark upon the search for spiritual truth and union with THAT from which they came forth.

Interestingly, in this verse the prodigal son as the microcosm speaks for the first time and, moreover, uses the first personal pronoun. This may indicate that in man universal life has attained to that self-consciousness and individuality which enable it to embark deliberately upon the upward way. In the mineral kingdom the indwelling life unconsciously changes from the path of forthgoing to that of return. Plant life only dreamily reaches upwards and outwards. Animals, especially when domesticated, instinctively reach upwards towards self-consciousness. Man, self-impelled and of self-choice, yearns for the heights (says " I will arise "), generally of the physical Himalayas at first and eventually of the Everest of the Soul. " God sleeps in the mineral ", says the Kabbalistic aphorism, " dreams in the plant, stirs in the animal and reaches self-consciousness in man."

If the parable be applied to physical life, then the going forth represents the descent of the Ego into incarnation, physical birth

the feeding of the swine, famine the discovery that self-centred and
sensual desire can never be satisfied through form (the husks), whilst
the yearning for the husks would indicate the constant attempt to
become satiated by means of contact with the objects of the senses,
typical of late adolescence and of adult life.   The prodigal son's
repentance is descriptive of that stage of maturity at which the discovery is made that nothing that is outside of him can spiritually
satisfy or " save " any human being.   The search for fulfilment then
begins to be directed inwards and upwards, away from the particular
to the universal and from the lesser, human self to the greater, divine
Self of the Universe as a whole.   Symbolically, the prodigal son
repents of his former errors, discovers the true path and begins the
journey home.

In the Initiatory meaning, which now begins to apply, passage
through the Grades of the symbolical or Lesser Mysteries (husks)
has brought the neophyte to the outer court of the Greater Mysteries.
There he contemplates the Sanctuary, with its promise of greater
light and deeper knowledge, and aspires to gain admittance.   This
phase of human development, referred to in the parable as the decision
of the prodigal son to forsake the lower and embark upon a higher
and nobler mode of life, susceptible of interpretation in terms of both
normal and hastened evolution, is also allegorically described in the
Old Testament in such instances as: Joseph is raised from the pit; [1]
the Exodus from Egypt is foreshadowed; [2] Samson is released from his
prison; [3] and Daniel is freed from the lions' den. [4]   This development
is also implied in injuries to the head, and decapitation; for the head,
in one sense, is the symbol of the materialistic, intuition-destroying,
prideful, power-seeking aspects of the formal mind, and these attributes
of the outer, mortal man must " die " (decapitation) before the Inner,
Immortal Self can be revealed and the intellect become illumined
with the light of wisdom and intuition.   Jael thus drives the nail
into the head of Sisera, [5] David cuts off the head of Goliath, [6] and John

[1] *Gen.* 37: 28.
[2] *Ex.* 13: 17.
[3] *Judges* 16: 25.
[4] *Dan.* 6: 23.
[5] *Judges* 4: 21.
[6] 1 *Sam.* 17: 51.

the Baptist is beheaded.[1]   To be without a head is a symbol for that spiritualised condition of consciousness in which the limitations of the formal mind are overridden.   The faculty of spiritual intuitiveness can then be freely exercised, unhampered by undue and premature analysis of its fruits.

In the Sacred Language the symbol of bodily death is used to indicate the attainment by the soul of freedom from the limitations of the personality, and especially those of the mind.   Christ is thus crucified and dies, a very clear suggestion of the true meaning being given by causing the Crucifixion to occur on Golgotha, *the place of a skull*, the seat of the mind-brain.

In this more mystical sense, the prodigal son's confession of having sinned against heaven and before God is descriptive not only of sensual indulgence, but also of realisation of the limitations of the argumentative mind and of disputation as means of discovering truth.   When this realisation is achieved, those methods are relegated to a subordinate, but still important, place.   In the sense that his search for truth and light is henceforth directed to those spiritual levels of consciousness wherein alone they are to be found, the prodigal son thus makes his way back to his father's home.

[1] *Matt.* 14: 10.

CHAPTER III

THE PATHWAY OF RETURN

"AND HE AROSE, AND CAME TO HIS FATHER"[1]

THE outpoured, Monad-bearing life of the Solar Logos, which has now become fully self-conscious as man, completes the involutionary and evolutionary journey. All the component cycles of the one major cycle of forthgoing and return have run their course. A description of some of these sub-cycles would seem to be appropriate at this point, both as additions to this interpretation of the parable and in explanation of terms used throughout this work.

According to the philosophy upon which this book is based, Solar Systems, in obedience to universal cyclic law, perpetually emerge, pass into obscuration and re-emerge. Each new " creation " continues the involutionary and evolutionary processes from the stage reached at the close of the preceding era. These periods of obscuration and manifestation are known respectively as " nights " and " days ".

The matter of our Solar System is arranged in seven degrees of density, generally called planes of Nature. The subtlest, most refined or most spiritualised condition of matter forms the first plane, and the densest, least refined, least spiritualised condition forms the lowest or seventh plane of Nature. These must not be thought of as strata or planes in the usual sense of the term, for they interpenetrate and, as the scale of refinement is ascended, extend further away from the physical Globe.

Each of these seven planes is in its turn composed of matter of seven degrees of density, called sub-planes. The names given to those worlds are: the physical and the etheric, which combine to form the densest plane; the emotional; the mental (also dual); the intuitional; the spiritual; and two others as yet beyond the range of

[1] *Lk.* 15: 20.

human consciousness.   This is the sevenfold evolutionary field through which the Monads (prodigal sons) pass on their involutionary and evolutionary journeys, as a result of which their latent powers germinate and develop.   At the opening of the major cycle of manifestation, the Monad-bearing life-wave (the cosmic " prodigal son ") emerges from the divine Consciousness, which is established at the highest of these levels, and descends through the seven planes to the lowest, as heretofore explained.   Thereafter the return journey is begun, culminating in reabsorption into the Source.

The Solar System to which our humanity belongs consists of ten Planetary Schemes, each composed of seven Chains of Globes, some superphysical and some physical.   Each Chain is composed of seven Rounds, during each of which the life-stream (the prodigal son), bearing with it the evolving beings, journeys once round the seven Globes.   The period of occupation of one of the seven Globes, on which seven Root Races develop, is called a World Period.[1]

The identical process of the emergence of the life-stream from the highest level, its descent to the deepest depths and its return (the journey of the prodigal son), is repeated in all sub-cycles.   In any particular cycle the outward journey begins at the least dense or most subtle manifestation of a Chain, a Round, or a Race.   This is invariably followed by the return from the densest to the most refined plane of Nature and the most spiritual condition of consciousness.   The powers contained in the Monads, or seeds of life, are latent at the opening of the cycle and active at its close.   Such is a Macrocosmic or universal interpretation of the great parable.

The microcosmic application of this principle of forthgoing and return—the theme of the parable—is that each single Monad completes all the sevenfold cycles of the Planetary Scheme which has been appointed as its evolutionary . field.   The shortest, but not the least important, of all these cycles consists of a single physical incarnation.   The journey of forthgoing refers to the process of the descent of the human Ego from the plane of the abstract intellect, through those of the formal mind, the emotions and the ether, into the physical body.   The return home begins at the death of the physical body and the gradual withdrawal of the personal soul, or

---

[1] q.v. *The Solar System*, A. E. Powell.

incarnated Egoic power, life and consciousness, back into the reincarnating Higher Self.

In the Initiatory reading of the parable the permanent realities have been chosen, the Path of Discipleship entered upon, and the evolutionary process deliberately quickened to the limit of the individual's power. This occurs only at a certain phase (" I will arise ") of the pathway of return, when materialism is outgrown and the " husks " are known for what they are. Conscious reabsorption into the one life, light and power of the Universe is then known and sought as the true goal of human existence. The illusion of self-separateness begins to be outgrown. Universalisation of consciousness is achieved in due course and, since it is the natural, inborn condition of the Monad, this state is correctly described as " the father's home ". Such, briefly stated, appears to be the central message of the Parable of the Prodigal Son, and such are some of its major and minor applications.

HIS FATHER RUNS TO MEET HIM, WARMLY WELCOMES AND KISSES HIM

Profoundly occult Macrocosmic and microcosmic processes are allegorically described by the father's haste to meet his son and by his compassion, affection and kiss. In general, the continually exerted, spiritualising influence of the First Aspect of the Logos (the father) upon the whole Universe and its evolving life (the son) is described. More particularly, the forthgoing life-stream emanates from the Second Aspect of the Blessed Trinity, the Cosmic Christos or " Son ". When the pathway of return has been followed to a certain point, a descent of spiritualising power occurs from the First Aspect of the Deity (his father runs to meet him).

A Macrocosmic example of this descent of spiritual power is found in the process known as the individualisation into a human Ego of the hitherto universalised life and consciousness ensouling the physical bodies of animals. Although this life is indwelling in every animal and during its physical life takes on a pseudo-individuality, a Monad-Ego is not incarnated in every single animal body. On the contrary, many Monadic radiations are included within what is called a " Group Soul ", which in its turn finds embodiment

in large numbers of animals. In the case of wild beasts, particularly
of the smaller variety, some thousands of bodies may be thus ensouled.
As an animal's evolution proceeds and domestication is entered upon,
the number of such bodies comprising a Group Soul decreases. This
culminates in the development by a single domesticated animal of a
high degree of intelligence and devotion, usually evoked by close
contact with the animal's evolutionary senior, which is man.

At this stage the Group Soul itself, within its superphysical
envelope, begins to be divided by partitions, until the condition is
approximated of a single Monadic Ray being manifest in a
single domestic animal. Thereupon the process called individualisation occurs. As the animal "reaches up" in devotion, love and
effort to understand and obey its master or mistress, a descent of power
from the First Aspect of the Blessed Trinity is evoked or induced.
This power "rushes down" to meet the upreaching feeling and
thought—the simile of the formation of a water spout over the sea
is used to describe the process—and the two become conjoined (the
father kisses him). The Group Soul envelope is then disrupted,
and its substance used to form the Causal Body of the human
Ego which has been "born" or brought into existence by this
process.[1]

Thus, as is also the case in all inspired allegories in which similar
reunions occur, the father's haste to meet the returning prodigal
son, and especially his kiss, refer Macrocosmically to the conjoining
of the returning life-stream of the Second Logos with the descending,
fructifying power of the First Aspect of the Blessed Trinity. In the
Sacred Language, Macrocosmically the kiss of love is an oft-used
symbol for the intimate touch of the power of the First Aspect of the
Logos (the father) upon the returning life of the Second Aspect
(the son).

In the Initiatory interpretation the kiss symbolises the descent
into the Candidate of the Monadic will-force, both directly and
through the Hierophant, his voice and the Thyrsus, at valid Rites of
Initiation.

To return to the process of the individualisation into a single,
human Spiritual Soul of the hitherto non-individualised Group

[1] q.v. *The Causal Body*, A. E. Powell.

Soul of the sub-human kingdoms, the Macrocosmic projection of a ray of will-force (the father runs to meet the son) produces a microcosm, a Spiritual Soul of man, which thereafter continues its evolutionary journey ("I will arise") on the upward arc or pathway of return as an individual entity. In the bodily sense, after death the Ego (father of the personality) "meets" the purely personal soul (the prodigal son) and draws all that is Egoic into itself and its body of light, the Causal Body (the father's home).

In the Initiatory sense, for every step which an aspirant to discipleship takes towards his Master, the Master takes two steps towards him. At Initiation the Monadic power flashes down into the Ego in the Causal Body, as heretofore described. As stated in Part Three of this Volume, there resides within the physical body of man a normally latent, fiery power which, when awakened, moves through the body along a serpentine path. This power is referred to, therefore, as the Serpent Fire. At a certain stage of evolution, and at a certain phase in the Rite of Initiation, this fire is aroused into supernormal activity. When such awakening is about to occur, this Monadic will-force descends through the crown of the head and spinal cord to the sacral *chakra*. By its fiery touch or "kiss" the will-force awakens the sleeping Serpent Fire which, as previously described, divides into three differently polarised currents which ascend along three appointed etheric canals associated with the spinal cord. When they reach and vivify the brain and certain organs in it, the personal soul is freed from the limitations of the body, which it can thereafter leave at will to ascend into full experience of its true Egoic life in the higher mental world, its "home". The touch of the descending will-force upon the sleeping Serpent Fire is also symbolised by a kiss. Indeed, all kisses and unions, legal or illicit, used in the Sacred Language refer to these various spiritual and occult actions and experiences, and more especially to those which occur on the Initiatory Path.

A purely mystical interpretation is possible of the father's haste to meet his son, and of his kiss. In the spiritual life of man every sincere prayer, aspiration and invocation meets with a full response, a descent of grace. No sincere cry for light is ever uttered in vain.

15

Christ has already " run to meet " every human soul, as is indicated by His words:

> " *For where two or there are gathered together in my name, there am I in the midst of them.*" [1]

> "*. . . Behold, the bridegroom cometh; go ye out to meet him,*" [2]

> " *. . . lo, I am with you alway, even unto the end of the world.*" [3]

> " *. . . for the marriage of the Lamb is come, and his wife hath made herself ready.*" [4]

> " *Behold, I stand at the door and knock. . .*" [5]

In these several ways, Macrocosmic and microcosmic, the Power Aspect of the Logos " runs to meet " the Life Aspect, which it " kisses " with its spiritually fructifying ray of will-force or *Atmic* fire.

THE PRODIGAL SON CONFESSES UNWORTHINESS

The returning Macrocosmic, pilgrim life, having descended into the deepest depths of matter and become " stained ", symbolically says: ". . . I have sinned against heaven, and in thy sight, and am no more worthy to be called thy son." [6] This metaphorical confession reveals that when at last the cycle of forthgoing and return is nearly completed, and so comprehended, the staining effect upon Spirit of the descent into matter is realised. Whilst Spirit may be regarded as being stained by matter from the point of view of the finite, it can never be so regarded from that of the Infinite, where Spirit is eternally pure. From below, however, one may say with Shelley:

> " Life, like a dome of many-coloured glass,
> Stains the white radiance of Eternity." [7]

The confession of the prodigal son is, perhaps, a recognition of this inevitable taint, rather than merely an admission of guilt; for no

---

[1] *Matt.* 18 : 20.
[2] *Matt.* 25 : 6.
[3] *Matt.* 28 : 20.
[4] *Rev.* 19 : 7.
[5] *Rev.* 3 : 20.
[6] *Lk.* 15 • 21.
[7] *Adonais*, St. 52.

blame can possibly attach to Spirit, meaning in this case the one life and its component Monads, for the inescapable consequences of the involutionary and evolutionary journey.

At a certain phase of its evolution the Monad, as a microcosm, reviews and realises the evolutionary cycle and its effects. Similarly, when the Inner Self of man attains to a certain degree of both self-conscious awareness in its own world and interior, spiritual development, and when it is able to convey their effects to the mind and brain of the quaternary or mortal man, then preceding unspiritual motives and conduct are deplored and renounced. Full responsibility for past errors is recognised and accepted, and an irrevocable resolve is made that a new life shall begin (" I will arise "). Idealism, both spiritual and practical, then dominates thought, word and deed.

The natural adoption of this attitude of recognition, renunciation, surrender and resolve marks an exceedingly important phase in the unfoldment of the Spiritual Soul. Indeed, it is an essential precursor to self-emancipation from past limitations, the attainment of a new and higher level of consciousness, and the effective expression of the resultant spiritual, intellectual and cultural powers.

If the life of Christ is interpreted as the interior experiences of one person—the Initiate (Nativity) becoming an Adept (Ascension)[1] —the preparatory mission of John the Baptist is susceptible of the same interpretation; for in the microcosm all the incidents of all inspired narratives are allegorically descriptive of both natural experiences of individuals and Races and the development attained by those who, entering in at " the strait gate ",[2] tread the way of swift unfoldment.

The prodigal son's confession of unworthiness may also be applied to a single human life cycle of birth, maturity, death and the withdrawal of consciousness to its Source, for it corresponds to a certain experience on the returning arc. As death approaches, the chief incidents of the physical life just ending begin to pass in review before the mind's eye, all being seen in clear perspective. Successes and their results, failures and their outworkings, are noted by the reincarnating Ego, which thus distils the essential wisdom from the

[1] q.v. Part Five of this Volume.
[2] *Matt.* 7: 13.

experiences of the life now drawing to a close. Although this is less a voluntary confession than an enforced recognition of facts, a correspondence between the acknowledgement of errors and failures then perceived and the confession of unworthiness of the prodigal son does, it is suggested, exist.

The humility, the surrender and the confession of the prodigal son may be interpreted as descriptive of the qualifications necessary for passing through the First Great Initiation. Before the final ascension out of the human into the Superhuman kingdom of Nature, typified by the Ascension of Christ, the last remaining *karmic* debts to Nature and fellow men must be paid, and as swiftly as possible, lest final liberation be delayed. This voluntary precipitation of *karma*, as it is called, is not accomplished without great suffering which, like that of the prodigal son, is largely psychological. The Passion of Christ, which began in Gethsemane and ended with His death on Golgotha, is descriptive partly of this process and partly of the forceful dissolution of the last remaining vestiges of the illusion of self-separated individuality.

The Apostle Paul, thought to have been an Initiate of the Eleusinia, partly on the grounds of occult tradition and partly on internal evidence contained in his writings, in which he uses phrases from Mystery Rituals, also expresses contrition in his words: " For I am the least of the apostles, that am not meet to be called an apostle, because I persecuted the church of God." [1] This humility is repeated in his Epistle to the *Ephesians*: " Unto me, who am less than the least of all saints, is this grace given, that I should preach among the Gentiles the unsearchable riches of Christ." [2]

THE FATHER SAID, "BRING FORTH THE BEST ROBE"

New garments are symbols of a renewed and expanded state of consciousness. Existing clothing is used to symbolise such limitations as egoism, prejudice, intolerance, blindness and other fetters of the mind. These must be cast aside before a new evolutionary phase, whether Macrocosmic or microcosmic, can be entered upon. Thus blind Bartimaeus removed his clothing before approaching

[1] 1 *Cor.* 15: 9.
[2] *Eph.* 3: 8.

Jesus as a suppliant for the restoration of his sight.[1] Thereafter his spiritual-mental sight was restored.

Robes, dresses and garments are also used as symbols for vehicles of consciousness at any level. The seamless coat of Christ [2] may be interpreted as the garment of the Cosmic Christos, which is physical Nature, and more especially its etheric counterpart which binds all atoms into a unity. The " parting " of the garments of Christ refers to the apparent division of the one life to become the ensouling principle of innumerable forms. To the spiritually unillumined observer —in the sacred Language a blind man—variety and individuality appear to characterise physical Nature in all her Kingdoms. *Illuminati*, however, perceive also the oneness of the indwelling life. The dividing of the garments of Jesus into " four parts, to every soldier a part ",[3] also refers to the fourfold nature of the physical Universe, which is composed of the four elements of earth, water, air and fire and, in addition, extends to the four quarters of the compass.

Clothing is a symbol, too, of the limitation which every vehicle inevitably puts upon consciousness. This fetter can be accentuated by the development of erroneous ideas, theories and habits. It can be cast off by obtaining and accepting true knowledge, which produces right conduct. Symbolically, new robes are put on. The limiting, cloying garment is then transformed into " garments of salvation ",[4] a new " robe of righteousness." [4]

In the Hindu Scripture, *The Bhagavad Purana*, the Lord Shri Krishna, as a child of nine, steals and hides the clothing of the bathing shepherdesses or *Gopis* (personal souls), and forces them to come to Him for its return. Garments here symbolise passions, desires and pridefulness. These errors must be laid aside before clear vision can be attained. This self-denudation is aided by the illuminating influence of the Spiritual Soul (Shri Krishna), when once its interior presence has been realised and surrendered to. The action of Shri Krishna in permitting the *Gopis* to receive the garments from His hands indicates that the lower vehicles and their undesirable qualities had been purified and transmuted by being submitted to His influence.

[1] *Mk.* 10: 50.
[2] *Jn.* 19: 23.
[3] *Jn.* 19: 23.
[4] *Is.* 61: 10.

In general, a new or cleansed robe signifies the reconstituted body in which consciousness is clothed after having attained to fruition at any level. This new dress or vehicle then displays, in terms of colour, radiance and form, the new powers to which the Self within has attained. The new garments of Saviours and heroes usually represent the *Augoeides*, the Causal Body, which is renewed (greatly expanded) after each complete cycle of Initiation, the expanded condition constituting the newness.

This Divine Robe, or " Robe of Glory ",[1] is also symbolised as a veil, a tabernacle, a house and a city. " For we know ", writes Paul, " that if our earthly house of this tabernacle were dissolved, we have a building of God, an house not made with hands, eternal in the heavens. For in this we groan, earnestly desiring to be clothed upon with our house which is from heaven." [2]

Macrocosmically, in the Parable of the Prodigal Son the bestowal of the best robe by the father indicates that when the closing phase of any cycle is entered upon, only the finest veil of matter enrobes Spirit-Life. The new dress also indicates the highest spiritual state of consciousness in which, after submission to the privation of matter and the illusion of diversity, realisation of oneness is fully reattained.

In the Monadic sense, the Innermost Self is now consciously clothed in the matter of its own world, the second of the seven planes counting from above—that known as *Anupadaka*, the " parentless ".

The Ego, now purified of the illusion of self-separateness and illumined by the light of the Monad or father, is clothed in the " Robe of Glory ", the purified and fully developed Causal Body, radiant with solar and zodiacal powers. At the end of each personal life cycle the Ego is temporarily out of incarnation, bodiless as far as the three lowest planes are concerned, being then clothed in the Causal Body or " best robe ". After the first Initiation, the Initiate is robed in a white, silken garment which both expresses and symbolises purity, a new life, the second birth, being " born again " [3] and becoming " as a little child ".[4]

---

[1] q.v. *The Hymn of the Robe of Glory*, G. R. S. Mead; a Gnostic version of the parable.
[2] *2 Cor.* 5: 1-2.
[3] *Jn.* 3 : 3.
[4] *Mk.* 10: 15.

The phrases " new born ", " child ", " children " and " little ones " are used by writers in the Sacred Language to designate those upon whom Initiation has been newly conferred. The title is appropriate, since the true Path has been newly entered upon, and pure wisdom and spiritual intuitiveness both rejuvenate and simplify the intellect, rendering it childlike, motive-free, spontaneous. A condition of spiritual and intellectual directness and simplicity is attained. This can cause such people to be regarded by the worldly-minded as fools, worthy only to be scorned and despised. The mystical child-state is, however, a condition and an attitude towards life of unswerving integrity, of self-free, instantaneous obedience to spiritual laws. Under these conditions the faculty of spiritual intuitiveness, already highly developed, manifests with great freedom and fruitfulness, to bestow upon the mind wisdom, comprehension, implicit insight.

All Initiates, and especially those who have newly attained, become somewhat vulnerable to the criticism, scorn and hostility of worldly-minded men and women, and in this sense they resemble the defencelessness of the new-born babe. These " little ones " receive, however, the special affection and care of their seniors in the occult life, and particularly of their own Masters, their Adept Sponsors and other Initiates with Whom links have been formed during the present and preceding lives. The occult step which they have taken, its accompanying expansions of consciousness, and the high ideals of purity and beauty of life by which they are now inspired, elevate them into an important position amongst the rest of humanity. Not only do they shed many blessings upon the world, but they are potential World Saviours, whilst in addition their own evolution has reached a highly critical phase. For these reasons an exceedingly stern warning is uttered by Our Lord against harming both new aspirants to spiritual wisdom and the spiritual life and, in the terms of the Sacred Language, those newly born or " born again ". Thus He said: " But whoso shall offend one of these little ones which believe in me, it were better for him that a millstone were hanged about his neck, and that he were drowned in the depth of the sea." [1]

---

[1] *Matt.* 18: 6.

THE FATHER SAID, "PUT A RING ON HIS HAND"

This incident is of such very great symbolical significance that a number of possible interpretations are required to be given to do justice to the symbology. It has been found desirable, in consequence, to dwell at some length upon the symbol of the ring and the allegory of its placing upon the finger of the recipient. The circle, being without beginning and without end, is a symbol of eternity and of eternal power, truth and wisdom. Its shape and completeness signify both the consummation of a cyclic journey of forthgoing and return and, by implication, such powers as have by that time been attained. In terms of consciousness, the circle refers to the realisation of the Eternal Now by the Adept and of duration, or time without limits, by illumined man.

A gift of a ring from an elder could also symbolise the attainment of timelessness, now-ness, here-ness, all-ness, or unity in time and space. One who has thus attained is " ringed ", or lives in the Eternal. Movement is also suggested by the gift of a ring, which symbolises that a cyclic journey has been made outwards from a point and back again. Thus Monads as prodigal sons travel round the great Circle, whilst human Egos repeat the " Cycle of necessity ", or are bound to the wheel of birth and death. Bodies, in their turn are born, reach maturity and die. Throughout the period of bodily existence night is followed by day, which leads to night again, and sleeping is succeeded by waking, after which the body must fall asleep once more. Thus existence is cyclic. It follows a circular path and obeys the rule of forthgoing and return, typified by the ring.

This principle is so fundamental as to be worthy of a more detailed exposition, even at the risk of some repetition. A ring and the gift of a ring are of very great significance. When symbolically regarded, some of their possible interpretations are:

Endlessness; eternity and the eternal.

The completion of a cycle and the attainment of the relative perfection which is the standard set for that cycle, major or minor.

The end of one period of manifestion, whether of Solar System, Planetary Scheme, Chain, Round, World Period, Root Race, sub-Race, civilisation, nation, and the beginning of their successors.

The principle of evolution by cycles of forthgoing and return in eternal progression.

One cycle has been completed and a new one *must* then be entered upon. *The Secret Doctrine* states that this orderly progression is without conceivable beginning or imaginable end. The return home of the prodigal son is inevitably followed by a setting forth again. So, by presenting a ring the father both commemorates the son's completion of one cycle and points to the next, in which still greater evolutionary heights will be attained. The circle, when formed of a serpent with its tail (positive) in its mouth (negative), typifies generation and regeneration in endless succession, the wisdom which is thereby attained, and the Wise Ones, the Adepts, Who are the embodiments of that wisdom.

The Monad has completed one life cycle and must embark upon its successor.

The Ego has completed one cycle of birth and death and must enter upon its successor. After a sufficient number of such Monadic and Egoic cycles and personal sub-cycles, a major cycle of human evolution is completed. Nature has produced a perfect man.

The Macrocosmic emergence of the first active, objective Creative Intelligence, and the first action of the Great Breath, set up conditions under which the law of eternal, cyclic progression comes into operation.

The prodigal son thus represents manifested life, finite existence, in contra-distinction to the Unmanifest, the Infinite in quiescence. The seed-bearing life-wave is a "son of necessity", as are all the seeds (Monads) and the forms they inhabit at every stage and phase of their active self-expression; for all are subservient to the law of cycles or of endless, cyclic progression, which "has neither conceivable beginning nor imaginable end." [1] The father with the ring is a personification of that law.

THE FATHER SAID, PUT "SHOES ON HIS FEET"

In the Macrocosm all substance, and more especially the densest, as symbolised by the shoes which are put upon the nethermost portions of the body, is at this concluding phase of the cycle thoroughly

[1] *The Secret Doctrine*, H. P. Blavatsky, Vol. I, Adyar Edition, p. 115.

permeated with Spirit, rendered completely malleable and obedient. It is therefore duly prepared to be used in the new cycle which is about to open as the substance of vehicles for the ever-journeying Spirit-Life. The process of transubstantiation has been completed. All Nature has become as a Consecrated Host.

In its Macrocosmic significance, the action of the Christ in washing the disciples' feet [1] is susceptible of a similar interpretation. Microcosmically, the feet partly represent both the foundation of human life and progressive day-by-day activities. When these are purified, or " washed " by the inspiring and enlightening action of the Christ Principle within, then complete self-purification has been achieved. Since the feet are the means of physical progress and desire is the driving force of many human actions, the allegory extends the process of purification into the realm of emotion.

The ancient writers would appear on occasion not to be above the use of a play on words. Thus the feet, by their supporting function as members of the body, refer to " understanding " or the intelligent comprehension, and so conduct, of life. The attainment of this clear understanding is aided by the interior influence of the awakened Christ-nature, allegorically portrayed in the incident of the purification or washing of the feet of His disciples by the Lord Christ. This incident will be more fully interpreted from this point of view in its proper place in the progressive study of the Bible, of which this work consists. It is hoped, however, that the symbols, the methods of interpretation and the examples contained in this Volume, will enable students to apply the principles to the great allegories of which the Bible consists.

The possession of new shoes might also suggest that the power to move onwards into a new cycle has been developed. The incident therefore suggests that throughout the Universe the inertia of matter has been overcome, or rather changed to mobility. The father's action in celebrating the return of the prodigal son by providing new shoes, refers to the fact that there is no ultimate, final cessation of cyclic activity. Eternal progression is the order of Creative Day. After the close of every cycle, forces are set in motion to carry the harvested fruits as seed-powers on into the next cycle.

[1] *Jn.* 13: 1-15.

When the vehicles of the preceding cycle have been laid aside at its completion, the Monad-Ego or microcosm receives a new set as means of further material progress (shoes). The left and the right shoe may possibly refer to feminine and masculine incarnations respectively. The provision of new shoes suggests that both forms of Egoic self-expression, the negative and the positive, have become purified, spiritualised, or renewed. The harmonising or balancing of the components of the pairs of opposites in human nature and conduct might also be indicated by the gift of two slightly differing objects which compose a pair.

At Initiation, which marks both the completion of one phase of human evolution and entry upon its successor, the existing Causal Body is disintegrated, a new one being instantly formed to serve as a vehicle to convey the Monad-Ego through its next evolutionary phase. In addition, those Initiates Who on the attainment of Adeptship decide to retain physical bodies, subject them to an occult process of purification and rejuvenation, so that the normal onset of death is delayed. When, however, physical death does occur, certain of the subtler vehicles are materialised to the physical level. This provides the Adept with a relatively immortal physical body. Although the appearance of such renewed bodies may not be greatly changed, their substance and condition are so altered, and the change is so carefully maintained thereafter, that longevity far beyond the allotted span is achieved. Since the attainment of Adeptship marks the completion of the purely human cycle of existence, the return of the prodigal son may analogically be compared to it. Similarly, the putting on of new shoes may symbolise the process of bodily renewal.

THE FATTED CALF

Bulls, oxen, cows and calves are, in general, symbols of the masculine and feminine divine creative potencies. Bulls, with their immense virility, are appropriate physical symbols for Spirit, or the masculine creative potency, and for the male participant in all generative processes. Cows, with their fertility and their production of the nutrient substance of milk, are appropriate physical symbols for Substance, the matter of Space, the feminine creative potency, and for the female participant in all generative processes. The cow thus suggests both the infinite reproductiveness of matter and the fertility of Nature, which perpetually provides an abundance of food. The cow is therefore regarded as the prolific image of the earth, or Mother Nature, who provides food, strength, health and happiness.

The calf potentially possesses one or other of the above-mentioned attributes, but more especially symbolises the product of the creative interaction of the Father-Mother, and is therefore a symbol of both the Universe and all to which it gives birth.

Macrocosmically, eating the fatted calf indicates absorption into the divine Source of all the powers resulting from the involutionary and evolutionary processes at the close of a major cycle. When a calf is new-born, Creative Dawn is implied. When it is grown and fattened, approach to the close of an evolutionary cycle is indicated, and eating it symbolises the final garnering of all the fruits of the period of manifestation.

In man, the microcosm, the calf is a symbol of the intuitive wisdom which is " born " from the fructifying descent of spiritual will (the bull) into the vehicle of abstract intelligence, the Causal Body (the cow). From this union the intellect becomes illumined by the light of pure reason and spiritual intuitiveness (conception), whilst from then on the higher vehicle, the body of intuition, develops into an effective instrument of supra-mental cognition, of direct perception and implicit insight into first truths and first causes.

The fattened condition also signifies the fulness of comprehension and of knowledge which the awakened principle of spiritual intuition bestows upon the mind of man. The enrichment of soul which comes from the accompanying upwelling of divine life and love is also implied. In the human interpretation, then, the fatted calf indicates that phase of Egoic evolution at which the intuition, or *Buddhic* vehicle, has developed into an effective instrument of consciousness, its efficacy having been enhanced by the transmuted personal forces of love and desire.

The process of eating the fatted calf—and indeed all symbolical feasts—indicates that the centre of awareness has been raised above the lower quaternary and established at spiritual levels above the intellectual principle, and that it there absorbs (feasts upon) the enriching fruits provided by the exercise of the faculty of intuition.

The molten calf [1]—to digress briefly—would signify the development and expression of the forces of desire, chiefly through the emotional and physical bodies. The Psalmist says: " They made a calf in Horeb, and worshipped the molten image. Thus they changed their glory into the similitude of an ox that eateth grass." [2] Acceptance of the literal reading of the Scriptures, apart from the undermeaning, and insistence upon the efficacy of mere outer forms and ceremonies, apart from the inner life, are symbolised by a molten calf. Whilst at first there must be reliance upon external guidance, even authority, and upon outer observance (the molten calf), the spiritual truth and power behind the veil of symbolism and ceremony must eventually be perceived. The molten calf symbol therefore describes the condition of the man who has not yet begun those interior processes of spiritual alchemy whereby the forces and faculties of desire and generation become trasmuted into the powers of spiritual will, spiritual wisdom and intellectual creativeness, or genius.

" LET US EAT, AND BE MERRY "

In the spiritual sense a feast symbolises absorption of the fruitage of any cycle of activity, Macrocosmic and microcosmic, major and minor. Eating and drinking refer to assimilation, whether of power, wisdom, knowledge or, in the larger sense, of the now active and well developed powers which were latent at the beginning of the process. Thus the fruits of the voyage, the pilgrimage, the journey, are said to be gathered, prepared, and enjoyed as a feast. The powers, the faculties, the wisdom and the knowledge developed when the end of any cycle is reached are absorbed and assimilated in a state of blissful fulfilment. For the time being nothing is lacking, all is attained. The journey of forthgoing and return has come to an end.

In this sense Isaiah wrote: " And in this mountain shall the Lord of hosts make unto all people a feast of fat things, a feast of wines on the lees, of fat things full of marrow, of wines on the lees well, refined." [3] Indeed, the whole of the twenty-fifth chapter of *Isaiah*

[1] *Ex.* 32: 4.
[2] *Ps.* 106: 19-20.
[3] *Is.* 25: 6.

abounds in descriptions of Macrocosmic and microcosmic attainments written in the symbolical language.

To sum up, all banquets symbolise the completed, "fulfilled" state which has been reached at the end of a cycle. In terms of one human incarnation, full majority is implied. The rich experiences of life, and the wisdom and the understanding obtained from them, have all been absorbed by the mind-brain. If applied to the life of the Sanctuary, the eating of the fatted calf, the feasting and the merry-making are all descriptive of a state of consciousness entered into as the final Initiation draws near—that act of self-liberation which makes a man an Adept.

The Last Supper,[1] and the accepted invitation to "Come and dine"[2] given by Our Lord to the disciples on the occasion of His third appearance after the Resurrection, may refer to this consummation, also symbolised by the Ascension of Christ. St. John alone narrates this incident and since his Gospel is full of mystic allusions, the Macrocosmic and microcosmic significations of *agape* may have been in his mind. The wedding feasts of Jacob,[3] of Samson,[4] of Esther,[5] and at Cana,[6] are especially susceptible of this interpretation.

THE ELDER SON WAS ANGRY

The suggestion of jealousy between different aspects of the Divine Nature, and between Monads evolving through the angelic and the human kingdoms, is unacceptable. The anger of the elder son may therefore be taken as a deliberate blind or cover to distract the attention of the profane from the deeper aspects of the secret wisdom, and the power which follows from their discovery.

Microcosmically, the two brothers may be regarded as the two aspects—the Higher, abstract (the elder) and the lower, concrete (the younger)—of the human mind. In the earlier phases of human evolution the concrete, mental principle becomes enmeshed and entrapped in the transient phenomena of the ephemeral physical

---

[1] *Matt.* 26: 20-29.
[2] *Jn.* 21: 12-13.
[3] *Gen.* 29: 22.
[4] *Jud.* 14: 10.
[5] *Esther* 2: 18.
[6] *Jn.* 2: 1-11.

body and world, wasting (being prodigal) its faculties in the acquisition of spiritually worthless, worldly possessions (husks). Eventually however, their illusory, transitory and so unsatisfying (famine and hunger) nature is perceived and they are outgrown and forsworn (" I will arise "), later to be replaced by the true riches of the soul. These consist severally of spiritual powers, wisdom, knowledge, and the enduring happiness and satisfaction (merrymaking and feasting on the fatted calf) which their possession and exercise bestow. Thus, that which hitherto was lower, prodigal (wasted by riotous living), worldly, is transformed into a purely selfless and spiritual state of consciousness and mode of life (fed from the paternal Source).

When this sublimation has occurred, the Higher and the lower minds are united to become one intellectual principle. This is then capable of awareness and action in both the " formless " [1] worlds of abstract truths and laws and the " form "[1] worlds of mental analysis and separate evolving forms. Thus, at the end of the great pilgrimage the younger and the elder brother are correctly brought together in the father's home.

The terms of the evolution of the Spiritual Soul and its successive personalities, the union of the two brothers refers to the fusion of Egoic and personal consciousness. When this has been attained the reincarnating Ego, represented by the elder brother, becomes fully aware of all the experiences of its projected Ray (younger brother), which has made the pilgrimage through the worlds of form (successive reincarnations), has received the stain or imprint of matter, and has now become self-purified from it. The personal soul is then consciously united with its Higher Self (the father). The prodigal son has returned home.

Although it may appear to some minds to complicate unduly the beautifully simple parable, this interpretation is supported by the reply of the father to the elder son: ". . . Son, thou art ever with me, and all that I have is thine." [2] The divine and immortal Self

---

[1] *Rupa, arupa.* (*Sk.*) Form and formless, referring to the levels respectively below and above the fourth sub-plane of the mental plane. In the former the tendency to assume shape preponderates over rhythm, and in the latter rhythm, or the free flow of life, predominates. Angels of the *rupa* planes present more definitely to human consciousness the idea of bodily form than do those of the *arupa* levels.

[2] *Lk.* 15: 31.

of man (the elder brother of the mortal personality) is, indeed, both immune from the stain of matter and at one with its Monadic Source (" thou art ever with me "). When the cycle of human evolution is complete, this at-one-ment of man-Spirit and God-Spirit is fully and continuously realised. The Adept abides in this " Promised Land ", or Nirvanic state of existence, and is able to say, as did Our Lord, " I and my Father are one." [1]

" THY BROTHER WAS DEAD, AND IS ALIVE AGAIN; AND WAS LOST, AND IS FOUND "

In the Sacred Language the words " dead " and " lost " have various meanings, as also have the words " alive " and " found ". In meanings applicable to the Parable of the Prodigal Son, states of consciousness rather than bodily conditions are described. Death implies complete, though temporary, loss by the present, mortal man of experience of the divine and immortal nature of his true Self. Resurrection, or being alive again, is descriptive of rediscovery of this knowledge and re-entry into that experience. Similarly, being lost in no sense implies finality, but only a state of mind in which the delusion of being a self-separated personality temporarily inhibits spiritual experience and comprehension, particularly of unity with God. To have been found again is to have been delivered from this delusion or " heresy " of separateness, and once more to have become aware of identity with God, and through Him with all that lives.

FALL AND REDEMPTION

The ideas of the " fall " of man, the curse of Eve, the brand of Cain, and the equally erroneous concept of original sin, have arisen from a misunderstanding, if not complete ignorance, of the theme of the Parable of the Prodigal Son. As suggested throughout this interpretation, the parable describes the journey of Spirit outwards from the Source on the path of forthgoing, and inwards to the Source on the path of return.

Spirit, whilst remaining perfect in its own world, inevitably becomes marked or stained by contact with matter, especially in its grosser densities. Incarnation in the mental, the emotional and the

[1] *Jn.* 10: 30.

physical aspects of the human personality causes Spirit temporarily to lose its pristine purity and universality. The illusion of self-separateness, individualism, pride, sensuality and sexuality—these constitute the inescapable price which, in the current period of the evolution of the planet Earth and its inhabitants, must be paid for the attainment of Adeptship.

This price—the descent and the resultant staining—is referred to in many ways by writers who use the allegorical language. Some of the Biblical symbols used to denote it are: the " fall ", the sin of Adam and Eve, the brand of Cain, the bruised heel, the descents into Egypt and Babylon, the pit and the prison into which Joseph was thrown, the idolatry of David, the surrender of Samson (the Ego) to Delilah and the Philistines (the emotional and the physical natures of man), the accusations of the elder brother of the prodigal son, and the death and burial of Christ.

Mythology contains many allegories susceptible of a similar interpretation. Amongst them are: the temporarily earth-binding errors of Lucifer, and the vulnerability both of Achilles, whose mother failed to allow the water to wash the heel by which she held him head downwards (symbol of the path of forthgoing) in the sacred waters of the River Styx, and of Siegfried at the place where the leaf fell on his back whilst he was bathing in the dragon's blood. Although the Spiritual Soul of man is eternal and immortal, his bodily nature (heel and place on the back) is mortal and eventually dies. The " accidental " arrow wound of which Shri Krishna died, and the wounds of Balda, Adonis and Osiris, as well as the shirt of Nessus which brought about the agonising death of Heracles, are all symbols of the temporary ill-effects upon Spirit of its intimate contact with matter.

These and the many similar stories are instructive examples of the use of allegory to conceal, preserve, or reveal to intuitive minds, profound truths concerning the underlying laws which govern cosmic and human existence. Similarly, as stated in an earlier chapter, human procreative activity, whether legal or illicit, has two symbolic meanings. One of these is the same as that given to the above allegories. The descent of Spirit (the male) into matter (the female), of the Monad into the Ego, and of the Ego into a human personality, are all implied by scriptural and mythological references to sexual

16

intercourse.   Another meaning of such unions applies to experiences upon the path of return, when the personal consciousness (the male in this sense) becomes fused with that of the Ego (female), and that mystical union occurs which is also referred to as the " heavenly marriage ".

If it be asked why the ancient authors should thus introduce the obscene into their writings on spiritual subjects, it is replied that to them human procreation was in no sense obscene.   On the contrary, they regarded it as a perfectly legitimate and natural human enactment of the divine creative procedure by which, in the larger sense, the Universe was created.   In modern man, passing through the present mental cycle, such references admittedly tend to evoke the blush of shame and the altogether unjustified sense of obscenity. Such, however, was not the case amongst earlier Races of mankind, and in the days when many such stories were written.

If the necessity for this veiling be questioned, it should be remembered that the discovery of the unity of the microcosm (man) with the Macrocosm (the Universe) could bestow very great theurgic powers upon the discoverer.   These could be misused with grave detriment to both the transgressor and all others adversely affected. Black magic is, in fact, one example of such misuse of knowledge. Further reasons for secrecy concerning occult knowledge and power are presented in an earlier Chapter.

" ALL THAT I HAVE IS THINE "

The father's gentle reproof, and his attempt to appease the elder son by assuring him that " all that I have is thine ", constitute an affirmation of the eternal truth that fundamentally all beings are expressions of the one divine life.   In consequence, all the apparently separate manifestations of that one life participate in each other's attainments.   Furthermore, the human Monad receives all the fruits of Egoic evolution, whilst the Ego, in its turn, absorbs into itself and stores the powers, the wisdom, the knowledge and the faculties developed by its successive physical personalities.   Therefore the Deity can rightly say to every human Monad, and each Monad to its Ego, " Son, thou art ever with me, and all that I have is thine."

The father's affirmation of unity rightly comes at the end of the story, which allegorically describes the completion of all cycles of progression, major and minor; for at all such consummations the unity of the human Monad with its spiritual Source is fully and consciously realised. This is the evolutionary goal, the crown of Him who has been crucified, whether He be the Cosmic Christos, the historical Christ, or the Christ Principle indwelling in every man. When the great mystical coronation [1] occurs, the elevated and liberated one is able to say with the Christ: " I and my Father are one ",[2] and with the prodigal son's father to his elder son: ". . . thou art ever with me, and all that I have is thine."

Such are possible interpretations of the great parable, particularly when it is regarded as an exposition of the law of cycles by which all existence is governed.

---

[1] The unillumined masses see only the trials and ordeals through which, in his purely human nature, the triumphant Initiate must pass. Fellow Initiates, however, perceive the exaltation of the human spirit, a coronation into spiritual Kingship indeed. This attainment is possibly hinted at in the inscription which Pilate wrote and had nailed over the head of the crucified Christ: " JESUS OF NAZARETH THE KING OF THE JEWS." When asked why he did not write, " but that he said, I am King of the Jews ", Pilate replied " What I have written I have written." (*Jn.* 19 : 19-22).

[2] *Jn.* 10: 30.

PART FIVE

THE LIFE OF CHRIST SPIRITUALLY
INTERPRETED

CHAPTER I

THE NATIVITY

THE NATIVITY AS A SPIRITUAL RE-BIRTH

In the course of the foregoing Chapters many examples of the use of symbols to reveal and to conceal portions of esoteric knowledge which are pregnant with power have been given from the Christian and other Scriptures. In this Chapter three possible interpretations of certain incidents in the life of Christ are offered. The narrative is treated as a record of universal truths and mystical experiences passed through by Races and individuals. The immortal story is considered from three points of view: the universal, in which the Christ personifies the Creative Deity and His outpoured life; the human, in which Christ represents the Spirit of man on its pilgrimage towards perfection; the spiritual, in which the progress of the man Jesus through the five Great Initiations to Adeptship mirrors the self-same experiences through which every Initiate has passed and must pass when treading the Way of the Cross. Of these the last-mentioned, referred to throughout as the Initiatory interpretation, is the most fully expounded and most frequently repeated—because considered to be of especial interest and importance.

A study of the Gospels from these points of view indicates that they were written by men who knew the Ancient Wisdom and were skilled in the language of allegory and symbol. These inspired authors would seem to have been Initiated members of one or other of the still-operative Sanctuaries of the Mysteries of their time and, knowing the Sacred Language, they used actual people and temporal happenings, substances and forms as symbols of eternal truths.

Whilst for many Christians the Gospel story in its wonder and beauty is all-sufficient, there are others who, noting certain mysterious events and words of Our Lord, perceive in the narrative a mystery, a light and a truth greater even than those of the historical account. Our Lord said, for example: " I and my Father are one " [1]; " Before Abraham was, I am " [2]; and in the Book of *Revelation* He is made to say: " I am Alpha and Omega, the beginning and the end, the first and the last." [3]   These words can hardly refer to the man Jesus who was born in Bethlehem.   Indeed, St. John opens his wonderful Gospel by referring to Him as the Creative " Word " which was in the beginning,[4] and later was made flesh and dwelt among us, " and the life was the light of men." [4]

That a mystery is hidden deep within the Gospel story and in the nature of the Lord Jesus Christ is evident.   Thus, whilst the historicity of the Bible is not contested, the idea is advanced that the related incidents have both a temporal, historical significance and a timeless meaning, universal and human.   The great central Figure in the Gospels thus assumes a cosmic grandeur and universality.   Mystically He represents the divine life and Presence in all Nature and in all men.   The main events recorded of Him are seen also as events occurring in the whole Universe and within the Spiritual Soul, or Christ, in man.   In a mystery beyond human comprehension, the Christ story is that both of the Cosmos and of every human being.   It tells of the birth and the evolution to relative perfection of the whole Universe, the human Race, and every human individual.

Indeed, three Christs can be discerned in the Gospel narrative These are: the cosmic—the deific life and Presence in all Nature and all things; the mystical, or the Christ-Presence in every human being; and the historical, the great Figure who appeared on Earth some 2,000 years ago in Palestine.

In the cosmic interpretation, the major cycle of forthgoing and return is portrayed.   At the cosmic Nativity the life of the Creative Deity is outpoured into the newly formed, or new-born, Universe. At the Baptism a deeper descent occurs.   At the Crucifixion, death and burial, the divine life is most deeply imprisoned in the densest

[1] *Jn.* 10: 30.
[2] *Jn.* 8: 58.
[3] *Rev.* 22: 13.
[4] *Jn.* 1: 1-5.

substance of the Solar System, the matter of the mineral kingdom, symbolised by the rock tomb. The Resurrection portrays embarkation upon the Pathway of Return, which is followed to its end in Ascension to the right hand of God.

Every human Spirit, or Monad, pursues the same outward and returning path upon its pilgrimage from innocence or sleep (as in the incident of the stilling of the tempest), outwards and downwards into conflict with matter and the elemental tendencies of the substance of the mental, the emotional and the physical bodies (the storm on Galilee and the temptation in the wilderness), overcomes them, and moulds them into the wings of the soul whereby it ascends to that peace from whence it came forth.

The Dweller in the Innermost of every man is represented and expressed through the outer man as the human Ego, the immortal Spiritual Self in its body of light, the *Augoeides*, the storehouse of all the faculties and capacities attained as a result of life's pilgrimage. This Ego repeats the great cycle, lives out the story of the life of Christ, every time it descends into incarnation as a divine visitant to the physical world. Thus the Inner Self of man is born (Nativity), reaches puberty (Baptism), is tempted and when successful overcomes, is crucified by suffering, and knows the death of the body and its own resurrection and ultimate return to the Egoic world. Thus the Christ-life is indeed a universal life. The Christ Himself composed and related a wonderful epitome of the life story of Cosmos, Solar System, human Race, human individual and human Initiate. It has come down to us as the Parable of the Prodigal Son, an interpretation of which has already been offered in Chapters I, II and III of Part Four of this Volume. The gnostics possessed another version which has come down to us as the *Hymn of the Robe of Glory*.[1]

THE APPROACHES TO THE WAY OF THE CROSS

In offering an exposition in outline only of this last (the Initiatory) application of the life of Our Lord, we find that three main types of men and women are introduced into the Gospel story. First there were the good but unheeding work-a-day people of the world, without any comprehensible mystical experience as yet, unawake to idealism,

[1] G. R. S. Mead.

and uninterested in the possible existence of the superphysical worlds and in a spiritual mode of life.   This was the contemporary population of Palestine amidst which the Lord Christ moved.

The second type consisted of those people who were gradually awakening to spiritual realities, and were beginning to hear the call to the spiritual way of life.   These would gather round the Master and listen attentively to His teachings as He moved through the cities and the countryside.   The rich young ruler who approached the Master in search of eternal life is an example of those who are spiritually awakened but are not yet ready to meet all the conditions necessary for the life of discipleship.   In answer to his first question as to how he could attain to eternal life, he was told by Our Lord to keep the commandments.   He protested that this he had done from his youth up.   Then came the acid test.   Our Lord said to him: ". . . sell all that thou hast, and distribute unto the poor, and thou shalt have treasure in heaven: and come, follow me."   Then follows what is surely one of the most poignant sentences in the whole of our Scriptures: " And when he heard this, he was very sorrowful: for he was very rich." [1]   We need not regard this decision as final, however.   Perhaps, later on in life, the rich young ruler may have found himself ready to forsake the world, or rather the purely worldly motive and mode of life, and follow the great spiritual ideal.   Reincarnationists would doubtless say that, even if not in that same life, the opportunity of discipleship would again present itself and in due course be accepted.

The third type of men and women introduced into the Gospel narrative are those who were ready to dedicate themselves wholly to the spiritual life.   These were the awakened ones who had answered the inner call to the higher life and who were determined, even amidst worldly duties, to enter in at the strait gate and tread the narrow way of which Our Lord spoke—" The way of Holiness ", as Isaiah called it.   These were the disciples and other immediate followers of the Lord, and it is they who afterwards transmitted part of His message to the world.

These three types of people have always existed.   They exist today and for all of them, whatever their outlook on life, the

[1] *Lk.* 18 : 18-23.

Christ-life is a pattern and example. His teachings provide the most perfect guidance, especially for the spiritually awakened, the seeking and the aspiring ones amongst men and women, of whom there are so many today.

A very wonderful experience comes to those who accept the example of Christ and try to live by His teachings. A mystery begins to be enacted both within and around them. They commence to pass through the major incidents in the life of Our Lord and His disciples. Whenever a man sincerely and genuinely seeks to live according to the highest that is within him, his true Teacher appears. As is described in Chapter II and Part Six, of this Volume, physically or superphysically, or both, a meeting occurs between the ardent aspirant and one who has reached the summit of human evolution, a perfected man, an Adept, a Master of life and death. Not only the rich young ruler,[1] not only the disciples and immediate followers of Our Lord 2,000 years ago, but throughout all time every strong, sincere, aspiring, self-dedicated human being finds his Master's feet. Then the mystery to which I referred begins to be enacted within them.

THE PHASES OF THE INTERIOR UNFOLDMENT

The five major stages in the life of Our Lord are passed through by every aspirant to perfection; for the Nativity, the Baptism, the Transfiguration, the Crucifixion and the Ascension of Christ, as recorded in the Gospels, portray by allegory and symbol the experiences of every human being who at any time finds the Master's feet. Trained by Him, they are presented for what is called Initiation or occult dedication to the swift ascent of the evolutionary mount, the attainment of the stature of a perfect man [2] in a relatively short space of time.

This mystical view of the Gospel narrative as a description of events occuring within the soul of spiritually awakened man may seem strange, particularly to those who are learning of it for the first time. It is, however, by no means new. Even at the time of Our Lord, a certain group of Neo-Platonists of Alexandria were studying the Scriptures of the world, and especially the Old Testament, from

[1] *Lk.* 18 : 18-23.
[2] *Eph.* 4 : 13.

this point of view. They were called, in consequence, the Analoge-ticists. Prominent among them was the great Alexandrian sage and contemporary of Christ, Philo Judaeus, to whom this work is respectfully and gratefully dedicated. The words of Angelus Silesius already quoted [1] indicate the continued prevalence of this view of the Scriptures during the Middle Ages, whilst modern literature contains expositions of this mystical approach.

The first Biblical symbolical references to the historical birth of the Christ-child consist of the prophecies in the Old Testament of the coming of Messiah. These correspond to the early stirrings of spiritual power within a man or a woman who has hitherto been living a normal, natural, and perhaps rather worldly, life. After a time what has been called a "divine discontent" is experienced, and an inexpressible longing of the Inner Man for the Infinite begins to be felt. The voice of conscience becomes stronger and stronger, until at last it is irresistible.

Such experiences are promises, prophecies or foreshadowings of the interior mystical "birth" or awakening of the inherent Christ-powers within man of which the Apostle Paul wrote: "I travail in birth again until Christ be formed in you." [2] The prophecies in the Old Testament are followed by the mission of John the Baptist, whose call to the people of his time to repent is interpreted as the voice of the Higher Self of man; a voice which, if heeded, eventually becomes the impelling summons of a fully-awakened conscience. The daily life is then purified of selfishness, sensuality and self-indulgence. Possessiveness begins to be outgrown and service on behalf of others assumes an increasingly large place in the life of the aspirant. Eventually the Inner Self rules the outer man, and a spiritual mode of life amidst worldly duties is embarked upon.

An interior Annunciation then occurs. From the very Highest Self of man a mighty spiritual power descends, a veritable creative fire which produces profound psychological and spiritual awakenings and developments. Within the Soul a veritable "birth" of new powers and new faculties occurs and a new, Christlike attitude to-wards life is quite naturally adopted. A deepening sense of unity

[1] q.v. p. 47.
[2] *Gal.* 4 : 19.

with God and with all beings is developed, and this leads to a Christlike life of self-surrender and sacrificial love. Thereafter, this new-found realisation dominates thought, motive, word and deed of the outer man, whose life thus becomes completely reformed, reorganised. Mystically he is said to be reborn or, as Our Lord said, " born again ".[1]

THE IMMACULATE CONCEPTION

Who then, from this mystical point of view, is Mary the immaculate Mother of Jesus? If one may say so, with deepest reverence for Her as an historical personage, She is also a personification of the Immortal Spiritual Soul of all men, the maternal matrix or womb from within which the Christ-power and Christ-consciousness, or child, is interiorly born.

This reading of the story, as being descriptive of interior experiences and developments of one person, is borne out by the statement that Joseph, the husband of Mary, was not the father of Jesus, who was immaculately born of a virgin mother.[2] Many earnest Christians find this doctrine of the immaculate conception difficult to accept. The difficulty vanishes, however, if the story is regarded not as history only, but also as an allegorical description of changes and developments occuring within the mind and heart of every human being.

THE ANNUNCIATION

The Archangel Gabriel represents the innermost Spirit in man. Mary is the Immortal Soul, receptive to the power of the Spirit; and the Christ-child Who is born of Mary is the Christ-consciousness within man, the newly awakened powers of universal love and spiritual intuitiveness which reveal to the mind the oneness of all life and all living things. Thus the Annunciation is an interior experience, a descent from the Dweller in the Innermost—the Monad, the source of creative will (Gabriel)—of fructifying power, sometimes pictured as a lily, symbol of generation and regeneration. This produces in the Ego, in its vehicle of the abstract mind (Mary), a profound intellectual and psychological development, a veritable birth within the

[1] Jn. 3 : 3,5,7.
[2] Matt. 1 : 18, and Lk. 1: 31.

Soul of new spiritual powers and intellectual capacities. After this mystical conception, its fruits are conveyed through the receptive mind and the purified emotions to the outer man in his physical body. Within that body the whole wonderful transformation occurs. The symbolism here is especially interesting, as it would seem that the Evangelists deliberately introduced personification of the bodies of man. The prepared and receptive mind is represented by Joseph; the purified emotions by the tamed domestic animals; and the physical body by the inn and its stable.

Indeed, all of the seven principles of man are thus personified and present in the allegory of the Nativity of Christ. This is the universal virgin birth in the advanced individual and Race, the First Great Initiation, the true Christmas of the Soul. It is beginning to occur in the more advanced elements of the humanity of this day, those men and women who are responsible for World Movements which seek international collaboration for the welfare of the Race as a whole. As ever, a Herod appears, in the guise of those dark fanatics of selfishness, the ruthless tyrants in every field of human endeavour who seek to frustrate and destroy the dawning impulse to world unity, even as King Kamsa sought the death of the child Shri Krishna, Seth of Horus, the Titans of Bacchus, and Herod of Jesus. As all of those Personifications escaped and rose to greatness, so will the great allegories prove to be true descriptions of the successful birth of the Christ-consciousness in twentieth century man. Such is the racial interpretation of which all allegories are susceptible.

THE MYSTICAL ACCOLADE

In the Ancient Mysteries, as stated elsewhere, the physical body was entranced. The Inner Self in its vehicle of light, the Causal Body, was thus freed and thereafter elevated to a level of awareness at which the existence of the one Source of all life, and unity with that life is recognised. At that level of awareness, this unity is no longer an intellectual conception, but is now a living truth, felt and known from within rather than seen from without. The real significance of the mystical Nativity is interior, intellectual, psychological self-identification with others in various states of happiness, sorrow and suffering. These experiences are shared, actually felt to be one's own. " The flight of the alone to the Alone " [1] has been made, and the hitherto individual focus of universal power and light becomes consciously merged in the resurgent life of the whole Universe.

In recording these profound mysteries of Initiation, the Evangelists revealed them in terms of analogy and symbol. The secrecy to which all Initiates are pledged, as indicated by the posture of Horus Harpocrates, is thus preserved: whilst at the same time, and with consummate skill, a measure of the truth is presented to " those that have eyes to see and ears to hear." The actual revelation, however, consists not of imparted information but of direct, personal, interior experience, and this is for ever incommunicable. The way to it can, however, be indicated and this is the great value of the inspired Scriptures of the world.

The great Ceremony of Initiation eventually draws to a close. The Soul returns to its body. The expansion of consciousness and its results must be transmitted to mind, emotion and brain, through which they must be made manifest in the conduct of daily life.

THE HOLY FAMILY

The interior birth is indeed immaculate; for in this reading of the Gospel story Joseph represents the formal, logical, concrete mind of an advanced human being, experienced and wise [2] before, and spiritually illumined after, the mystical Nativity. Valuable though the formal mind with its powers of logic can be, it cannot give birth to the intuition. By its very nature it is mentally analytical and factual. The intuition, represented by the Christ-child, brings swift realisation of underlying principles and accurate premonitions which are independent of the action of the formal mind. The Immortal Self, personified by Mary, with its capacity for abstract thought, can receive, comprehend and convey to the formal mind (give birth to) this intuitive power. Thereafter the revelations of the intuition are justified at the bar of the intellect, their expression in action being guided by a wise and balanced mind. Joseph, then, personifies the developed mind of the Candidate for Initiation and is rightly only the putative foster-father of Jesus.

[1] *Plotinus.*
[2] *Matt.* 1: 19.

Domestic animals were present at the Nativity. They represent the controlled and purified emotions. The manger as a container of food may be regarded as an emblem of the vital or etheric body which contains, preserves and distributes throughout the physical body the life-force from the sun. The stable in its turn represents the physical body. Thus, in the language of symbols and with the greatest skill, the whole of man—his spiritual, intellectual, emotional, vital and physical principles—is introduced into the wonderful story of the historical Nativity. This story is so related as to reveal in addition profound mystical truths of universal significance.

THE SHEPHERDS AND THE MAGI

The shepherds refer to those great Shepherds of Souls who are the perfected men of our Earth, humanity's Elder Brethren, the rare efflorescence of the human Race. The Apostle Paul writes of Them as the " just men made perfect ",[1] and displays in many ways a knowledge of the mystical meaning of the Gospel story. The shepherds are rightly introduced into the story of the Nativity; for whenever a human being reaches the evolutionary stage at which the Christ-power is born within him, he is drawn into the presence of these Great Ones of the Earth, man's Seniors in evolution. A great ceremonial is performed in Their presence after divine assent has been received. The shepherds are therefore included in the story to make of it also a description of what is called the Initiation of man, which occurs in the presence of the Perfected Men of our Earth, our planet's Adept Shepherds of Souls.

The Magi or Kings from the East, traditionally three in number, are variously interpreted by Biblical scholars. In one sense they refer to the three aspects of the Inner, Immortal Self of man, which are spiritual will, spiritual wisdom and spiritual intelligence. Each of these parts of the Soul of man is at that time sufficiently awakened to contribute its special powers or gifts to empower, guide and inspire the Initiate in the new life into which he enters. In another rendering, the three Magi refer to the purified mind, emotions and bodily powers of the Initiate, whose sublimated faculties (the gifts) are offered or surrendered to the Christ-power which is now awake

[1] *Heb.* 12: 23.

within him. Symbolically, the three gifts are laid at the feet of the newly-illumined Soul, or Christ-child newly born. The Star of Bethlehem is the white and fiery pentagram which flashes out above the head of the Hierophant when a valid Initiatory Rite is to be performed. It is the sign and symbol that the necessary powers and qualities, especially selflessness, have been attained and that Initiation may be conferred.

THE MASSACRE OF THE INNOCENTS

Herod represents the past, the infant Christ represents the future, and between these two a measure of warfare is inevitable. Old appetites, habits, self-indulgences, selfishnesses, and a materialistic and purely worldy and acquisitive attitude towards life, are incompatible with the life of loving and sacrificial service which will now be lived. The Initiate may therefore, at first, experience some difficulty in subduing the clamorous demands of the body and the jealous, prideful, possessive attributes of the mind, which are symbolised by Herod. This aspect of human nature (the Herod in man) will lose its power if the Christlike attitude is allowed to develop. The loss is subconsciously resented by the outer man, who makes every endeavour to prevent the dominance of the new, spiritual ideal. Symbolically, Herod massacres the innocents in an endeavour to destroy the new-born Christ-child.

THE FLIGHT INTO EGYPT

The flight to Egypt is of great interest to symbologists, for again the whole make-up of man is present, all the seven parts of human nature being portrayed. Joseph, Mary and the Christ-child here personify the threefold Spiritual Self of man, the human reflection of the Blessed Trinity of Father, Son and Holy Ghost. The four lower parts of human nature—mind, emotion, vitality and flesh (the lower quaternary, as it is called)—are frequently symbolised by a quadruped.

The normally stubborn ass is chosen as the beast of burden, both for the flight to Egypt and the entry into Jerusalem on Palm Sunday, thus fulfilling the Old Testament prophecy: ". . . shout, O daughter of Jerusalem: behold, thy King cometh unto thee: . . .

17

lowly, and riding upon an ass. . ." [1]   This is a very apt choice from the symbolical point of view; for the more material aspects of man's nature, the lower quaternary, tend stubbornly to resist the will of the Spirit within him.   When once the Spiritual Self has become dominant, however, then the obstinate and self-willed attributes are transformed into docility.   The outer man becomes obedient to the will within.   This tamed, fourfold personality is well represented by the symbol of a domesticated quadruped, the hitherto stubborn donkey now trained to willing service.

Why was the so-called flight to Egypt made? The suggestion of a flight may be regarded as a cover for the true purpose of the journey.   Although a spiritually minded man may ignore his enemies, both without and within, and may even make tactical withdrawals in order later to advance, he would not be likely to fly from them.   The journey from the danger which in Palestine threatened the light of the Sanctuaries of Egypt, may be interpreted as descriptive of the process of the transmutation of spiritually dangerous personal attributes and tendencies, personified by Herod, into their sublimated, positive expression as spiritual and intellectual powers.   Occult tradition records that Jesus did actually make a journey to Egypt. This is one of the many instances where historical fact and mystical interpretation are formed into a narrative where both local, temporal facts and eternal truths are revealed; for Egypt is regarded by some modern students of occultism as a still-operating Sanctuary of the Greater Mysteries, where Initiations continue to be conferred and inspiration bestowed by the still-living Masters, Who form the Egyptian Branch of the Great Brotherhood of the Adepts on our planet. Egypt was one of those sacred places on Earth where Sanctuaries of the Greater Mysteries had long been established.   So it was to one of these that Jesus repaired, after some years of training by the Essenes in Palestine, in order to have consummated that mystical experience which is described in allegory and symbol in the narrative of the Nativity in Bethlehem.

---

[1] *Zech.* 9: 9.

CHAPTER II

FROM BAPTISM TO ASCENSION

THE WATERS OF JORDAN

The Baptism of Jesus in the Jordan at the hands of John the Baptist [1] refers to the second of the five Great Initiations, and is of both occult and mystical significance. A second, solemn Ceremonial is performed, a new level of consciousness is attained, and a new spiritual power and authority is the result. The intellectual principle in man receives an evolutionary stimulus, and this makes dangerous the period which immediately follows. The analytical faculty is greatly enhanced and can for a time shut out from the mind the spiritual wisdom derived from the supra-mental, intuitive levels of consciousness. The outer personality can then become hypercritical, scornful, and even materialistic. This is symbolised in the Gospel story by the wilderness into which Jesus was led after His Baptism to be tempted of the Devil,[2] who then symbolises the prideful, scornful, materialistic aspects of the formal mind, as also does one of the thieves at the Crucifixion.

The interior, mystical interpretation of the Baptism of Jesus indicates that it refers to an important phase in the unfoldment of man's higher faculties; for spiritually minded people, and the disciples and Initiates amongst men, are all of them potential servants and saviours of mankind. In order that they may be able to teach man the way of happiness, health and harmony, and so that they may have the power and the knowledge to heal the sicknesses of human bodies, hearts and minds, they must themselves experience those sufferings. Symbolically, the waters of this world's sorrows (the waters of Jordan) must engulf them. Voluntarily they must submit

[1] *Matt.* 3: 13-17.
[2] *Matt.* 4: 1-11.

themselves to full experience of unity with all who suffer; they must share the pains and woes of all mankind and know them as their own.

If this experience is steadfastly endured, then indeed, as the story tells, the man emerges from it with a new vision and a new power to understand, to help and to heal. The heavens opened,[1] meaning that a new and higher level of spiritual awareness is attained. A voice from on high proclaims the one who is thus baptised as a Son of God [2] and a deliverer of men, meaning that as this phase is passed through, the awakened and empowered spiritual will within man bestows upon the outer personality divine attributes and capacities.

THE TEMPTATION IN THE WILDERNESS

The story of the temptation of Jesus by the Devil in the wilderness [3] portrays in part only, and in the language of symbols, the experiences of the Initiate of the Second Degree. Just as, after the Nativity, the attack was made by Herod, symbolising the clamour of past habits and desires, so now the remaining vestiges of pride, egoism, self-satisfaction and desire for power, personified as Satan, tend to spring to life and tempt the Initiated One to abandon his divine mission. Allegorically, in the wilderness—representing periods of spiritual aridity, to which all mystics bear testimony—the Devil tempts Jesus to abandon the great quest and to use his new-found power to gain personal possessions and prestige. It is said that under this great test many aspirants fall. The sense of heightened power is so very strong, the intellectual capacity is so wonderfully enhanced by passage through this degree in the Greater Mysteries, that egoism and pride (personified by Satan) can reach monstrous proportions and lay the Candidate low in gratification of the lust for power, and the sense of personal pride.

Eventually victory is attained. The tempted one says to the Tempter: " Get thee behind me, Satan ".[4] The permissible use of the new-found powers enables him to heal, to teach and to draw

---

[1] *Matt.* 3: 16.
[2] *Matt.* 3: 17.
[3] *Matt.* 4: 1-11.
[4] *Lk.* 4: 8.

around him those who become disciples, and are themselves helped to find and tread the self-same Way of Holiness, " the strait gate " and " the narrow way ".

" EVERY ONE THAT IS OF THE TRUTH HEARETH MY VOICE "[1]

The inspired story, thus interpreted, is found to describe not only processes of cosmic evolution, and the experiences of highly developed individuals in the final stages of their evolution to Adeptship. It describes also the life of every human being; for, as has been previously suggested, all men experience on occasion their spiritual or inward awakenings or " births ". There are times in the lives of most people when they know a dissatisfaction with themselves as they are; when they experience what has been described as an inexpressible longing for the infinite, a divine discontent. This almost universal human experience corresponds to the Nativity of Christ. Most people also have their Baptisms in the waters of sorrow, when grief, pain and despair can overwhelm them even as the waters of Jordan closed over Jesus. If, like Him, they are steadfast, they emerge stronger, wiser, and able to heal the pains of others. Temptations in the wilderness, states of consciousness when spirituality seems far away, also assail mankind. The lower nature tempts man to betray the highest for personal gain, prestige and power. Again, those who conquer, as did Our Lord, and use their powers rightly, will bring about a renewal of the spiritual impulse. Sometimes this is so strong as to transform people's characters and lives, even as Our Lord was transfigured on the mount.

THE TRANSFIGURATION

The temptation of Jesus, and His embarkation upon a life of ministration, were followed by ascent of the mount of Transfiguration. As previously stated, in the Sacred Language the mount, upon which so many wonderful things are made to happen in the Bible, is a symbol for an exalted state of full, waking consciousness. So it is that the third of the great Initiatory Degrees is taken on the "mount", or lofty altitude of the higher consciousness. Again, as at the Nativity,

[1] *Jn.* 18: 37.

those Perfected Ones Who have gone before are present to honour the great occasion and there, upon the mount of Initiation, the Initiate experiences a brief time of illumination and peace, attains a new and wider vision of the great plan of the creation, the vitalisation and the perfecting of a Universe and all that it contains. There also, whilst thus exalted, the fulfilment of his own destiny as man, the attainment of the stature of the perfect man, is envisaged.

Severe trials follow, amongst them those dark nights of the soul in which the quintessence of loneliness is experienced. Such Gethsemanes are not unknown to many human beings who, in their time of great need, have found fast asleep those upon whom they had relied. In the darkest hours of human life, hours of solitude, isolation, defamation and betrayal, men have felt crucified, cut off from man and God, and as if their hearts were dead within them. Resurrection and Ascension from this darkness will follow, however, for those who endure faithfully to the end.

In this way the life of Jesus the Christ is indeed a universal life, portraying the experiences of every human being. Thus it was that in the darkness of the Garden of Gethsemane, in the hour of His great need, Jesus found his disciples asleep. He knew then all that was before Him; the betrayal, the mockery of the trial, the Crucifixion and the cruel death. Naturally He turned to those He loved and who loved Him best, seeking some support from them in the great ordeal. But, as had to happen in order that He might learn to rely upon His own inward strength alone, all outer help was seemingly withdrawn. Allegorically, His disciples were sleeping around Him, no hand being outstretched to help Him in the hour of His need. Rarely, it is said, does a soul pass through this trial without uttering the cry: ". . . could ye not watch with me one hour?"[1] Then, despite a momentary shrinking of the human nature from the cup, it was accepted. Already His face had been set steadfastly towards Jerusalem, symbol of the world that He was then to enter, in order that mankind may be delivered from sin and selfishness, and so from the suffering which under compensatory law they inevitably bring.

[1] *Matt.* 26: 40.

THE CRUCIFIXION

The Fourth Portal then opens before the dedicated and consecrated soul. It is symbolised by the betrayal, the trial and the Crucifixion of Christ. Whilst attaining and passing through this lofty stage the Initiate experiences a still deeper darkness and loneliness, when a gulf seems to open up between the Father and the Son, between life infinite and life embodied. It is the bitterest of all ordeals, as is portrayed by Christ's passion on the Cross. He seemed to be deserted by such friends as still remained. He saw His enemies exultant around Him. He drank the bitter draught [1] (which is another wonderful symbol for the bitterness of defamation and betrayal). The Father, Who was still realised in Gethsemane, was veiled on Golgotha in the passion of the Cross. From the heart which felt itself deserted there then rang out the cry: " My God, my God, why hast thou forsaken me? " [2]

" I AND MY FATHER ARE ONE " [3]

Why this last, dread ordeal? It is said to be necessary because the goal of human evolution is fully realised unity, and even identity, with God. The Adept-to-be must learn, and does learn, even in the agony of loneliness—indeed because of it—that he *is* the Eternal and the Eternal is himself. Then he can say with full realisation, as on a former occasion did Our Lord: " I and my Father are one." [3] Thereafter, he remains beyond the possibility of any more falling under the illusion of separateness. He now knows, and will forever know, that the life of God in all beings is one life, and that life in him and the Spirit in him are identical with the life and the Spirit of the Universe, which is God. Thus he is one with God, and through Him with all that lives. As far as earthly life and human limitations are concerned, he can also say those final words of the Christ upon the Cross: " It is finished " [4] and ". . . Father, into thy hands I commend my spirit ".[5]

[1] *Matt.* 27: 48.
[2] *Matt.* 27: 46.
[3] *Jn.* 10: 30.
[4] *Jn.* 19: 30.
[5] *Lk.* 23: 46.

The death and the burial are also figurative, allegorical. They refer not to the death of the body, but rather to that of the personal sense of self-separateness; for now, at last, the old Adam is completely outgrown. The Resurrection follows naturally, for the freed and crowned Soul is no longer entombed within the limitations of body and mind. He can leave that earthly tomb at will and, without a break in consciousness, enter the higher regions of the heaven world. At last the great consummation is achieved. The Initiate can transcend the limitations of the formal, personal mind, can perceive truth direct by the developed and consciously used faculty of spiritual intuitiveness. Thus, at last, the Fifth Portal, the Ascension, is passed through. All human weaknesses are left behind. Divine powers are developed and employed. Symbolically, the Perfected One ascends in clouds of glory to the right hand of God.[1] The divine power in man, first born as a little child, has then attained to " the measure of the stature of the fulness of Christ." [2]

Such, in part, and from one point of view, (the Initiatory), is the immortal Gospel story. Thus regarded, the narrative is not only an account of the passage of the man Jesus through the five Great Initiations to perfection. It is not only the story of the descent of the Second Aspect of the Blessed Trinity upon Jesus for the three years of His ministry; it is also the story of every human being who finds and treads the Path of Discipleship and Initiation. For they are allegorically and mystically new-born, baptised and crucified. They have buried their human nature for evermore and ascended to the full powers of Christhood.

[1] *Acts* 1 : 9-11.
[2] *Eph.* 4 : 13.

PART SIX

"THE STRAIT GATE"
AND "THE NARROW WAY"

CHAPTER I

THE WAY OF HOLINESS [1]

MANY symbols are used to describe the mystical experiences passed
through by those who successfully find and tread the Path of Discipleship and Initiation.   One such symbol is the cure of disease.   Another
is the return of plenty after famine.   A third is the discovery of the
way of escape by those who had hitherto felt lost, as in a desert or a
wilderness, and a fourth is the attainment of safety from ravening
beasts, either by their destruction or by their taming.   Thus interpreted, chapter thirty-five of the Book of *Isaiah*, verses five to ten, may
be read as an allegorical description of such interior experiences:

> " *Then the eyes of the blind shall be opened, and the ears of the deaf
> shall be unstopped.*
>
> *Then shall the lame man leap as an hart, and the tongue of the dumb sing:
> for in the wilderness shall waters break out, and streams in the desert.*
>
> *And the parched ground shall become a pool, and the thirsty land springs of
> water: in the habitation of dragons, where each lay, shall be grass with
> reeds and rushes.*
>
> *And an highway shall be there, and a way, and it shall be called The way
> of holiness; the unclean shall not pass over it; but it shall be for those:
> the wayfaring men, though fools, shall not err therein.*
>
> *No lion shall be there, nor any ravenous beast shall go up thereon, it shall
> not be found there; but the redeemed shall walk there:*
>
> *And the ransomed of the* LORD *shall return, and come to Zion with songs
> and everlasting joy upon their heads: they shall obtain joy and gladness,
> and sorrow and sighing shall flee away.*"

The well-known passage from chapter eleven of the Book of
Isaiah, verses six to nine, is susceptible of a similar interpretation:

> " *The wolf also shall dwell with the lamb, and the leopard shall lie down
> with the kid; and the calf and the young lion and fatling together; and a
> little child shall lead them.*

[1] *Is.* 35: 8.

And the cow and the bear shall feed; their young ones shall lie down together: and the lion shall eat straw like the ox.

And the sucking child shall play on the hole of the asp, and the weaned child shall put his hand on the cockatrice' den.

They shall not hurt nor destroy in all my holy mountain: for the earth shall be full of the knowledge of the LORD, as the waters cover the sea."

These passages may be read literally as prophecies of a future Golden Age on Earth, when peace shall reign between man and man and animals and men. They also aptly describe in the terms of the Sacred Language the transformations and exaltations of the human soul through which disciples and Initiates pass on their swiftly trodden, upward journey to the stature of the perfect man.

Animals represent human attributes, desirable or undesirable according to their nature and degree of wildness or domestication. The little child that shall lead them is the " new-born " spiritual power and unifying wisdom, the newly awakened Christ Principle within the Inner Self of man, by which all predatory and hostile characteristics are subjugated and sublimated, and all the varied forces and aspects of the human character integrated into a harmonious, co-operative unit. This regenerated or " reborn " condition is constantly described as being essential to success in the ascent of the Everest of the Soul, one example being the words of Our Lord: ". . . Whosoever shall not receive the kingdom of God as a little child, he shall not enter therein." [1]

This interior change comes about as a result of two agencies. One is the normal evolutionary process, which will bring it about quite naturally. Tagore would seem to have referred to this in his words: " He who can open the bud does it so naturally." [2] The other agency consists of the concentrated efforts of the disciple himself combined with the help of his Adept Master, Who long ago achieved complete unification of all His powers, to become a single instrument in the service of the omnipotent will, the enthroned King, within.

When the Master sees that the disciple has reached a sufficient degree of development—in the Egyptian Mysteries *mer kheru*, " true

---

[1] *Mk.* 10: 15.
[2] *Gitanjali.*

of voice ", and in esoteric Buddhism *Gotrabhu*—He presents him to an assembly of His brother Adepts for the purpose of rendering still further assistance by means of a ceremonial procedure known as Initiation into the Greater Mysteries. Passage through five such profoundly secret, potent and power-bestowing Rites marks the progress of the soul from the limitations of a preceding phase into the freedom of its successor. At each, a plane of Nature and a level of consciousness are entered and gradually mastered by means of the development, as an instrument of consciousness and action, of the human vehicle or body in which the inmost Spirit is clothed at that level. As already stated in Part Five of this Volume, a description of these five Initiations is included in the Gospel narratives of the life of Jesus the Christ, the symbols for each of them being respectively Nativity, Baptism, Transfiguration, Crucifixion and Ascension.

SOME FUNCTIONS OF THE HIEROPHANTS OF THE ANCIENT MYSTERIES

Information concerning the Mysteries referred to in the literature and religious art of ancient peoples may usefully now be given. At least seven functions would seem to have been performed by the Institutions known as the Ancient Mysteries: to establish centres of research and scholarship, exoteric and esoteric; to maintain centres of spiritual power and light; to provide Schools of the Prophets, or secluded Sanctuaries wherein special training and teaching could be given to those amongst the contemporary population who applied for it; to provide the public with religion and religious worship; to compose allegory and myth in which to enshrine the esoteric wisdom perceived in the Sanctuary, " the pattern . . . in the Mount ";[1] to keep open the way leading from the outer world, through the lesser to the Greater Mysteries and the experiences beyond them; to confer Initiations.

The word " Initiation " has the same root as the Latin *initia*, which means the basic or first principles of any science. This suggests that Initiates were—and still are, for the process continues—consciously united with their own first Principle, the root of their existence, the Monad or Immortal Germ from which they emerged. The word

[1] *Heb.* 8: 5.

" Initiation " also means a new birth, a new beginning, a new life. The Temples of the Ancient Mysteries were presided over by appointed senior Initiates known as Hierophants. These officials were installed by their predecessors using a prescribed Rite of Installation. The hierophantic power by virtue of which Initiations were conferred, was then transmitted to them. Certain of the Patriarchs, prophets and kings of Israelites are said in the Old Testament similarly to have transferred their powers to their successors. Such passages will be interpreted in later volumes of this work in this Initiatory sense.

The title of " Hierophant " is derived from the Greek word *heirophantes*, " one who explains sacred things ", the discloser of secret learning, the chief of the Initiates. The Greek word *teletai* means both deaths and finishings or Initiations. Candidates passed through the experience of bodily death, though the body still lived, whilst the soul was freed, trained to act and to observe in the superphysical worlds, and elevated to that level of consciousness at which oneness with the all-pervading divine life is known. The soul was loosened from the body by the Divine Trance, in which complete self-consciousness in the higher worlds was attained and the occult senses opened. The soul of the Candidate was elevated and absorbed all the wisdom, power and purifying energy it could assimilate. It returned to the body, generally after three days and three nights, bridging death by means of the mystic Elixir of Life thus acquired. This experience was constantly repeated, higher levels of consciousness being reached and greater powers obtained on each occasion. In occult alchemy this was symbolically called " the augmentation of the power of the sun ", and in all these procedures the aid of a Master Alchemist was obtained.

Veiled reference to the Rite of Initiation, and to the secret knowledge imparted and acquired on passing through it, occurs in both the Old and the New Testaments. In the incident of Jonah and the great fish,[1] certain symbols are used which suggest the description of an Initiatory Rite. The ship refers to the physical body out of which Jonah (the soul) was cast into the underworld portion of the plane of emotion (the sea), to be swallowed by a great fish (the Christ-consciousness of oneness with all beings) and there to remain

---

[1] *Jonah* 1: 17.

for three days and three nights, afterwards to be deposited on dry land (returned to the physical body and world). The universality of this experience of Initiates is indicated by the words of Our Lord: " For as Jonas was three days and three nights in the whale's belly; so shall the Son of man be three days and three nights in the heart of the earth." [1] An indirect reference to Initiation as the way of salvation from sin may also be implied by Our Lord's later reference to Jonah.[2] These references will, however, be more fully considered in the later Volumes of this work, wherein the Books of the Bible in which they appear are interpreted.

[1] *Matt.* 12: 40.
[2] *Matt.* 16: 4.

CHAPTER II

STEPS ON THE PATHWAY TO DIVINE MANHOOD

As stated earlier in this Volume, amongst possible interpretations of the Bible there is one which provides guidance in treading " The way of Holiness ",[1] the Pathway of Discipleship and Initiation leading to the hastened attainment of perfected manhood. As this interpretation has been included amongst others in this work, it is therefore desirable to offer a brief exposition of the ancient ideal, the laws governing its fulfilment and the experiences passed through in the process. Throughout this work such interpretation has been named " the Initiatory ".

The evolution of man into the Superhuman Kingdom of Nature can apparently be consummated in the two ways referred to on page 228. The first of these consists of those natural processes by which all life is gradually brought to a greater degree of unfoldment, and all forms develop into increasingly sensitive and suitable vehicles for that life. To man this method appears to be slow for it occupies a long period of time, requiring at least seven hundred human lives, it is said, with a general average for post-primitive peoples of seven hundred years between death and the succeeding rebirth.

The other means of attainment is referred to as " treading the Path ". This implies self-conscious participation by man in the fulfilment of Nature's plan. Evidently there comes a time in human evolution when some people become extremely dissatisfied with the slowness of their progress, with their faults and limitations, and especially with their inability to give effective help to others in times of great need. This mental condition has been described as " the divine discontent " and " the inexpressible longing of the inner man for the Infinite."

[1] *Is.* 35: 8.

From the earliest days of human life on this planet, men and women have known this discontent and have set forth upon the path of swift unfoldment, the way of life which will bring them rapidly to their goal.   Some of these early aspirants succeeded, but only at the cost of tremendous effort and great suffering.   In consequence, they discovered ways or rules of life by means of which both the effort and the sufferings could be reduced to a minimum.   Eventually all this knowledge became formulated into sets of rules, which were made available for the guidance of all who similarly aspire.   These rules are known as the Laws of the Higher Life.

In this Chapter, however, I shall consider not so much the rules of the occult life as another codification, that of discipleship and Initiation, also designed for the guidance of spiritually awakened men and women.   This divides the process of deliberately hastened attainment into stages, at certain of which special laws come into operation and the aspirant is particularly susceptible to guidance from Seniors.   This systematisation, for which Tzong-ka-pa was largely responsible in more modern days, has proved to be of immense value, if only in the avoidance of pitfalls, the reduction of suffering and the increase of the speed of attainment.   Thus have come to be recognised what are known as official Steps upon the Path.

These evolutionary phases and the experiences usually associated with them are not, however, limited to the life of the Path.   They are also rehearsed throughout the period of man's normal, natural evolution.   In Christianity, for example, as described in Part Five of this book, the five major Steps on the Path are portrayed by means of allegories describing experiences through which Jesus passed— namely Nativity, Baptism, Transfiguration, Crucifixion and Ascension. Every human being repeatedly passes through these self-same experiences before " The way of holiness " is entered upon.   True, the degrees of expansion of consciousness, as also of strain and of suffering, are far less than when the Path has been finally adopted as the only possible way of life.   Nevertheless, all human beings have their conversions or new births, their baptisms in the waters of sorrow, their temptations and trials, as also their temporary upliftments when both they themselves, and the world in which they live, seem to be transfigured or transformed.   Gethsemane, the dark night of the

18

soul, is frequently experienced by both individuals and nations, as also are betrayal and unjust condemnation.

These tribulations can culminate in a sense of veritable crucifixion, when the quintessence of loneliness is known, as also are agonies of heartache and even bodily pain. Wonderful recoveries, ascensions from darkness, can lead to great happiness, whilst death itself, which comes to all, marks the ascension of the Inner Self from the limitations of earthly life. These universal human experiences may perhaps be usefully regarded for what they really are; for they are both results of the operation of the law of cause and effect and preparations for the time when, as Steps upon the Path, they will be lived out in full, even as they are portrayed in the Gospel stories of the life of Our Lord.

There are, however, more than five stages on the pathway which leads out of the purely worldly life, with its material and rather self-centred motives for living. The change begins with a sense of frustration, and with a growing feeling of dissatisfaction with one's own limitations and the hollowness of the purely material and worldly life. So many problems, interior and external, remain unsolved, so many questions remain unanswered, when guidance is sought from the formal religions of the day. The result of these experiences is a growing determination to conquer one's weaknesses, to develop one's powers swiftly, to find esoteric truth and to live a more spiritual kind of life.

When this stage is entered upon external help begins to be received. Persistent effort attracts the attention of both the Adept Head of the Ray [1] and the great Official Whose assent must be gained before advancement into pupilage of an Adept is sanctioned. This Official is known as the *Maha-Chohan*, part of Whose Office is to keep the Record (said to be imperishable and preserved in a Golden Book) of the progress, the successes and the failures of every human Ego on this planet who, from the remotest times, has entered upon the path of swift unfoldment. Thus Adept consideration is given to every aspirant and, in due course, recognition of evolutionary stature is granted. Sometime during this phase the outer man in his personal nature is guided to the discovery of a satisfying system of philosophy.

[1] See footnote 1, p. 106.

The outer circumstances of his life may even be moulded to assist his evolutionary progress, so far as *karma* permits.

The next phase consists of the discovery of a valid [1] occult school, application for admittance, acceptance, and the receipt of the necessary guidance and training which will help in the passage through the later phases of the life of the Path. These experiences are of the first importance; for they mean that the Ancient Way has been found by another pilgrim on Earth, sometimes for the first time and sometimes as a repetition from former lives. As a consequence, a marked change of outlook upon life is likely to occur. This may be described as both the universalisation of consciousness and the diminution of the sense of self-separteness and of self-importance. Realisation of oneness with the larger Self of the Universe and with the life of all Nature is also deepened. This continues until the fifth of the Great Initiations, when conscious " oneness with the Father " is obtained or " the dewdrop (of individualised self-consciousness) slips into the Shining Sea " [2] (of the life of the Universe as a whole).

THE FIRST INITIATION

The first official Step on the Path follows in due course. It is known as " Probation " and refers to the presentation of the neophyte, generally during bodily sleep, to his Master-to-be. In full self-consciousness and with the higher senses alert, he finds himself in the Presence of a perfected Being, full of majesty and power, and yet also of kindliness and friendliness. The significance of the experience is then explained by the Master. The inevitable tests and trials are described, and the Candidate who accepts is taken as a pupil on Probation. Sometimes needed changes in character are pointed out, special work indicated, and the so-called " living image " is made and kept by the Master. This image is in some form of superphysical radio or radar contact with the outer man, wherever he may be in the world. Somewhat as upon a television screen, thoughts, experiences and actions are reflected in it hour by hour and day by day. The Master, Who regularly examines the living image, is thus able to keep a watchful and kindly eye upon His new pupil.

[1] *Valid*—accepted and used by the planet's Hierarchy of Adepts.
[2] *The Light of Asia*, Sir Edwin Arnold.

When the time is ripe, official "Acceptance" as a disciple follows. The pupil's aura is intimately attuned to that of his Master, Who absorbs him into Himself for a time and charges him with His Adept power, life and light. Thereafter, wherever an accepted disciple may be in the outer world his Master can always use him as a channel of His power and His blessing and, on occasion, as a vehicle for His very Presence.

The next Step is described as "Sonship of the Master", and after this inexpressible privilege has been granted an even closer attunement is established between both the auras and the Inner Selves of disciple and Master. When the necessary progress has been made the First Great Initiation follows, though on occasion this Step may precede that of Sonship. In Buddhism the Initiate of the First Degree is called *Sotapatti* or *Sohan*—meaning " he who has entered the Stream." In Hinduism he is referred to as *Parivrajaka* —meaning " wanderer ". In recognition of the advancement which has been achieved under the Master's guidance a powerful Initiatory Ceremonial is performed, the " Path proper " is entered upon, and admission to membership of the Great White Brotherhood of the Adepts and Initiates of this planet is granted. A powerful descent occurs of the Monad-Atma into the Ego, and later into the personality, and the Star of Initiation thereafter shines out in the upper part of the aura of the Initiate. Increasingly close attunement with the Master and with the consciousness of the Great White Brotherhood itself is thereafter experienced, as also is a deepening sense of responsibility for the evolution of life and form upon this planet. After this great Step the Ego of the Initiate is said to have reached a degree of development which will ensure his safe passage through the Day of Judgment, which will occur on this planet during the next, the Fifth, Round.[1] Such, in part, is the mystical Nativity, meaning the awakening of the *Buddhic* consciousness or the " birth " into activity of the Christ-nature present in every man.

THE SECOND INITIATION

The Second Great Initiation follows, and during this phase three fetters must be outgrown and cast aside. They are doubt, superstition,

[1] q.v. *The Solar System*, A. E. Powell.

and the delusion of self-separated existence. A very rapid development of the mental body usually occurs during this evolutionary phase and this can prove to be a great test under which, it is said, many aspirants may fail. The mind, whilst a mighty instrument in the hands of the Ego, is also the vehicle of *Ahamkara* or self-personality, with its concomitants of pride and desire for power, position and prestige. These temptations assail everyone who steps out of the worldly into the spiritual life and, in consequence, acquires powers somewhat greater in certain directions than those of the man of the world. Whilst the ordeals and tests are accentuated at certain phases, they are not restricted to those " temptations in the wilderness " which follow spiritual " Baptism ". The occult life as a whole is a great ordeal, a great test, made up of many ordeals and many tests. All must successfully be passed through before the higher Initiations are granted.

The Second Great Initiation brings the aspirant to that phase which is known in Buddhism as *Sakadagamin*—" the man who returns but once " (before Arhatship). In Hinduism he is known as *Kutichaka* —" the man who builds a hut " (has reached a state of peace). The psychic faculties generally develop rapidly during this phase, which corresponds to the Baptism of the Lord Christ, since the particular difficulties through which the Candidate must pass are portrayed in the temptation of Jesus in the wilderness.

THE THIRD AND FOURTH INITIATIONS

An Initiate of the Third Degree is referred to in Buddhism as *Anagamin*—" He who does not return " (or takes the Fourth Initiation in the same life). In Hinduism he is known as *Hamsa* or *Soham*— a mystical word meaning " That am I " or " I am He ". This would seem to imply that self-identity with the Supreme Lord of Life has begun to be known; hence the power, in full consciousness and with truth, to make this great affirmation: " I am He ". The Transfiguration of Christ portrays this phase, and it is said that the manifestation of the Inner Spirit through the outer form of the Initiate of the Third Degree can be so powerful and so full that, on occasion, what would appear to be a physical transfiguration takes place. The shining *Augoeides*, the immortal Initiate Ego, frequently descends upon the outer man—indeed, the two are now almost one—to bestow upon him transcendental powers and veritable genius. In this Initiatory Degree presentation before the One Initiator, the great Lord of the World, occurs and the Initiation itself is said to be conferred by one of the Lords of the Flame. When the Initiate is out of the body at night *Buddhic* consciousness is available to him, whilst by day he is able to be fully aware in the higher mental worlds and to use the powers of Causal Consciousness.

The Fourth Great Initiation generally follows the Third in the same life. In Buddhism the Initiate of this Degree is known as an *Arhat*—meaning literally "one worthy of divine honours". In Hinduism the Sanskrit title *Paramahamsa*, meaning "above *Hamsa*", is bestowed. This is the phase of Crucifixion. The sufferings of the Christ before Pilate and on Golgotha allegorically describe the interior experiences of the Initiate of the Fourth Degree, for whom the axiom "no cross, no crown" becomes true. Indeed, if he seeks to throw down his cross it will crush him in its fall. An extremely interesting if somewhat terrible experience is associated with passage through the Fourth Initiation. The *Arhat* descends into Hades or *Avichi* (the waveless) and attempts to rescue souls who are self-imprisoned there. This is part of the meaning of the statement that Our Lord preached to the spirits in prison.[1] The Initiate now enjoys *Buddhic* consciousness while awake in the body, and when asleep can enter *Nirvana*, this being part of the meaning of Christ's Resurrection.

THE FIFTH AND HIGHER INITIATIONS

The Fifth Great Initiation is known in Buddhism as that of the *Asekha*—"no more to learn". In Hinduism the Adept is known as a *Jivanmukta*—"a liberated life". Human existence has now come to an end and the Superhuman Kingdom has been entered. The Sixth Great Initiation brings the title of *Chohan* or Lord, the Seventh that of *Maha-Chohan* or Great Lord, and at the Eighth *Buddhahood* is achieved. The very highest attainment possible to man on this Earth—and then only on the First Ray—is to take the Ninth

[1] I Peter 3: 19.

Initiation, which brings the Ego to the inconceivably lofty stature of the One Initiator sometimes called the Lord of the World.[1]

Such are the heights which, as immortal, unfolding spiritual Souls all human beings will one day ascend, whether naturally or as a result of self-quickening, " taking the kingdom of heaven by force."

Such is one part of the esotericism of world religions, such is the Pathway which leads direct to the attainment of theurgic powers. Since, as stated, these powers are susceptible of grave misuse, instructions concerning them and their attainment are given direct under a vow of secrecy from Master to disciple and by inspired authors to humanity under the veil of the symbolic language.

[1] The great Being responsible for the evolution of life and form on this planet. He is referred to in the Bible (*Daniel* 7: 22) as " The Ancient of Days ", and in the Hindu Scriptures as *Sanat Kumara*, " the ever Virgin Youth ".